WITNESSES

OF THE UNSEEN

WITNESSES

OF THE UNSEEN

SEVEN YEARS IN

GUANTANAMO

LAKHDAR BOUMEDIENE

AND

MUSTAFA AIT IDIR

WITH DANIEL HARTNETT NORLAND, JEFFREY ROSE, AND KATHLEEN LIST

REDWOOD PRESS
Stanford, California

Stanford University Press
Stanford, California

Printed in the United States of America on acid-free, archival-quality paper

Library of Congress Cataloging-in-Publication Data

Names: Boumediene, Lakhdar, 1966- author. | Ait Idir, Mustafa, 1970- author.

Title: Witnesses of the unseen : seven years in Guantanamo / Lakhdar
    Boumediene and Mustafa Ait Idir, with Kathleen List, Daniel Hartnett
    Norland, and Jeffrey Rose.

Description: Stanford, California : Redwood Press, 2017. | Includes
    bibliographical references and index.

Identifiers: LCCN 2016052475 (print) | LCCN 2016055459 (ebook) |
    ISBN 9781503601154 (cloth : alk. paper) | ISBN 9781503602113 (electronic)

Subjects: LCSH: Boumediene, Lakhdar, 1966---Imprisonment. | Ait Idir,
    Mustafa, 1970---Imprisonment. | Boumediene, Lakhdar, 1966---Trials,
    litigation, etc. | Ait Idir, Mustafa, 1970---Trials, litigation, etc. |
    Guantánamo Bay Detention Camp--Biography. | Detention of
    persons--Cuba--Guantánamo Bay Naval Base. | Prisoners of war--Abuse
    of--Cuba--Guantánamo Bay Naval Base. | Prisoners of war--Legal status,
    laws, etc.--Cuba--Guantánamo Bay Naval Base. | War on Terrorism,
    2001-2009--Prisoners and prisons, American.

Classification: LCC HV9467.8 .B68 2017 (print) | LCC HV9467.8 (ebook) |
    DDC 355.1/2960922729167--dc23

LC record available at https://lccn.loc.gov/2016052475

Typeset by Bruce Lundquist in 12/16 Adobe Garamond Pro

For our families

"[W]e do not bear witness except to what we have known, and we could not keep watch over the unseen."

The Sura of Youssef, Qur'an 12:81

CONTENTS

FOREWORD

Guantanamo has been described as a "legal black hole." This is the story of two men who emerged from that black hole, and whose U.S. Supreme Court case, *Boumediene v. Bush*, shone a light into the darkness.

Lakhdar Boumediene and Mustafa Ait Idir were living in Sarajevo, Bosnia, with their wives and young children when, shortly after September 11, 2001, they were arrested and accused of being members of a group plotting to attack the American Embassy in Sarajevo. They maintained their innocence, and after a three-month-long Interpol investigation found no evidence linking them to terrorism, the Supreme Court of the Federation of Bosnia & Herzegovina ordered that they be released. It was then that their nightmare truly began.

As Lakhdar and Mustafa exited the jail, relieved to have finally been exonerated and eager to be reunited with their families, they were instead met by American special forces who threw bags over their heads. Unbeknownst to them, Bosnia's prime minister had been given an ultimatum in a meeting with General David Petraeus, General John Sylvester, and Deputy U.S. Ambassador Christopher Hoh: turn over Lakhdar and Mustafa, or "let God protect Bosnia." Instead of going home, Lakhdar and Mustafa were beaten, strip-searched, shackled, and flown to Guantanamo, where they were confined in outdoor cages while a military prison was built around them.

For years, Lakhdar and Mustafa had no meaningful opportunity to establish their innocence. This was by design. The Bush Administration had built its prison in Cuba, not on American soil, precisely because their lawyers had advised them that this would ensure detainees had no constitutional protections, including the *habeas corpus* right to challenge one's detention in federal court. That was exactly what Judge Richard Leon, the Bush-appointed judge who first heard Lakhdar and Mustafa's case, ruled when they tried to challenge their detention: they had no *habeas corpus* right to appear in his court and argue their innocence. Guantanamo detainees were not American citizens, and they were not on American soil, so the American Constitution did not protect them.

Lakhdar and Mustafa's lawyers appealed their case to the U.S. Supreme Court, and in June of 2008 they won their appeal. In the landmark *Boumediene v. Bush* decision, the Supreme Court ruled that Guantanamo detainees do in fact have a constitutional right to challenge their detention in federal court. Even in Guantanamo, the Constitution still had force. Because of *Boumediene*, Guantanamo was a legal black hole no longer.

Of course, this did not mean that Lakhdar and Mustafa were free to go. It merely meant that Judge Leon was required to hear their case. For the first time, the government would have to offer some reason to believe that Lakhdar and Mustafa actually belonged in Guantanamo. And it could not. After reviewing the government's evidence, including classified documents, Judge Leon ordered Lakhdar and Mustafa's release. He even went so far as to urge the government not to appeal, given the weakness of its case and the amount of time Lakhdar and Mustafa had already spent in Guantanamo. Seven years, Judge Leon told the government, was "more than plenty."

Months later, Lakhdar and Mustafa were released, Mustafa to Sarajevo and Lakhdar to France. After reuniting with their families and rebuilding their lives, Lakhdar and Mustafa decided to share their stories with an American audience. They feel that by sharing their stories together, they can paint a fuller picture of what happened in Guantanamo and what it took to survive and ultimately recover. They believe that most Americans would have opposed their mistreatment if they had known about it, and they hope to ensure that what happened to them does not happen to other innocent people in the future.

PREFACE

DANIEL NORLAND

In July of 2011, Kate List and I flew to Nice, France, and Lakhdar Boumediene met us at the airport. We apologized for keeping him waiting after our flight had been delayed.

"I waited in Guantanamo for seven years and four months," he replied with a wry smile. "Half an hour is not a problem."

Lakhdar spoke in a soft voice, carrying himself with a grace that belied what he had been through. He looked nothing like the man in the photograph I had seen, a photograph taken in Guantanamo, where he wore an orange jumpsuit and a bushy beard that he had not been allowed to shave. That man appeared dejected, bitter, broken, his eyes bottomless pits, his frame gaunt. The man who stood before us now, two years after Guantanamo, was wearing a pressed dress shirt and khakis. His beard was neatly trimmed. His eyes sparkled. He was of slight build, but he no longer looked hollow. There was life in him now.

Lakhdar led us to a nearby bus stop, where we made small talk underneath a billboard for the new Smurfs movie. I showed Lakhdar a picture of my four-month-old daughter. Lakhdar had a son who was almost one year old, so we discussed diapers and sleep schedules and other details that captivate new parents and no one else. Mostly we conversed in English, but sometimes Kate spoke with Lakhdar in his first language, Arabic. Kate had studied Arabic in college, and then spent a year in Syria for a fellowship program and a year in Morocco as a Fulbright scholar.

After a twenty-five-minute bus ride, we found ourselves in Carros, Lakhdar's new hometown after Guantanamo. Carros is picturesque, nestled among trees on a hillside above Nice, dotted with pink and yellow apartment buildings that are well-worn but not yet rundown. As we walked from the bus stop to our hotel, Lakhdar paused at each intersection, waiting for the walk signal even when there were no cars in sight. He rolled our largest suitcase behind him, carefully wheeling it around the puddles left behind by the previous day's rain.

Over the next two weeks, Kate sat down with Lakhdar and interviewed him in Arabic for several hours a day. After a few days of interviews, Lakhdar invited us over to meet his wife, Abassia, and their three children. They live in a snug three-bedroom apartment on the sixth floor of a pale yellow high-rise. Lakhdar welcomed us and led us into the living room, where Abassia had set out a tray with tea, cookies, and fruit. A children's cartoon played on the television in front of Lakhdar's toddler, Youssef, whose eyes flitted back and forth between the cartoon and his family. Lakhdar's daughters, fifteen and eleven, made faces at their brother and laughed softly at each other's jokes. At one point, Youssef pointed skyward and Lakhdar scooped him up, a game that brought delight to all involved.

It was impossible, watching Lakhdar play with his son while his two daughters giggled and egged him on, not to think about how his daughters' young childhoods had been stolen from him, and their father from them. I retreated to the bathroom, looked at a picture of my daughter, and fought back tears at the idea of spending seven years apart from her.

Then I returned to the living room. The scene, still heartbreaking, was heart-mending too. Watching this man with his playful grin and the wife he adores and the kids he cherishes, a family not only at peace but truly happy despite everything they have been through, I couldn't help but be filled with hope and an abiding belief that with enough patience, endurance, courage, and love, nearly anything can be overcome. Nothing can ever erase what happened—what we did—to this man. But neither can anything erase the moments of transcendent joy he somehow made his way home to.

.   .   .

While we were in Lakhdar's apartment, we Skyped with Mustafa Ait Idir. Mustafa had been Lakhdar's friend back in Bosnia, before Guantanamo, when they were both young men. Like Lakhdar, he had been born in Algeria and had moved for work, first to Croatia and then to Bosnia. He had repaired computers for a charitable organization that helped orphans of the Balkan conflict, and he and Lakhdar had played soccer together on the weekends.

Like Lakhdar, Mustafa had been arrested by Bosnian police, imprisoned until the Bosnian court ordered his release, and then handed over to American troops. Like Lakhdar, Mustafa won his freedom when finally, after seven years in Guantanamo, he got his day in court. Unlike Lakhdar, Mustafa returned to Sarajevo and lives there now. Mustafa and Lakhdar talked for a while, and Mustafa showed off his infant son, whose gurgles eventually gave way to fussing that demanded his father's attention and ended our call.

Five months later, Kate and I traveled to Sarajevo. Mustafa met us at the airport and accompanied us in a taxi to our hotel. As we drove through Sarajevo, Mustafa pointed out some landmarks. The jail where he had been imprisoned, right next to a law school. The elementary school his son had attended. The American Embassy, which he mentioned but was careful not to actually point toward, lest that seem suspicious. Mustafa showed us a fairly new mosque and said, "That wasn't there before I went to Guantanamo," using the same tone of voice as someone describing how their neighborhood had changed while they were away at college.

"In Guantanamo," Mustafa later told us, "the world is moving forward, and you are standing still."

Kate interviewed Mustafa in Arabic over the next week. One afternoon, Mustafa was feeling ill and Kate suggested that he stay home and get some rest.

"By God," Mustafa said, his voice tinged with both mirth and earnestness, "I wish my interrogators had been more like you."

During the interviews, Mustafa listed the men he bears a grudge against. The Bosnian officials, chief among them Foreign Minister Zlatko Lagumdžija and Deputy Interior Minister Tomislav Limov, who disregarded his innocence and handed him over to the Americans. The American soldiers who tortured him. The American political leaders who oversaw all of it. Like Lakhdar, his is a narrowly targeted anger, directed not at Bosnia or America but at specific Bosnians and specific Americans.

Unlike Lakhdar, Mustafa wears his emotions on his sleeve. He snaps when angry. He speaks animatedly, in rapid bursts punctuated by sharp jabs of his finger. He is a louder, more gregarious sort. He called everyone "brother," be it a hotel valet or a college professor, and he joked with the cashiers while shopping at stores where he was clearly a regular.

When he was not sharing his story with us, Mustafa showed us the places in Sarajevo that had been his and Lakhdar's stomping grounds. He took us to the outdoor soccer field where they had played in the summer, and the gym where he still plays soccer every Tuesday night. He showed us the mall where he and Lakhdar would shop for presents for their families, and the coffee shop where they would relax after soccer.

One evening, Mustafa brought us to the gym where he is a karate coach, and we watched him lead a class. His students, ranging from five to fifteen years old and including his own son, were a diverse group: male and female, Eastern Orthodox and Roman Catholic and Muslim, novice and advanced. All of them, it appeared, were having fun, and everyone treated each other with genuine respect. Mustafa was clearly in his element.

Lakhdar and Mustafa's stories, as told to Kate in the interviews in Carros and Sarajevo, appear in the pages that follow. In addition to their own accounts, we have provided an appendix with some relevant materials, including the never-before-published account of the intelligence officer who first recommended bringing them in for questioning. Readers can draw their own conclusions, but these materials strongly suggest that the incarceration of Lakhdar and Mustafa was a mistake.

If so, it was a mistake that nearly destroyed their lives. It was a mistake that made some people question the extent to which we as a nation live up to the principles we hold self-evident. It was a mistake that ultimately led to *Boumediene v. Bush*, one of the most important modern-era Supreme Court decisions on executive power in wartime. And perhaps, if we pay attention, it is a mistake we will not repeat.

NOTE ON THE TEXT

Lakhdar Boumediene and Mustafa Ait Idir are eager to share their stories with an American audience, but they are not fluent English speakers. This book was therefore compiled as follows.

First, Kate List interviewed Lakhdar and Mustafa for several days, as described in more detail earlier in the Preface. Next, Kate List and Felice Bezri, a professional interpreter who had worked with Lakhdar and Mustafa's lawyers, translated the recorded interviews into English. Lakhdar and Mustafa's words were then edited for narrative flow by Dan Norland and Jeff Rose. At Lakhdar and Mustafa's request, Dan and Jeff also inserted portions of judicial opinions and other public records, and provided brief explanations of complex legal proceedings. Finally, Lakhdar and Mustafa carefully reviewed the text.

Unless indicated otherwise, the quotes in the text are based on Lakhdar and Mustafa's best recollection of what individuals said. Given the length of time they spent in Guantanamo and the systematic effort to disorient them, their memories may not be perfect, and many of the government documents detailing what happened to them have been classified, misplaced, or destroyed. Hopefully more documents will emerge in the fullness of time.

WITNESSES

OF THE UNSEEN

BEFORE GUANTANAMO

Lakhdar Boumediene

LONG BEFORE I WAS AN ALLEGED TERRORIST, I was a child.

I was born on April 27, 1966. I grew up in Saida, Algeria, a mid-sized city a few hundred miles southwest of Algiers. Most of my family still lives there. When I was growing up, we lived in a house with three bedrooms: one for my parents, one for my five sisters, and one for my four brothers and me.

Our home was in a working-class neighborhood, and our family was fairly poor. My father earned a modest paycheck as a night watchman. But modest becomes meager pretty quickly when a paycheck has to support so many people.

My father is a gentle, soft-spoken man whose slender frame conceals a fierce spirit of pride. He wouldn't borrow money and he wouldn't ask for help. I saw him turn down food at mealtimes so that there would be enough for his kids. As a child, I never once heard him complain.

My father often went out of his way to try to help people who were even less fortunate than we were. When we came across someone in town begging for money, my father would press a few coins into my hand and say, "Give these to him." Sometimes we would bring bread with us on our walks to give to people in need.

That was the kind of community in which I grew up. People looked out for each other. When someone died, the neighbors would take turns preparing meals for the grieving family for at least a month. Our corner of Saida could be a chaotic, hardscrabble place, but we were in it together.

. . .

When I was six, I started going to school. I'll always remember my first teacher, a kind, sympathetic man who understood my family's situation and did what he could to make sure it didn't keep me from getting a good education. He convinced the school administration to give me pens, notebooks, and other supplies for free. If it weren't for him, the simple fact of being poor might have made me hate school. Instead, I loved it. I was an enthusiastic, hard-working student all through elementary school. When people asked me what I wanted to be when I grew up, I told them I wanted to become a teacher.

Every year, the school gave out books as prizes to the top students, and I usually came in first or second. My favorite subjects were history and geography—I liked to read stories about the past, and it was fun to think about all the places I might travel when I grew up.

In the afternoons and on weekends, my friends and I played in the mountains a short walk outside of Saida. There was a forest where we could run and climb and hide, fields where we played soccer for hours, and a river where we swam and caught fish. We also tried, without success, to catch rabbits.

A few times, we came across a nest of baby doves whose mother had abandoned them, and we took them home and raised them as pets. They spent most of their time in the rafters of our house, and my pet cat Za'iim ("Chief") had the same experience with them as we did with the rabbits.

In the summertime, I lived with my grandparents in their village. It was just fifteen miles outside of Saida, but it felt like a different planet. The houses were spread out instead of crammed together. The roads were dirt instead of asphalt. There was no electricity or running water—we had canisters of gas for the stove and we fetched water from a nearby well with our donkey's help. The biggest difference was the silence. Except for the occasional bark or bray, the village was completely calm.

I loved the peacefulness of the village. I loved spending time with my grandparents and learning about farming from my grandfather and my uncles. Most of all, I loved riding the horses. My grandfather had a few white horses, and I went riding every chance I got. I would climb on the horse, grab its mane, and off I went. I'll never forget how good that felt, galloping bareback across the open fields.

When I reached the sixth grade, they stopped giving me school supplies. And in middle school, money mattered more. The other kids had new backpacks, new clothes, new shoes, new books and notebooks—and I didn't. For the first time, being poor made me feel inferior.

I did what I could to earn some money—I would buy trinkets in the neighborhood souk, where everything was cheap, and resell them at a higher price—but I wasn't able to make enough to afford all the school supplies I needed. Everything came to a head one day in math class.

Our teacher had told us to buy a specific type of ruler and bring it to class. It wasn't an expensive ruler, but it cost more than my parents or I could spare. So when the teacher walked over to my desk and asked where my ruler was, I meekly told him that I hadn't been able to afford it. Disdainfully, the teacher took two dinars out of his pocket and tossed them on my desk.

"There," he spat, as the coins clanked down in front of me. "Go buy one."

The classroom erupted in laughter. I sat there, my ears burning, as the teacher, my classmates, and the two coins stared at me. I still don't know why he did that. He could have taken me aside after class and given me the two dinars, and I would have been grateful for his generosity. Instead, I'll never forget how humiliated I felt that day.

For the next week and a half, I skipped school. I couldn't bring myself to face the other students. I eventually dragged myself back, afraid that my father would find out, but the enthusiasm I had once felt for school was gone. Instead of devouring books and dreaming about college, I counted the days until I turned sixteen, and then I dropped out of high school and signed up for a year-long course in mechanical maintenance at a trade school near my house. I figured it would be a more direct path to a paying job.

At the trade school, my professors appreciated my seriousness. A lot of the students would goof off or skip class, but I wasn't there to waste time. I learned as much as I could, as fast as I could, so that I'd be able to find work. I got along well with a few of the more serious students, and we had a friendly rivalry to see who would earn the highest grade in the program. On the final test at the end of the year, I came in second or third. I had learned a lot, and I was ready to start looking for a job. There was just one thing I had to do first.

In Algeria, before you could get a job, you were required to complete two years of mandatory military service. I really didn't want to be a soldier, but I didn't have a choice, so I enlisted.

Basic training was tough. I wasn't especially comfortable holding a Kalashnikov, no matter how much they trained me. And I was a skinny, frail teenager, so the push-ups and sit-ups and long jogs in the heat were more than I could take. I became very ill, and during Ramadan, when I was fasting, my health got worse. I felt dizzy whenever I stood up.

I was ordered to go to a military hospital for medical exams to determine whether I was fit to serve. If I wasn't, I'd receive a letter exempting me from the two-year requirement. When the doctor came in to speak with me, I saw that he didn't have a letter for me.

"Is that everything?" I asked him.

"I don't know," he answered. "Do you have anything else for me?"

I wasn't sure what he meant, so I shrugged, confused. I was too naive to realize it at the time, but looking back, I'm sure he was hinting that he wanted a bribe.

Since I didn't pay the bribe, I didn't get the letter, and I wound up back at training camp a few days later. I toughed out the last couple of months of basic training. The more sympathetic officers saw how sick I was and didn't make me run or do push-ups. They let me walk while the others jogged.

After basic training, I was assigned to a base in a city not too far from Saida. I was in charge of distributing uniforms and other gear to soldiers. The job itself was fairly boring, but I liked being in the city. After work, I could go to the souk or the café. Best of all, I could go home on weekends to see my family. Sometimes, I went home without first asking my supervising officer for permission, afraid that he would deny my request for no good reason. He may have had his suspicions, but I got away with it for five or six months.

On the holiday of Eid, when several soldiers were given leave permits, my supervising officer told me that he needed me to stay on the base, and that I would be severely punished if I went home. I obeyed his order and missed Eid with my family. I was so sad about it, though, that I went home to see my family the following weekend without asking for permission first. My supervising officer found out and was furious. As punishment, I was transferred to the border patrol.

The border between Algeria and Morocco, or at least the part that I was sent to, was a desolate, barren place. Four other soldiers and I were in charge of a five-mile stretch of border. We patrolled the area with our Kalashnikovs and made sure no one came in or went out. Our stretch of border was in a mountainous region without roads or power lines, and in my year there, I didn't see a single person try to cross.

Because it was a military zone and civilians weren't allowed in, I didn't really see anyone other than my fellow soldiers and the driver who brought us food every few days. It was a dull, lonely year.

In the evenings, we passed time playing cards by candlelight. On days when we weren't on patrol, some of the other guys hunted hyenas and snakes, but I never did. The area was crawling with scorpions. I would stay inside and whittle—I could fashion pretty good-looking birds out of a block of wood, which I would send to family members and friends as gifts. It wasn't much, but it was a scorpion-free way to fend off the boredom.

After about a year at the border, my two years were finally up. I was relieved to get my military ticket and go home, where I could get a normal job and not have to worry about soldiers or scorpions or grueling physical exercise ever again.

After recuperating from service, I started looking for a job. I went to a coffee shop near my house with a pen and notebook, and I sat for hours each morning writing cover letters. "To Whom It May Concern: I am Lakhdar Boumediene. I have a diploma in mechanical maintenance. I am seeking employment as. . . ." I sent letters to dozens of companies looking for work.

A few weeks later, one of them wrote back. I was excited when I saw the Cement & Lime Factory logo on the envelope. It was a factory ten miles outside Saida. The letter invited me to come to the factory and take a test. If I passed, they would hire me.

I was so nervous that I had trouble sleeping the night before, but the test was fair and I managed to do well. About a week later, I started working as one of the factory's repairmen. Finally, I had a respectable job.

At 7:30 every morning, a company bus picked me up at a bus stop not too far from my house. I worked on a four-person team that went around the factory fixing various machines that broke down throughout the day. The key was to keep the factory running without interruption.

It felt good to have a regular job and a regular paycheck, to provide for myself and help my family with some of the bills. I also was fortunate to have a great group of co-workers whom I got along well with.

One of my friends at work was a religious man who encouraged me to join him in his prayers and at the mosque. My parents had always taught me to believe in God, and we were faithful Muslims— we fasted during Ramadan, never drank alcohol, celebrated Eid with large family gatherings where everyone brought different desserts, and slaughtered a lamb on the Feast of the Sacrifice to share with people in need—but we hadn't been regular mosque-goers. My grandparents' village where I spent my summers didn't even have a mosque.

With my friend's encouragement, I began going to the mosque more often, and I always found it to be an uplifting experience. The imam would read words from the Qur'an or the hadith,* and deliver sermons on themes like the importance of doing good deeds and the need to look out for one another. I know that some imams twist the words of the Qur'an and hadith to incite anger or even violence, but my mosque was a place of peace.

After several months working at the Cement & Lime Factory, I had saved up enough money and enough vacation days to take a trip. I took a steamboat to Alicante, a tourist town on Spain's Mediterranean coast. The glistening beaches, the bright colors, the happy crowds—it was like nothing I'd ever seen before. I determined, then and there, that I wanted to see more of the world beyond Algeria.

For a while, I thought that I could have a comfortable, happy life working at the cement factory, exploring the world when I had vacation time, and growing old in Saida with my family, my friends, and my faith. The longer I worked at the cement plant, though, the more I realized that it was a pretty dangerous place. There was dust everywhere, and the older workers complained that after years of inhaling it all day, every day, their lungs were shot. "You're still young," they told me. "Get out while you can."

And there were frequent accidents. In my first year there, I heard about a few deaths. One man was repairing the industrial-size sintering oven when part of it fell on him, killing him. The danger didn't really sink in until I saw one of the accidents myself.

Every day, trucks would arrive from the quarry with large limestone boulders. The trucks dumped the boulders through holes in

---

* Translator's Note: *Hadith* refers to the collection of various accounts of the prophet Muhammad's teachings, sayings, and deeds.

the ground onto a conveyor belt that carried them to the crusher. One day, a young co-worker of mine was standing too close to the hole as boulders were being dumped in. I don't know why he was there, and I don't know if he tripped, or was startled, but he fell into the hole with the boulders.

We stopped the conveyor belt, and dozens of men began frantically pulling away rock. Some workers pulled boulders away from the top; I went with some others down to the conveyor belt and tried to get to him from below. As the rock shifted, he fell through the hole, and a few of us caught him. I could tell right away that he was dead. An ambulance came, but it didn't matter. The paramedics pronounced him dead on the spot. He had been crushed.

Between the dust and the deaths, I started to think that I should try to find a new line of work. In 1990, when I was twenty-four years old, I ran into a childhood friend who was back in Saida on vacation from his job in Pakistan.

"How can you keep working here, in the dust?" he asked. "There are tons of jobs in Pakistan. Come to Pakistan, stay in my home for a few weeks, and I'll help you find work."

It was an appealing offer. I didn't want to work in a cement factory for the rest of my life, and I wasn't sure what else I could do if I stayed in Saida. And my trip to Spain had made me interested in travel. I decided to go to Pakistan and see what it was like—if I didn't like it I could always come back. I hoped it would be like Alicante.

It wasn't. I was shocked, when I arrived in Pakistan, by the grime, the poverty, the oppressive heat, and the general unpleasantness of the place. After two weeks, I was ready to turn around and go home.

There was just one problem—at some point during those two weeks, I was bitten by a mosquito carrying malaria. I became quite ill and was hospitalized. By the time I recovered and got out of the hospital, months later, I didn't have enough money for a plane ticket home.

So I looked for work. I heard about a job opening at the Hira Institute, a boarding school for Afghan refugee children who had lost their fathers in the war against the Soviets. I could see why the position hadn't been filled—the pay was low, the hours were long, you were expected to live at the Institute, and the nearest large city was twenty-five miles away. Whoever took the job wouldn't get to have much of a life outside the Institute.

The job appealed to me, though. I actually liked the idea of living at the Institute. I wouldn't spend any money on restaurants or rent, so I could save up everything I was paid. That way, if I didn't like the job, it wouldn't be too long until I could afford a flight home.

Also, I loved the idea of working with orphans.* I would be continuing my father's tradition of doing good deeds, and I'd always had a soft spot in my heart for orphans. One of my older brothers had divorced his wife when she was pregnant and refused to have anything to do with his son. I felt terrible for the poor child, growing up without a father. I would give him candy whenever I saw him, and clothes for Eid, but I never felt like it was enough. And here was a chance to help dozens of children whose circumstances were even more difficult than his.

So I went to the Hira Institute and told them I was interested. I had a brief conversation with the deputy director, who asked me if I drink (no), if I care about doing charitable work (yes), and if I minded spending all of my time at the Institute (no). I was hired on the spot.

It was a demanding job. I supervised about seventy kids, ages six to sixteen. I'd get up at 5:00 a.m., wake the kids, lead them in some not-too-demanding exercises, and then, after they showered, get them to the cafeteria for breakfast at 6:30. Then I helped them pre-

---

* Translator's Note: In Muslim cultures, any child who has lost their father is referred to as an "orphan," even if their mother is still alive. The mother remains very present in the child's life, but typically there are programs that attempt to fill in some of the gaps traditionally filled by the father, including boarding-school-type institutions like the Hira Institute.

pare their book bags, and I'd have them lined up in neat rows by 7:30 so each teacher could come collect his class.

After the kids had gone off to their classes, I went with the driver to the village souk to buy meat and vegetables for the kitchen. We got back around 11:00, I rested for an hour or two, and then the kids came back. I took them to the cafeteria for lunch, then to study hall for a few hours, and then at 5:00 we played sports—soccer mostly, but sometimes volleyball or cricket. They loved cricket! We just had to be careful not to hit the cows that the Hira Institute kept on the grounds to provide a fresh supply of milk and butter and cheese.

After sports, the kids washed up, observed Maghreb (sunset prayers), and then it was time for dinner. They studied for a while after dinner, and then we'd either watch a video or play games. I made sure the games were always educational—math games, for example, or memory games. Then it was bedtime. After all seventy kids fell asleep, it was my turn. A few short hours later, it was 5:00 a.m., and we'd start the routine all over again.

The work was hard, and sleep was scarce, but I loved it. The kids were great. They'd been through so much—there was one six-year-old I was particularly fond of, and I remember thinking how sad it was that he didn't have anyone to call "Daddy"—but they were full of energy and hope and resilience. And they were smart. There were two twelve-year-olds whose heads were always buried in books. If you asked them to play, they would say, "I don't have time. I want to read."

While I was working at the Hira Institute, civil war broke out in Algeria. I kept in touch with my family and knew they were safe, but I was reluctant to go home—especially since I loved my job. I was doing something that really mattered. I began to think I could stay at the Hira Institute for quite a while.

When I was twenty-seven years old, it all fell apart. One morning in 1993, after I had been at the Institute for two-and-a-half years, there was a knock at my door. There were three men whom I'd never seen before. I couldn't tell where they were from, but they were definitely Arab. They started with pleasantries, but the conversation quickly grew serious.

"You're from Algeria, right?" one of them asked.

"Yes," I answered, not quite sure how he knew where I was from. Maybe he could tell from my accent?

"What do you think of the jihad in Algeria?"

"What do you mean?" I replied, a bit taken aback. "Whose jihad?"

They didn't like that answer. They told me that every Muslim had a responsibility to fight with the revolutionaries in Algeria against the "non-believers." They talked for ten or fifteen minutes about the jihad in Algeria and how important it was that I go back to Algeria right away to join in the struggle.

I didn't want any part of their jihad. To kill someone in cold blood and say, "Well, he deserved it, he doesn't share my beliefs"—that's not how I was raised. But I was scared to tell them that, so I hemmed and hawed.

"I'm not sure that's really necessary," I said.

"Well, think about it," one of them told me. And then, a bit more ominously: "We'll be back in a few days." With that, they left.

I was terrified. Pakistan was not a place where you wanted to be accused of non-belief. It didn't matter how devout a Muslim you were—if someone thought you weren't devout enough, he'd kill you and think he'd done a good deed. If I refused to join these men in their jihad, I figured there was a good chance they'd beat me to death. At the very least, they would take my money—"for the cause"—and keep coming back every few weeks for more. So I resolved that when they came back, I wouldn't be there. I didn't want to kill or be killed, so I left. I hated the idea that I'd never see any of the orphans again. But I had no choice.

I had to leave Pakistan, and because of the war, I couldn't go back to Algeria. Where would I go next? I figured that with my mechanics degree, I could get a job in an oil refinery, and I knew there were lots of refineries in the Gulf countries. I tried to get a visa to Saudi Arabia, but they turned me down—they were afraid of Algerians because of the war. Same thing with Kuwait and the Emirates. There was one Gulf country, though, that didn't require a visa: Yemen.

I landed in Sana'a, Yemen, in the pre-dawn hours. I was expecting Yemen to be like the other Gulf countries I had heard about—prosperous, modern, clean. As the sun rose over Sana'a, I realized how wrong I had been. I immediately regretted leaving Pakistan.

Sana'a was a dirty, impoverished city. There were no asphalt roads, so the cars kicked up dust everywhere. It reminded me of the cement factory. And just about everyone chewed qat leaves. Everywhere you looked—the streets, the sidewalks, even on the floor of the bus—there were wads of chewed-up qat.*

I called my mother and told her that I was thinking about coming home. "Don't," she warned me. "The situation here is terrible. Go anywhere—go to the moon!—but don't come here." The fighting in Algeria, she said, had gotten to the point that she was afraid of opening the door in the morning and finding corpses on the doorstep.

So I decided to make a go of it in Yemen. I rented a room on the second floor of a friendly Muslim family's home with some of the money I'd saved at the Hira Institute, and I started looking for work. Unfortunately, Yemen was a far cry from the bustling, oil-producing nation that I'd hoped it would be. There weren't a lot of jobs to be had.

While I was out of work, I signed up for some courses at Sana'a University. Some of the classes were free, such as French. I knew a little French, having grown up in Algeria, but I was happy for an opportunity to improve. I also took a course on Macintosh computers. There was a small charge for it, but the class was interesting and seemed like it might prove useful in finding a job. I was enjoying being a student once again.

---

* Translator's Note: *Qat*, a flowering plant native to the Arabian Peninsula, contains the stimulant cathinone. Chewing qat is a social custom that dates back thousands of years in some places. While some countries list qat as a controlled substance, it is legal in Yemen.

In April of 1994, four months after I had arrived, war came to Yemen. Around 4:30 in the morning, I was startled awake by a loud boom, and I felt the house rattle. In the morning, one of the neighbors told me what had happened. The communists in southern Yemen had decided to secede, and they were launching Scud rockets on Sana'a. "Don't be afraid," the neighbor reassured me. "The rockets were nowhere near us." Apparently, two of them had struck the airport on the outskirts of town, and one had landed near the Presidential Palace.

The ground fighting never reached Sana'a, but for the rest of my time there, I worried about the Scuds. I was afraid to leave the house and afraid to stay there. Most of the rockets were fired at the airport or the palace, but there were exceptions. One landed next to the hospital, just a few blocks from my house.

It was around this time that my mother called me. She had recently been talking with the parents of one of my childhood friends, and she found out that my friend was now working in Albania. She had gotten his phone number, and she suggested that I give him a call to see if he could help me get a visa to Albania and a job there. So I did.

"I'm in a tough spot," I told my old friend. "I'm in Yemen. Even if the war ends, I can't find work. I've saved up some money, but I really don't want to be in Yemen when it runs out. Can you help?"

"Well," he told me, "I can't promise you a job, but I can promise you a place to stay until you find one. Come here, stay in my house, eat my food, and you can sort out your affairs and maybe find work."

Thankfully, the old Saida tradition of neighbors looking out for one another was alive and well, even years later and hundreds of miles from home.

My friend sent me a letter of invitation, which meant that I would be able to get a visa to travel to Albania. The only problem was that the Sana'a airport was under regular rocket fire. There were no flights in or out. I hunkered down in Sana'a, praying for a chance to leave.

In July, thank God, the communists were defeated. The war was over. On the day the airport reopened, I was there. I bought the earliest available ticket to Albania, and three days later, I was airborne. As I watched Yemen grow smaller beneath me, I felt an overwhelming sense of relief.

For the first time in my life, I walked out of an airport and didn't immediately want to buy a ticket back to where I had come from. Tirana, the capital of Albania, was a beautiful city, and the people were warm and welcoming to foreigners.

For the first couple of months, I lived in Tirana in my old friend's house. And he also got me a job interview. A friend of his was the director of the Albanian branch of the Red Crescent—a humanitarian relief organization—and my friend told him that I was a hardworking, reliable, trustworthy person.

When I went in for the interview, the director told me right off the bat that he had a job for me if I wanted it. There was just one problem: the job was to run an educational center in Patos, a town seventy-five miles south of Tirana, and the Red Crescent couldn't afford to hire an interpreter for me. I would need to learn Albanian. And the Red Crescent needed me to start right away—so I would have to get by as best I could while I learned the language.

I decided to take the job. I made my way to Patos and started looking for a place to live. I wandered around town as the residents stared at me, bug-eyed. Unlike Tirana, Patos wasn't accustomed to tourists or foreigners. I asked random strangers, using hand gestures, if they knew of anyone looking to rent out a room.

I found a welcoming family in a small two-bedroom house that rented me a room for the equivalent of about eighty dollars a month. We all got along quite well. We shared meals together—one of the first Albanian words I learned was *bukë* (bread), which the father would call out when it was mealtime. After the loneliness of Yemen, it was nice to feel like part of a family again.

My new job was wonderful. It reminded me of working at the Hira Institute. The educational center was a tranquil place overlooking a garden, where girls and boys ages six to sixteen could come and learn skills that would help them find jobs. We had a sixty-year-old woman who taught the children how to sew, and an English teacher, and after I'd been there awhile, we bought ten computers and brought in a teacher to show the children how to use Microsoft Word and other useful programs.

In addition to overseeing the center, I taught an Arabic class. While I taught the students Arabic, they taught me Albanian. I would point to something—a road, for example—and say the Arabic word, *tariiq*, and then one of the students would say the Albanian word, *rrugë*. After just four or five months of this, I had become a passable Albanian speaker. The hardest thing to get used to was that people nodded to say "no" and shook their heads to say "yes."

During that first year in Albania, there were times when I couldn't believe my good fortune. In less than a year, I had gone from being jobless, friendless, and in a war zone to feeling fulfilled, at home, and at peace.

When I was twenty-eight years old and comfortably settled, I began to think about getting married and having kids. There was a girl I had liked in high school, and as was customary, I asked my mother to speak with her mother. Then my father had a conversation with her father, and shortly after that, we got married and she moved to Albania.

I know that some people are uncomfortable with the idea of arranged marriage. I'm sure that it isn't for everyone, and I know it doesn't always work out well. On the other hand, that was the tradition in my neighborhood, and my parents and many of their friends had happy marriages. And as it turned out, Abassia and I were—and are—perfect for each other. She is my soulmate, and I can't imagine my life without her.

As Abassia and I began to build a life together in Albania, we made some close friends. One of my co-workers, Mohamed Nechla, often had us over to his house, which was in a village about ten miles outside of Patos. And on one of those occasions, Mohamed introduced us to a neighbor of his, a middle-aged widow named Houriyya, who had four sons and regretted that she'd never had a daughter. She practically adopted Abassia as her own child, and by extension, me as well.

Whenever we went to visit Houriyya, she would put bags of fruit and vegetables in our car. I would tell her, "No, that's not necessary," but she insisted. She cooked us meals and made tea for us. When I took off my shoes and socks at the door to be courteous, I would come back to find that she had taken my socks to wash them and had put clean ones in their place. I used to say, only half-kiddingly, that I had a mother in Algeria and a mother in Albania.

In 1995, a few months after we had gotten married, Abassia and I were overjoyed to learn that Abassia was pregnant. When the doctors told us we were going to have a baby girl, we were delighted. There are some people who only want sons, but I've never understood that. My mother, my sisters, my wife—they were all baby girls. Every child, male or female, is a gift from God.

When Abassia was six months pregnant, she traveled back to Algeria so that her mother and sister could help during and after the birth. I wished I could go with her, but I couldn't take that much time off from work. I called Abassia every day to see how she was doing.

I barely slept the night she gave birth. Talking to Abassia the next morning—learning that everything had gone well, that I was a father, and that we had a healthy baby girl—was one of the happiest moments of my life. There is an Algerian tradition, when a newborn arrives, of performing an *'aqiiqah*, a charitable act, to show your gratitude to God. I bought a lamb, slaughtered it, and gave the meat to needy people in Patos.

Abassia and our daughter, Raja—"Hope"—came back to Albania a few months later. I was thrilled to meet Raja. She was a bit frightened of me at first—she cried the first time I held her, and didn't stop until Abassia took her back—but she warmed up to me after a few days. She was fussy at times, in particular at 2:00 a.m. every night, when she woke up and cried until I rocked her to sleep. I adored her.

We had built a good life in Albania, and I had no intention of ever moving again. But in December of 1996, when Raja was one year old, the country devolved into anarchy and chaos.

Hundreds of thousands of Albanians had invested their savings in government-endorsed funds that falsely promised huge returns. When the funds collapsed and the government didn't take action, thousands of investors who had lost their life savings took to the streets in protest. The police and military were overwhelmed, and criminal gangs took advantage of the lawlessness to loot and kill. They smashed shop windows, broke into homes, and took whatever they wanted. No one was safe.

The educational center was shut down. Abassia and Raja and I stayed home with the doors locked and blinds drawn for days, afraid to venture out. We heard gunshots from time to time. We were running low on food, but a friend of mine who owned a bakery gave me a hundred pounds of flour—he couldn't keep his bakery open, so he didn't need it—and Abassia was able to make us bread.

I wasn't sure whether to flee Albania or try to tough it out. I hated the idea of leaving behind another group of students I'd grown close to, but I also hated the idea of Abassia and Raja being unsafe. My friend and co-worker, Mohamed Nechla, was torn as well. We decided to drive to the capital, Tirana, where things were a bit calmer. We would leave our passports and papers in the Red Crescent's main office for safekeeping, and while we were there, we would see what our options were. We took Mohamed's car.

While we were in Tirana, we stopped at a gas station to fill up. The attendant, a ten- or eleven-year-old boy, asked us about the fighting and what side we were on. "Get out of here," I told him. "You're young. You should be playing."

"Wait here," he responded. "I'll go home and get my gun and kill you."

The kid's bluster didn't scare me, but it helped me realize just how chaotic Albania had become. Even the pre-teens were threatening to kill you.

Mohamed and I told the Red Crescent director that we feared for our families, and we weren't sure we could stay in Albania. He told us that there were four countries we could relocate to: Somalia, Indonesia, Kazakhstan, or Bosnia. Of those, Bosnia made the most sense. It was close to Albania, close to Algeria, and the war there had ended two years ago. If we had to leave, that's where we would go.

When we got back to Patos, we stopped by the garage where I had stored my car and saw that it was bullet-riddled. When I looked at the damage and thought about what could have happened if Abassia and Raja had been in the car, I knew we couldn't stay in Albania any longer.

I suggested that Abassia stay with her family in Algeria while I got settled in Bosnia and made sure that it was safe. The country had been at war just two years earlier, after all. But Abassia insisted on staying by my side. "I go where you go," she told me. "We stick together in good times and in bad." And so we arrived, together, in Sarajevo in January of 1997.

The first few weeks were rough. It was snowy and bitterly cold, we didn't speak the language, and we didn't have a house or a car. Luckily, there was a kind man working at the Red Crescent, Hadj Boudella, who allowed us to stay in his house until we could find a place of our own. Hadj had also grown up in Algeria, and we quickly became good friends. After a short while in his house, we were able to find a nice apartment for rent within walking distance of my office.

Sarajevo still bore the scars of war: roads that were blocked by piles of debris, buildings that had been shelled, people whose families and lives had been ripped apart. Many of the survivors turned to the Red Crescent for help, so I found myself very busy right away. As in Pakistan, I mostly worked with orphans—children who had lost their father or both of their parents in the war.

On weekdays, I did paperwork and checked on the orphans on my list. If a kid was sick, I visited him in the hospital with a gift. If he was healthy, I visited his school and his home to see if there was anything the Red Crescent could do to improve his living situation.

I was also in charge of distributing a small stipend from the Red Crescent to the guardian of each orphan on my list. Sometimes, people with young children who weren't on the list would come by my office and ask for help. I gave them papers to fill out to try to get on the list, but I wished I could do more. I kept a stash of diapers and powdered milk behind my desk to give to needy parents. Every parent, I figured, could use diapers and milk. I knew it wasn't much, but at least no one left empty-handed.

Another one of my responsibilities was to run a daycare program for the orphans on weekends and holidays. At first, we rented space from a local school. We didn't have electricity—the school turned off the power on the weekends—but we had fun. We played sports, mostly basketball and soccer, and I hired teachers to lead Arabic and English classes. At lunchtime, I bought sandwiches and fruit for the kids, and in the afternoon each kid was picked up by his mother or uncle or grandparent.

After I'd been running the weekend daycare program for a while, I convinced the director of the Red Crescent that we should stop renting space from the school and rent a house of our own instead. We found a three-story house near a large park. We kept doing sports and Arabic and English classes, but we also bought computers and hired a computer teacher, and we got a ping-pong table, a foosball table, and a few small electric-powered cars that the five- and six-year-old kids could vroom around in. The house was a boister-ous, exuberant place.

I always carried candy in my pockets, and I often went on grocery runs to buy snacks for the house. Every time I got to the house, the same two boys would sprint up to greet me. One ran to my left pocket and the other to my right. The candy was gone in sec-onds. The two of them then demanded my car key, unlocked the back door, and carried the grocery bags into the house, usually exact-ing a small tax on the best-looking snacks. I got a kick out of those two pickpockets—their sense of mischief was exceeded only by their good nature.

Some weekends, I took the orphans on day trips into the Bosnian countryside. We would rent a bus, pack lunches, and go to a river or up into the mountains. I also brought the boys camping for a few weeks one summer—we set up tents near a river, close enough to a village that we were able to get electricity and put a lantern in each tent. The kids swam and played soccer in the daytime, and in the evenings they learned songs and played games.

Holiday time was often hard on the orphans—it was when they felt their parents' absence the most—so we made a point to throw a huge party every Eid. We had games and races and prizes and pres-ents for all the kids. They saw that there were lots of people who cared about them, and that there were other children going through the same thing as they were. They didn't have their fathers, but they had each other. In a very real sense, we were a family.

As Raja grew older, I often brought her with me to play with the or-phans. Sometimes she even came along on our day trips to the coun-tryside. I enjoyed her company, as did the orphans, and I was glad that she was getting to know, understand, and sympathize with kids whose childhoods were so much tougher than hers.

I doted on Raja. I was excited to give her all the things that I'd never had. My father hadn't been able to afford new clothes or a bike for me, but I could buy those things for her. I could take her to the sea. I could make sure that she had a playful, happy childhood, free of want or worry.

In 1999, we learned that Abassia was pregnant with our second daughter. Again, we were overjoyed, and again we decided that Abassia should give birth in Algeria so that her mother and sister could help out. We decided that we would all go to Saida during Ramadan, when Abassia was five months pregnant. We would spend the holidays with our families, and then Abassia and Raja would stay and I would return to Bosnia to get back to work. I was excited to see my parents and my brothers and sisters for the first time in almost a decade.

When we stepped off the plane in Algeria and went through passport control, airport police arrested me. I hadn't realized it, but I had been traveling on an expired passport. And it didn't help that the last time I'd gotten my passport renewed was when I'd been in Pakistan—the Algerian police were suspicious of all things Pakistani. They kept me in custody for three days while they sorted everything out.

The police were very courteous, and even brought me candy in the evenings—Ramadan tends to bring out kindness in people—but it was still a miserable experience. I was confident that they would realize I wasn't a criminal and release me soon enough, but I figured that Abassia would be nervous, and I was anxious to spend my few leave days with her and my parents and siblings before flying back to Bosnia.

After three days, the police told me that I was free to go. However, they said that to get a new passport and to make sure that I wouldn't run into trouble in the future, I needed to sign what they called a "Reconciliation" paper. Apparently, the government had recently passed a law offering amnesty to revolutionaries who renounced violence. Signing up for the amnesty, the police told me, would be the quickest way to get out and to get on with my life.

At first, I didn't want to sign the paper. I had never had anything to do with the Algerian revolution or with violence of any kind. But I needed a passport—without one, I wouldn't be able to go back to

Bosnia and I'd lose my job. And I was exhausted. So, against my better judgment, I signed the paper. I was given a temporary passport, told to contact an Algerian embassy overseas for a long-term one, and sent on my way. I spent a wonderful Ramadan and Eid with my family, and then I flew back to Bosnia and got back to work, eagerly awaiting good news from Abassia.

On April 29, 2000, Abassia gave birth to Rahma, who we named after my mother. I told my mother that I couldn't possibly thank her enough for everything she'd done for me when I was young, but I would name my daughter after her as a start. Again, as an 'aqiiqah, I bought a lamb and shared the meat with the orphans, their families, and other needy people I knew in Sarajevo.

Abassia, Raja, and Rahma stayed in Saida for a few months, until Rahma was old enough to fly. On their way back, I met them in Istanbul, where they had a layover, and we spent three days there before flying home. Getting to know Rahma was a thrill, and it was wonderful to see Abassia and Raja again. It had been incredibly difficult to be away from them for seven months.

After we got home, we settled into a nice routine. I left work fairly early, around 4:30 in the afternoon, and got home in time to meet Raja when the bus dropped her off from kindergarten. We took the elevator up to the sixteenth floor together, and she would tell me about what she'd learned in school. It was amazing how quickly she was picking up Bosnian. It got to the point that we'd be out shopping and she would correct my grammar.

In the evenings, Abassia and the children and I had dinner— either Abassia would cook or I'd pick up food from The Fountain, a little café owned by a nice couple who made good pizza and great coffee. After dinner, when it was warm enough out, we went for walks around town until bedtime. Unlike when Raja had been little, Rahma slept through the night, so we were a much better-rested family than we had been in Albania.

On the weekends, I often played soccer with friends after work. Hadj, whose house we lived in when we first arrived in Sarajevo, was a regular, as was Mustafa Ait Idir, another Algerian who did computer repair work for the Red Crescent and other local charitable organizations. Mustafa was the best athlete by far. One time, I was playing goalie—our regular goalie had left early—and I jokingly said to Mustafa, "Just try and kick one by me!" He lasered a kick so hard that when I got in front of it, it practically knocked me out. Off the field, though, he was a gentle soul. After soccer, Mustafa, Hadj, and I would meet up with our families at a restaurant or coffee shop and talk and laugh for hours.

That winter, Rahma had breathing problems, and our doctor told us that it could be because our apartment was too damp. I found a very nice apartment that was dry, warm, in a great neighborhood, and close to work. Our new home was beautiful. The fridge, the dishwasher, the living room couches—all were brand new. There was even a satellite television and a fax machine! And we were high up on a hillside, so we had a beautiful view of Sarajevo and the mountains.

On September 11, 2001, I left work, collected Raja, and went home. Abassia was upset. "Do you know what happened?" she asked. I shook my head.

"A big building just fell," she told me. "In America. An airplane flew into it."

"That's impossible," I told her. "Maybe it was a cartoon? Or a movie?"

"No," she insisted. "I saw it on the news."

I sat in front of the TV and saw that Abassia was right. It was shocking. I had no idea how someone could do something like that. Over the next few days, Al Jazeera was abuzz with speculation about who might have been behind the attacks. First, it was the Iraqis. Then, maybe the Japanese Red Army or a Yugoslavian group. After a week, it was someone I'd never heard of named Osama bin Laden. At the time, I didn't know what to think, other than that it was tragic so many innocent people lost their lives.

In late September, I got a call from the Algerian Embassy in Rome. When I had gotten back to Bosnia with my temporary passport, I had called the embassy in Rome—one of the closest Algerian embassies—to see about getting a long-term passport. Now, a year-and-a-half later, the passport was finally ready, but they told me that I had to come to Italy to pick it up.

I wound up having one day in Rome to sightsee, so I went to the Vatican. I knew that it was for Christians, but I was curious to see what it was like. I had always wanted to know more about religions other than my own, and I had many Christian friends and colleagues in Albania and Bosnia. This holy city at the center of Christian worship was strikingly beautiful. I wished I had brought a camera.

When I got back to Sarajevo, I was happy to have a long-term passport and to have the administrative hassle behind me. Hopefully, I wouldn't have to travel again anytime soon. That evening, I sat on our balcony, staring at the rooftops of Sarajevo and the mountains in the background, and felt at home and at peace. This time, I thought, maybe it will last.

Mustafa Ait Idir

I WOULD LIKE TO TELL YOU a bit about my life before it was ripped away from me, or rather, I from it.

I was raised in the town of El Madania, just a few minutes from Algiers, the capital of Algeria. My parents had moved to the city as young adults in the early 1960s, after growing up on subsistence farms in a rural Berber community. Neither one of them was literate, and my mother had not been able to go to school at all. Still, my father was able to find a job with a government company that did maintenance work for the city. He worked there for fifty years, and he always earned enough to provide for our family. I never wanted for food or clothes or schoolbooks or supplies, unlike some of my classmates.

I was the middle child, with four older siblings and four younger siblings, not counting one brother who, sadly, died in his infancy. We lived in a portion of a large, subdivided house, and we had one bathroom and three bedrooms for all of us. I shared a bedroom with my six brothers. It was a tight fit, but fortunately we all got along well.

I was a shy, quiet child. I treated all of my neighbors with respect, calling every adult "Uncle" or "Auntie" so-and-so instead of just using their first name.

From the start, I liked school. My first-grade teacher was a kind, motherly woman. I adored her so much that I still remember her name, Miss Sufiya, some forty years later. In middle and high school, my favorite subject was math. I also liked science classes, especially labs. I was always curious to learn more about the inner workings of things, whether that meant dissecting worms and lizards and various other creatures that our teacher instructed us to bring in, or going to the public library to read science magazines that I could not afford.

I enjoyed learning about foreign cultures, too. Even now, I love watching National Geographic and The Discovery Channel. I started studying French in third grade and English in eighth grade, and I liked them both. Really, the only classes I disliked were the ones that involved nothing but rote memorization, like geography and some of my music classes.

I attended El Thaelebi High School, which was located in what had once, centuries earlier, been the palace of the Turkish sultan in charge of Algeria. The sultan had built a school within his palace walls. Even though there was no longer a sultan, the classrooms were still there, and it was in those rooms that I learned how to do equations and dissections. There was a four-kilometer path, initially carved out as an escape route for the sultan, leading from my school to the Mediterranean Sea.

On my way home from school, I would stop to pray at our neighborhood mosque, Masjid Al Atiq, a beautiful building that was probably a hundred years old. My family was serious about our faith, as were most Berber families: none of us were clerics or experts on Islam, nor did we wear long beards, but we prayed routinely, behaved well, and never imbibed. I liked our imam's sermons because he was not a ranting extremist; he was a down-to-earth man focused on the practical realities of everyday life. The whole neighborhood respected him.

While I liked my school and the mosque, I lived for sports, especially soccer. There was a field between my home and school, and I would play pick-up soccer there for hours on end. I would play with one group, and when they left, I would stay and practice until another group arrived for me to play with. I did not own a soccer ball; I would fashion a makeshift one by stuffing an old milk bag with grass or paper or socks. It was never a perfect sphere, but as long as I had something to kick around, I was content.

Sometimes all of the children in the neighborhood would get together to play soccer against the children from a nearby neighborhood. For a while, each player would put in one dinar, and the winning team got to keep it all. We had to stop doing that when some parents found out and thought that it seemed too much like gambling. Instead, we decided to use the money to buy orange juice; the reward for winning would be getting to drink the juice. In reality, though, there always wound up being enough for both teams, so really we were just playing for fun, competitive pride, and the opportunity to sit around with friends and drink juice together.

I developed a reputation for being a talented soccer player, and sometimes when faraway neighborhoods played against each other, one team would recruit me for the day. It was a nice feeling to score a few goals and help a team win, and to have people all over the city know my name even though I was just a child.

I also liked watching Algeria compete in the Olympics, especially seeing the middle-distance runner Noureddine Morceli win medals and set world records. What I respected most about Morceli was his humility. Even though he was a world champion, he would walk casually around town, chatting with ordinary Algerians and never holding himself out as better than anyone else. He was also a man of faith, fasting during Ramadan despite his demanding training regimen.

I enjoyed watching some athletes from other countries as well. The Dutch soccer player Marco van Basten was a masterful, acrobatic striker, and his countryman Ronald Koeman was brilliant at turning defense into offense with gorgeous long-range passes. I admired the Japanese karate master Taiji Kase, and I watched and read everything I could about him. It was easier, though, to follow boxing, a much more prominent sport. I especially liked watching Muhammad Ali, a truly dominant boxer, and Naseem Hamed ("Prince Naseem"), a unique fighter who looked more like he was dancing than boxing.

. . .

When I was fourteen years old, I took up karate. It was becoming popular in Algeria, as were boxing and judo. I had just seen *The Karate Kid*, and one of my neighbors was often outside practicing his karate techniques. It looked like a lot of fun. I joined a club and started working my way from one belt to the next.

In 1988, shortly after I turned eighteen, my coach told me that I was ready to take the test for a black belt. Back then, everyone in the country took the test in the same place, in a city on the coast about five hundred miles from Algiers. Flying there with my coach, five other karate students, and some of our parents was the first time I had ever been on a plane.

After we landed, the coach brought us to our hotel, an elegant establishment overlooking the beach. I had never stayed in a hotel before. The next morning, I found myself in a giant hall with hundreds of other black belt applicants. Each of us went up, one at a time, before a two-judge panel who would tell us which techniques to perform. With the judges and everyone else in the hall watching, I completed each of the moves they asked me to perform. Performing in front of that many people was nerve-wracking.

I was even more anxious waiting to find out if I had earned the belt. The judges read out a list of all the applicants who had passed. Mine was the first name they read. When I heard it, I nearly fainted. I hugged my coach, and then my mother. She was so happy for me. Flying home, with my newly earned black belt in my suitcase, I felt a tremendous sense of accomplishment. It was one of the happiest days of my childhood.

After I graduated from high school in 1989, I decided to enroll in a two-year program at the nearby Asten Institute, to learn about computers and graphic design. I knew that a degree from the Asten Institute was widely respected by employers, and participating in the program would allow me to defer my compulsory military service. I had no interest in firing weapons or blindly following orders.

My first day at the Asten Institute was the first time I ever used a computer. I was sitting in a computer lab with several other students, and when our instructor told us to turn on our computers, I wanted to raise my hand and ask, "How do I do that?" Instead, I looked everywhere for an "on" switch, finally discovering it on the back of the computer. Once the Macintosh hummed to life, the instructor started explaining how to use it. She was an excellent teacher whose expertise and clear guidance made it fun to learn. I sat in front of a screen from 8:00 to noon, five days a week, and eventually became reasonably adept at graphic design.

Once I received my certificate from the Asten Institute, I enrolled in a business administration program at another institute. I was not interested in the subject and rarely attended class, but simply signing up meant that I could postpone military service for another two years. I was able to earn some money working with my older brother, who ran a business painting houses. I was not a painter, but I was able to help him with menial tasks like spackling a wall or mixing paint.

During that time, I started looking for work in graphic design, but employers were only interested in applicants with experience. To gain experience, I volunteered to work as an unpaid intern for a local newspaper, *Al-Salaam*. Newspaper layout involved more complicated, less intuitive software programs than the ones that exist nowadays. Journalists would give me their text, and I would arrange it into neat columns interspersed with pictures.

In 1993, I was still struggling to find paying work when I was offered a position with the International Islamic Relief Organization (IIRO). They were about to open an office in Split, Croatia, to assist Bosnian refugees, and they were looking for someone to help maintain the office computers. They were having trouble finding someone who was familiar with Macintoshes, and I had trained on a Macintosh, so they were eager to hire me.

I was reluctant to leave my family and Algiers, the only place I had ever known, but this was my only employment offer. And Algerians over the age of twenty-eight were exempted from military service; if I left and did not come home for five years, I would be able to avoid the military altogether. I took the job.

To get to Croatia, I flew from Algiers to Rome and then took an eighteen-hour train ride to Zagreb, the capital of Croatia. Seeing Croatia for the first time, I was struck by the country's natural beauty. And yet, it was not nearly as economically and technologically developed as Italy.

After two days of orientation at the IIRO headquarters in Zagreb, I flew to Split, a city on the Adriatic Sea approximately fifty miles from the Bosnian border. At first, I lived with three other Algerians, renting out the ground floor of a house from a landlord who lived on the second floor. The Algerians were students who had received a scholarship from the government to study in Split. I felt very fortunate to have housemates with whom I shared a language and culture.

I was homesick. I had never been away from Algeria before, and I missed my parents, brothers, and sisters. I spoke with them on the telephone whenever I could. I also mailed them a letter with some pictures of Split, but they never received it, so I stopped sending letters. At one point, my brother came to visit me for a few weeks, and it was wonderful to see him. In fact, I still have some of his pictures from that trip, more than two decades later.

Eventually, the three Algerian students moved out. I could not afford our whole floor by myself, so I rented a room in the home of a friendly middle-aged Croatian couple. We got along wonderfully. We sat down for meals together when we could, and my language skills improved rapidly thanks to our conversations. They were so hospitable that they refused to let me pay my share of the electric and phone bills; sometimes I would simply take the bills and pay them without permission.

In the evenings, I continued to do karate. I joined a karate club in Split where I coached children and trained and competed with adults, many of whom became good friends of mine. I was the only Muslim in the club, which mostly consisted of Catholic Croats and Orthodox Serbs, but I never felt out of place. I loved going there, and I practiced enough that I was able to win several competitions. For about three years, I was the champion of the southern region of Croatia.

At one point, the Croatian National Team recruited me, offering me Croatian citizenship so that I would be able to join the team and compete in international events. It was tempting, but I declined, fearing that Croatian citizenship would require me to fight in Croatia's military. In hindsight, I wish I had accepted the offer.

Instead of competing on the Croatian team, I continued to coach in the evenings and work for the IIRO during the days. My job mostly involved entering data into a system that tracked donations to make sure the money went to its intended recipient, rather than being siphoned off by bureaucrats. I also occasionally assisted with projects that did not involve computers, like distributing food to refugees or pitching tents for them to sleep under. I felt like I was doing important, worthwhile work.

In 1993, my work led me to meet the woman who is now my wife. She had been a schoolteacher in Bosnia before the war, and in 1993 she was teaching classes to Bosnian refugee children in Croatia. She and I are opposites in many ways. Where I can be somewhat impetuous and spontaneous, she is more patient and thinks things through before she acts. I can be quick-tempered and stormy; she is the calm. We fell in love, and I have been blessed to have her by my side, at least in spirit, ever since. I would tell you more about how I met her and fell in love with her, but in my culture, those sorts of details are for a husband and wife to talk about only with each other; they are a treasure not to be shared with the outside world.*

In 1995, after the conflict in Bosnia finally ended, the IIRO decided to shut down its office in Split. There was no longer a significant influx of new refugees, so the IIRO felt its resources could be better

* Translator's Note: Mustafa made it clear that his wife's privacy is extremely important to her, and also to him. For that reason, her name does not appear in this book.

used elsewhere. I was offered a position doing similar work at a similar organization, Qatar Charities, in Zenica, Bosnia. It seemed like a perfect fit, especially since I could not go back to Algeria until 1998 without being conscripted into the military.

After moving to Zenica, my fiancée and I were married in June of 1996. Our first son, Mohamed, was born the following year. We relocated to Tuzla when Qatar Charities promoted me to be the director of a small office there. Then, in 1997, when Qatar Charities closed down the Tuzla office, I took a position in Sarajevo with Taibah International, a charitable organization headquartered in Washington, D.C.

Taibah offered free courses for children who wanted to improve their English and computer skills, with some classes on specific programs like Word, Windows, and Autocad, and other classes on more general topics. Taibah also had classes for adults, usually charging a fee well below what most organizations charged for similar classes. Taibah's students came from diverse backgrounds. There were Muslims, Croats, and Serbs. There were even high-ranking officials from the Egyptian, Saudi Arabian, and Libyan embassies, as well as members of the Bosnian Federation Police.

I worked at Taibah as a computer technician. My job was to fix and maintain the hardware and to keep the software running. I was very happy to work at Taibah. My co-workers were friendly, and so were the students. I did not get to know anyone at Taibah closely, since my co-workers and I did not socialize outside of work and the students' courses only lasted a week or two, but everyone seemed nice.

Each morning, I would wake up before dawn to say my prayers. If it was early enough, I might doze for a bit before eating breakfast and heading off to work. My wife was not working at the time, so she was home with me in the mornings.

My workday usually ended around 4:00 p.m., but I could sometimes leave a half-hour early if I wasn't very busy. On some days, I played soccer in the evenings. I would come home from work and rest for a bit, then grab my bag and go to the field, which I could see from my home. Our games typically began at 5:00 p.m. and lasted until 6:30. After soccer, I would race home to drop off my soccer bag, change into my karate uniform, and head back out. I worked with two karate teams. From 7:00 p.m. to 8:30, I coached young children as they trained. Then, from 8:30 to 10:00, I received training as a member of the Bosnian karate team. I would get home around 10:30 or 11:00, and the next day I would wake up and do it all over again.

The routine was exhausting. Fortunately, the director of the karate team was understanding, and he let me try a few different schedules. I also cut back on soccer, usually only playing on weekends and Tuesday nights. The Tuesday night game was with a group of highly educated men, almost all of whom were professors, teachers, or businessmen. I have played with that group since 1997, and have almost never missed a game as a free man.

In 1998, I became good friends with Lakhdar Boumediene, who was working at another charitable organization in Sarajevo. On Saturdays, we played soccer with a group of men we both knew, and on Sundays I taught karate and soccer to some of the orphans being taken care of by Lakhdar. Our families would often spend time together on the weekends as well, and I would fix his computer when it broke.

In 1999, I performed the *hajj* to Mecca with several friends of mine. We drove there in two cars, and it was a seventeen-day road trip through Romania, Bulgaria, Turkey, Syria, and Jordan. Each day, we would drive until we came across an area that seemed like it would be a good place to camp, and then we would pitch our tents and make a campfire. The roads were pothole-riddled and every border crossing official demanded a bribe, but otherwise, it was an excellent trip.

My wife and I had another boy, Hamza, in 2000. On some Sundays in the winter, I would take my family to ski and play in the snow. In the summer, we often went to a lovely little spot on the edge of a forest outside the city, with ducks and a playground and nice restaurants. I also sometimes brought the kids to the swimming pool, and when Mohamed turned four, I started taking him with me when I played soccer.

On September 11, 2001, I was at the gym. I had just finished my karate training for the day, and I went downstairs to sit and have a cup of coffee. There was a television in the facility, near where I was sitting. On the screen, I saw images of a plane hitting a building, but I was not able to hear the television. Since they usually played movies on that television, I assumed it was a film. Other people were watching, and no one thought that it was real. Not a single person said something like, "My God, look what's happening."

I went back home and I turned on the television there. When I saw the exact same footage on Al Jazeera, I realized it was not a movie after all. The reporters said that a group of people had attacked the building with airplanes. It was real, it happened. The building collapsed and people died. Even today, when I think about it, I wonder how somebody could fly an aircraft into a building.

After everything that has happened to me since that day, some people probably think that I had some kind of connection with Al Qaeda. Anyone who actually knew me would have thought that was absurd. I had no connections with terrorism, nor with any terrorist groups. Many of my karate teammates were members of the Bosnian Special Police Force. They were not the kind of people a terrorist would associate with.

At the time, thanks be to God, I had never had any trouble with the law whatsoever. I had taken the proper steps to register myself and my sons with a nearby Algerian embassy, in Budapest, thinking that I would soon travel back to Algeria to see my parents and siblings for the first time in nearly a decade. I never had anything to hide or anyone I thought I needed to hide from.

Lakhdar

WHEN YOUR WHOLE LIFE IS UPENDED because of a phone call, there are things you wonder about. *What if I'd been in a meeting? What if my phone had been off?*

It was an otherwise uneventful autumn day when my cell phone rang. I answered it. The woman on the other end was stammering in Bosnian through tears. "My husband," she sobbed. "The police have taken him."

At my job, I'd developed a knack for distinguishing between genuine emotion and the crocodile tears of people trying to take advantage of the Red Crescent. This distress was real.

I tried to soothe her. "Calm down. Let's go back to the beginning. First of all, your husband. Who is he?"

She told me his name, and when I didn't recognize it, she reminded me how I knew him. He lived in Zenica, a city about forty-five minutes north of Sarajevo. He had come by the office in Sarajevo a couple of times with his daughters, looking for help, and I'd given him some Pampers and powdered milk. He was from Algeria too, and he had taken one of my business cards on his way out.

"Okay," I said. "So what's he in trouble for?"

"I don't know. I don't know!"

"Okay, then. Don't cry. Everything will be all right. We'll figure something out, Insha'Allah."

And that's how we left it. She hung up, mollified for the moment, and I sat at my desk thinking about how I might be able to help. A few minutes later, she called a second time, panic still in her voice.

"Please, there must be something you can do!"

"Okay," I said, hoping I sounded reassuring. "I can't do anything right now, but tomorrow, I'll try to find you a lawyer."

After all, I couldn't release her husband—I wasn't the government, and for that matter, I had no idea what he'd been charged with or what he had done—but everyone, I figured, is entitled to a lawyer. And I had to do *something*. He, like me, was an Algerian living abroad with two young daughters, and his wife, in her distress, had turned to me for help.

The next morning, I woke up early and drove to Zenica. I had driven through the city several times, since it was on the way to some of the schools and homes that I visited for work, but I had never spent much time there. I found a parking lot downtown, got out, and asked the first person I came across if he knew where I could find a lawyer. He pointed down a nearby street, which I walked along until I came to a door with a small rectangular placard: "Law Office."

I opened the door and was greeted by a friendly young woman. After we exchanged good mornings, I asked if she was a lawyer.

"No," she replied, "I'm a secretary. The attorney is out of town today. Is there something I can help you with?"

"Well," I explained, "I'm trying to hire a lawyer for someone."

"Who?"

"I don't know," I answered. I hadn't recognized the name when I'd heard it, and for the life of me I couldn't remember it. The secretary laughed.

"No, really," I protested, "I'm being serious." I took my cellphone out of my pocket and showed her the screen. "A woman called me from this number and told me that the police took her husband. She's distraught, she's poor, and I'd like to help her. Is that possible?"

"Sure," she said, sounding sympathetic. She told me that without knowing who the man was or why he'd been arrested, she couldn't be sure what his case would cost, but she thought that 250 marks (about $125) would probably cover it. I went to a nearby ATM and withdrew 500 marks. "Keep half of it for the legal fees," I told her, "and when you meet with this poor woman, give her the rest to buy food and whatever else she needs for her children."

The secretary took down the woman's phone number and promised to call her to arrange a meeting. I thanked her and headed out, feeling good about having done what I could to help. As I left, almost as an afterthought, I handed her my business card so she could call me if there were any problems.

It was still early when I got back to Sarajevo, about 8:30 a.m., so before going to work I stopped by a café and bought a coffee and the paper. One of the front-page stories jumped out at me—it was about an Algerian man arrested in Zenica. This, I thought, must be the man whose wife I had just helped. As I read on, I was startled by the accusation against him: that he was a terrorist with connections to Osama bin Laden. *What have I gotten myself into?* I wondered. But I reminded myself that I barely knew the man. All I had done was help a poor woman hire a lawyer. Surely, I reassured myself, there couldn't be anything wrong with that.

About ten days later, on October 19, 2001, the police came for me.

The night before, the wives of my good friends and coworkers Mohamed Nechla and Mustafa Ait Idir had both called me. Mohamed and Mustafa had been arrested. Their wives had no idea why, and I couldn't think of any reason either—Mohamed and Mustafa were the last people you would expect to run into trouble with the law. So, early on the morning of the 19th, before going to my own office, I stopped by the Red Crescent's central office in downtown Sarajevo to talk with my boss about the situation and what we could do to help.

"I'll look into it," my boss told me, and we scheduled a follow-up meeting for later that morning. I drove to my office and spent a few hours—my last hours of freedom, as it turned out, for almost a decade—doing paperwork. A bit before 11:00 a.m., I drove back to the central office.

As I walked toward the office building, one of the guards at the front gate asked for my ID. I was surprised—I was on a first-name basis with most of the guards, including this one, and it had been years since I'd been asked for identification. Seeing my quizzical expression, the guard explained, "I recognize you, of course, but just for today we're collecting them. You'll get it back on your way out."

"Okay," I shrugged, handing him my ID. As he took it from me, I noticed that there was another man standing slightly behind him—a uniformed police officer I had never seen before. The whole thing struck me as a bit odd, but I had a meeting to get to, so I turned away from the two men and started to walk in.

I made it about seven or eight steps before the police officer called after me: "Hold on a minute." I turned. The officer had taken my ID from the guard and was studying it intently. "Could you come with me for a minute?" he asked. "Of course," I replied.

The officer removed a piece of paper from his pocket. "Are you Boumediene?" He was polite, but still it sounded like an accusation.

"I am."

"Lakhdar Boumediene?"

"Yes."

"Born April 27, 1966?"

"That's me."

"Okay. I need you to stay here for a minute." The officer pulled out his phone, dialed a number, and said, "I have him. He's here with me."

Soon afterward, a white car pulled up—I didn't notice what kind, but it wasn't a police car—and three official-looking people (two young men and one young woman) climbed out. "Where is your car?" they asked, and I walked them to it. "We have a warrant to search it," one of them said, presenting me with formal-looking documents. I had no idea why they'd want to look in my Volkswagen, but I unlocked it and told them to go ahead. I had nothing to hide.

The search took quite a while. They looked under the seats, in the wheel frames, inside the steering wheel. I was bewildered. "What's this all about?" I wondered aloud, but they said they weren't allowed to tell me. "I have a right to know," I insisted. At one point, my friend Hadj Boudella walked by and asked what was going on. I told him I had no idea, and we chatted for a few minutes while the officials continued their search.

After they finished with my car, they wanted to look around inside the building, but my boss wouldn't let them. He pointed out that their warrant only mentioned me, and that my office was in a different building in another part of town. They said "Okay," put me in their white car, and started driving to my office.

As we drove toward my office, I thought more about what could possibly be going on. *Who are these people? What do they want from me?* I wondered if this had something to do with Mohamed and Mustafa's arrests, or with the Algerian man whose wife I'd helped the week before. Whatever it was all about, I was sure it was just a simple misunderstanding that would be resolved soon enough. I would go along with them, show them what they wanted to see, and they'd quickly realize that I was a decent, law-abiding man.

Once we got to my office, they started combing through it, looking at each item on my bookshelves and going through each drawer of my desk. I had a nervous moment when they got to a box of videotapes and I realized I had no idea what was on them—one of my co-workers down the hall had run out of space in his office and put a few boxes in mine. The videotapes, I was amused to later learn, were recordings of Saturday morning children's cartoons.

Less amusing was when the officials packed up my computer and the two-foot-high stack of CD-ROMs sitting next to it. "Hold on," I argued. "Don't take those. I won't be able to do my work without them." They told me that I would get them back shortly, as soon as they finished examining them. I worried about how I would be able to get anything done in the meantime, but there wasn't much I could do.

When they finished going through my office, I thought we might finally be done, but no: they wanted to search my house. "Fine," I sighed. "It's just down the street." On hearing this, one of the officials got agitated, whipped out his phone, punched in a number, and started swearing. From what I was able to overhear, I gathered that another group of officials had been assigned to stake out my house, but had gotten the wrong address—they were outside my old apartment, clear on the other side of town, carefully observing whoever was living there now.

The mix-up made me nervous: Bosnia had a strict law about updating your ID card every time you moved, and I didn't want the official to think that I hadn't complied. I showed him my ID, pointed out the address on it—which was current—and asked him if I'd done anything wrong.

"No," he laughed. "Not you. They're the idiots. They're the ones who went to the wrong address."

When we got to my house, I called up to Abassia on the intercom and let her know that we had guests, so she could put on her hijab—like most Muslim women, she didn't wear it in the house when it was just us and the kids. As we walked in and she caught sight of the officials, she was understandably startled, but I reassured her that it was just some sort of silly misunderstanding.

"Everything will be fine," I promised.

They searched our home. The female official patted down Abassia and went through her belongings while the others investigated the rest of our house. At one point, they started tapping on the walls and ceilings, I guess listening for hollow spots. "Are you looking for drugs?" I joked, baffled by what they were doing but trying to stay lighthearted. They didn't answer.

The hardest part was when they took Raja's computer. We had bought it a little while back—I would occasionally read the news on it, but mostly she used it to play games. She was watching when they picked it up and carried it out. She didn't say a word, and she didn't cry, but I'll never forget the glare she daggered at them through squinty eyes.

It was late afternoon when they finally finished their search. They told me that they needed just a little more of my time. "Come with us for thirty minutes, and then you can return home," one of them said. "Okay," I assented, relieved that the craziness would soon be over. As we were walking out, I told my wife not to worry: "They're confused about something, but I'm going to go with them and we'll get it all straightened out. I'll be back in about half an hour." There were other people in the room, so I didn't kiss her goodbye.

Immediately upon arriving at the central police station, they finger-printed and photographed me.

"No," I objected. "Why are you doing this?"

"It's routine procedure," I was told. "We do this to everyone. It doesn't mean anything."

After I scrubbed the ink off my hands, one of the officials, a Croat, brought me into a windowless office and sat down across from me. He was going to begin questioning me, he said, but first he needed to know if I wanted a lawyer.

"Why don't you tell me what this is all about and then I'll decide?" I answered. After all, why waste time and money getting a lawyer if this was just a simple misunderstanding that I could clear up myself?

It was then that I heard, for the first time, the allegation against me. "You are suspected," the Croat told me, "of conspiring to bomb the American Embassy in Sarajevo."

It was so absurd that I couldn't help but laugh. I had never con-spired to hurt anything, and for that matter, I only vaguely knew where the American Embassy was. *Maybe*, I thought, *I'm on* Candid Camera. I looked up at the spot on the ceiling where the hidden camera would be.

"I'm a family man," I said into the camera. "I have a busy job. If this is *Candid Camera*, I don't have time for games."

"No," the Croat said soberly. "Let's talk."

A million thoughts collided in my head. One was that I obviously wouldn't make it home in half an hour. Another was that I would definitely need a lawyer. With the Croat's permission, I called my boss at the Red Crescent and asked for help. He said he would contact the law firm that did most of the organization's legal work and have them send an attorney over right away.

As we waited for the lawyer, I thought more about the terrible crime I had been accused of, and my shock began to turn into anger. *How dare they?* I should have kept my mouth shut, but I couldn't. All day I had been patient, polite, good-natured—and then to be accused of *this*. It was too much.

"You people," I sputtered. "You shallow, busy people. You have no principles. How can you even say something like that to me?" As I went on, my voice grew louder. "Do you have a shred of evidence? Have I ever even entered the American Embassy? Is there a report? Show me the report. Tell me who said these awful things about me so I can—"

And then my lawyer walked in. "Calm down and let me do the talking," he said. "You're going to have a court hearing tomorrow"— this seemed odd, court on Saturday, but everything about the situation was odd—"and I'll do what I can." The lawyer and I spoke for a few more minutes, but it wasn't long before the officials ushered him out. "We'll talk more tomorrow," he said as he left.

The officials offered me dinner, but I was in no mood to eat, so I declined. They asked if I wanted to go to a prison cell to sleep for the night. "Prison?" I repeated incredulously. "Why prison? On what basis?" I figured I was entitled to at least one day in court before I should have to spend a night in prison. "I'll stay right where I am," I told them.

And that's what happened. My first night away from my wife and children passed with me sitting upright in an office chair in the middle of a windowless, soulless room, flanked by a guard on either side of me to make sure I didn't try to escape.

I couldn't sleep. It was my restless mind, not the chair or the guards, that kept me up. I tried to figure out why anyone might think I was involved in a plot to attack the American Embassy. *Have I ever had anything to do with the Embassy?* I asked myself. *I've never requested a visa. I don't have any friends who work there. I've never gotten into a fight with an American.* I spent all night thinking and came up with nothing.

In the morning, a new official came in, carrying himself as though he were important. "How are you?" he asked in an oily voice. I assumed the question was rhetorical, given the circumstances. "Tea?" he offered. I told him I drank coffee, and he sent a guard to get me a cup. Then he started questioning me.

"How do you know Belkacem Bensayah?"

The name sounded familiar, but it took me a minute to place it. It was the name I had heard on the phone and then hadn't been able to recall in the law office: the Algerian whose wife I had helped. I explained to the official that I didn't really know Belkacem—that I'd given him some diapers and some milk when he stopped by my office with his daughters, and that I'd helped his wife find a lawyer after she had called me in tears. That was it.

For at least a couple of seconds, I thought that maybe I finally knew what was going on. Maybe Belkacem was suspected of plotting to attack the American Embassy, and the officials had found my business card and thought I was involved. But then the official asked his next question.

"And how do you know Mustafa Ait Idir and Mohamed Nechla?"

I was shocked to hear their names. I knew they had been arrested, but I couldn't believe that they were suspected of the same crime as I was. After all, what did they have to do with the American Embassy or this Belkacem character? I answered the official's question honestly: "They're good friends of mine."

"And Hadj Boudella?"

This was too much. "Even Hadj is a terrorist?" I laughed.

"Yes."

"He's locked up here too?"

"No," the official answered. "We haven't found him yet."

This was surprising, since he'd been standing right next to me when the officials were searching my car. But it gave me an idea— one I'll always regret.

"Do you believe in logic?" I asked the official.

"Yes."

"One plus one is what?"

"Two."

"You say Hadj is a terrorist?"

"Yes."

"So if he found out that the police were searching for him, would he flee or would he stick around?"

"He'd flee."

"So if I call him and ask him to come in to the central police station, and he does, that means he's not a terrorist, right?"

"Right."

"Give me the phone."

The official hesitated. "For all I know, you could be saying anything to him."

"You can listen," I assured him. "I won't talk to him in Arabic. I'll only speak in Bosnian."

The official seemed satisfied by this. He handed me the phone and I dialed Hadj's number, eager to prove my point. Hadj picked up, we exchanged hellos, and I asked him where he was.

"At work," he answered.

"Okay," I said. "I'm being held by the police, and they're looking for you as well. Could you please come down to the central police station?"

"No problem." Hadj sounded a bit bewildered, but he was eager as ever to oblige a friend's request. It cost him seven years of his life. He walked into the police station on his own two feet and still they thought he was a terrorist.

I'm sure the police would have eventually found Hadj on their own, or at least that's what I tell myself. But it doesn't change the fact that he came in because I asked him to.

By the time Hadj got to the police station, I had been whisked away to the courthouse. I was hoping I'd have a chance to talk with my lawyer before my hearing, but instead I was marched straight into one of the courtrooms. Moments before we entered the courtroom, the officials put handcuffs on me for the first time.

Waiting inside the courtroom were my lawyer, the prosecutor, and the judge. Judge Jasminka gazed down from her bench at me and the two guards flanking me. She said a few words to one of the lawyers in Bosnian, and that's when it struck me that I ought to have an interpreter. My Bosnian was good, but I really didn't want there to be any misunderstandings. When I mentioned this, the judge and both lawyers agreed.

It being the weekend, finding an interpreter took time. Apparently, no one in Sarajevo was available, but after several hours they found someone in another city who was willing to come in. It was close to 5:00 p.m. when the hearing finally started.

The first question I was asked was how I knew Abu Zubaydah. That was easy: I didn't. In fact, I didn't even recognize the name. It's possible I'd seen it in the paper or heard it on the news, but it hadn't made any impression on me.

"That's the first time I've heard that name," I testified.

"And what about Belkacem Bensayah?"

"I barely know him," I said, and repeated the explanation I'd given at the police station about the few interactions I'd had with Belkacem and his wife.

Next, I was asked about three people I did know: Mustafa, Mohamed, and Hadj. It still surprised me to hear their names. *How could anyone think they had anything to do with such a horrible crime?* I said as much to the judge.

"They're good friends of mine. And let me tell you something about them: they're good men. I know they're not terrorists or criminals or anything like that. If one of them is, I'll gladly spend fifty years in prison myself—I'll promise you that right now, no problem."

After all, I worked with these men, played soccer with them, shared meals with them. I knew their wives and I'd watched their babies turn into toddlers. I trusted them.

I was asked a few more questions and the hearing came to an end. Hours later, the judge issued her ruling: I was to be kept in prison for one month while an investigation took place. Hearing this was, at the time, the worst moment of my life.

As the guards ushered me out of the courthouse, one at each arm, my lawyer told me not to panic. He promised to contact my family and let them know what was going on. (I hadn't been allowed to call Abassia since I had told her, the day before, that I would be home in half an hour.) My lawyer left, the guards put me in a car, and a short drive later we were at the prison.

I was processed. The guards took my watch, my ID cards, and what little money I had on me and placed everything in a manila envelope. They tried to take my wedding ring too, but I'd put on some weight since I'd gotten married, and they were unable to pry it from my finger. After taking my belongings, the guards deposited me in a holding cell with five other men.

That first night, I didn't sleep. I just sat there thinking, *What am I doing here?* I was apprehensive about my cellmates and sick at the thought of what Abassia and the girls must be going through. And I missed them. It was going to be a long month.

When day broke, I saw that the cell wasn't as grim as I had initially expected—most likely because it was a cell for people under investigation, not convicted criminals. The room was fairly large, with a table and chairs and a small television in one corner, a toilet and sink in the other, and beds in between. It was good that it wasn't too cramped, since I wound up spending almost twenty-four hours a day there. The guards would occasionally let us out to walk around a snowy little courtyard, but in the Bosnian winter, we could never stay outside for more than a few minutes at a time.

My cellmates, like my cell, turned out to be much better than I had feared at first. They saw me as an innocent political prisoner and treated me with respect. One of them, a graying, grizzled man, seemed genuinely perturbed by my arrest. "I know that you aren't guilty," he sympathized, "and the Bosnian government probably knows it too. But they aren't in charge. The way politics are in this country nowadays, the Americans and Europeans call the shots. They do whatever they want."

Family visits were allowed on Thursdays, so on October 25th, my fifth day in jail, I was finally able to see Abassia for the first time since I had been taken to the police station. She brought me clean clothes and a home-cooked meal. I wasn't able to hug her or even to hold her hand—there was a glass divider between us, just like in the movies, with four inmates in a row on one side, four visitors lined up on the other, and a group of guards listening in—but hearing her voice and her faith in me made me feel better about the future.

For the rest of my time in jail, Abassia never missed a Thursday visit. She also sent me a home-cooked meal as often as the prison allowed her to, which was once every few days. The prison food was awful, so I never ate it. Instead, I rationed myself tiny portions of the meals that Abassia sent, making each one last for the two or three days until the next one arrived. The visits and meals might not seem like life-changing things, but knowing that Abassia was there for me and believed in me was what made it possible to survive.

On some of the Thursday visits, Abassia would bring our baby with her. Rahma would play and coo and bounce and sleep, blissfully unaware of her grim surroundings. Seeing her was a delight. Abassia offered to bring Raja as well, but Raja was older—old enough to know what this place was, and old enough to remember it—so I said no. I didn't want her to have memories of visiting her father in jail.

My other regular visitor was my lawyer, who came in a few times a week to deliver a report from the court on the government's ongoing investigation. The report summarized what the police had looked at and what they'd found. "Examined CD #21: list of potential gifts for orphans," for example, or "Examined phone records: no calls to Afghanistan or Pakistan." The reports never contained anything even mildly suspicious, so as my fourth week in jail drew to a close, I was optimistic that the government would soon admit their mistake and let me go home.

Instead, on what I had expected to be my second-to-last day in jail, my lawyer informed me that the court had extended my sentence by two months—the government had requested more time to complete its investigation. "But," my lawyer reassured me, "that's the longest they can possibly keep you. Under Bosnian law, after three months, they either have to convict you or set you free. No matter what."

I was crushed to learn that the day I'd been counting down to was really just another day, another day in jail, and there would be sixty more just like it. But I steeled myself to be strong. I had survived it for one month, so I could tough it out for two more. No matter what, they couldn't keep me there any longer than that.

So I waited. Besides talking to my cellmates, reading the investigation reports, and seeing Abassia and Rahma on Thursdays, I mostly passed time by watching the news on the little television in our cell and reading the newspaper.

The news stories that I was most interested in, of course, were the ones about my co-defendants and me. "The Algerian Group," they called us, or "The Algerian Six." At first, the stories were almost all negative. "Algerian Six Plotted Bombings on Bosnian Soil," an early headline read. The press simply repeated the government's accusations as though they were fact.

In time, though, the media coverage began to shift. As the weeks passed and the government's investigation still hadn't turned up any evidence, I started seeing editorials that were skeptical about the case against us. And journalists who took the time to do research reported that we didn't have violent pasts, and were in fact family men who had worked for charities before our arrests. During my second and third months in jail, I even saw articles about protests and demonstrations on our behalf, held not only by our families and co-workers but also by everyday Bosnians we did not know. It was uplifting to know that so many people were on my side.

The authorities remained convinced that I was "the worst of the worst." I didn't fully realize this until the first time the guards brought me somewhere outside the prison. It was during Ramadan. I was fasting every day and never got enough food to make up for it at night, so I was having fainting spells, and the prison doctor insisted that I be taken to a clinic where they could run some tests. As the guards walked me out of prison and into a police car, handcuffed, I was surprised to see a large group of armed policemen and police cars cordoning off the area. There were police dogs everywhere. On the way to the clinic, we were escorted by what seemed like a dozen police cars, their lights flashing and sirens blaring. *Wow*, I thought. *All this for one person?* It was as though they expected something out of a Jean Claude Van Damme movie: a gang of my burly accomplices would swoop in and I would snap out of my dizziness and start kickboxing everyone in sight.

Finally, on January 17th, 2002, the three months were up. By the end of the day, under Bosnian law, the court either had to convict me—without a shred of evidence—or order my release.

That morning, I was feeling ill, and a medical officer gave me an injection of medicine. I don't know what it was, but it didn't help much. I perked up around noon, though, when Abassia visited.

"By the end of the day," I told her, "I will be a free man, Insha'Allah."

After Abassia left, I spent the rest of the day watching the television in my cell. I had become accustomed to learning about my life from the news.

At 8:00 p.m., the report came. "Good evening," the female news anchor said. "Our lead story tonight is the Bosnian Supreme Court's decision in the case of the 'Algerian Six.' The court has ordered their immediate release." I was elated, but most of all, I was relieved. Soon enough, I would get to go home to my wife, my daughters, and my normal life.

I spent the next fifteen minutes or so daydreaming about the future and all the little things that I would now appreciate even more. I said goodbye to a few of my cellmates and thanked them for their kindness. A guard came into my cell with a sheet of paper for me to fill out, and after I did, he told me that I should come with him to reclaim my belongings.

Unbelievable as it might sound, it was just as I was walking out of the cell that the television caught my attention. I heard my lawyer's voice. His tone was urgent. "I just tried to speak with my client," he told the reporter, "but I wasn't allowed in. I have been informed that my client is going to be transported from the Bosnian prison to a second site in Europe and from there to Guantanamo."

The guard ushered me downstairs, and we stood in a long, plain hallway near a door that led outside. Two other members of the "Algerian Six" were already there: Saber Lahmar, whom I'd never met before, and Mustafa.

After a minute or two, another officer walked in, tapped Mustafa on the shoulder, and gestured to the door. "Time for you to go," the officer said, and Mustafa walked out. The officer quickly shut the door behind Mustafa, but I was still able to hear Mustafa shout. "Lakhdar! Don't come out! There are police and dogs and—"

And then the shouting stopped. I will never forget that my friend's first instinct in that moment was to try to warn me.

Mustafa

OCTOBER 18TH, 2001, began just like any other day. As usual, I woke up, said my prayers, got in the car, went to work, and came home. As usual, I finished my karate training around 10:00 p.m. When I got home, I started working on a laptop that needed to be repaired.

It was less than an hour later when I was interrupted by a soft knock at the door. I opened the door to see a large group of police officers, maybe ten or so. Some officers were in uniform, others in civilian clothes. Three of the officers were members of the UN International Police Task Force;* one was from Ghana, one was from Argentina, and the third was from Jordan. The Jordanian told me, in Arabic, that they had a court order to search my home. Honestly, they were all very courteous. I told them they were welcome to come in, and I asked one of the officers what they were looking for.

"Weapons," he said. He did not elaborate.

The officers searched for hours. Our home was a tiny place to be searched by so many people, with just three bedrooms, one bathroom, and the kitchen, but they conducted an extremely thorough search. One policeman noticed I had a little jar of *Zamzam* water, which I had brought back with me from Mecca after performing the *hajj*.† I offered him some and he took a sip.

---

* Translator's Note: In December of 1995, in accordance with the Peace Agreement between Bosnia, Croatia, and Serbia, the UN Security Council established the UN International Police Task Force to monitor and assist Bosnian law enforcement personnel. Forty-seven countries contributed civilian police personnel. More information is available online at http://www.un.org/en/peacekeeping/missions/past/unmibh/facts.html.

† Translator's Note: The Well of Zamzam is located twenty meters east of the Kaaba, the most holy place in Islam, and is believed to have been created by God when Abraham's infant son was crying in thirst. Millions of Muslims visit the well each year and obtain water while performing their pilgrimage to Mecca.

Another officer asked me for my cellphone. I had turned it off because it was late at night, so he switched it on and asked for my password. I willingly wrote it down on a piece of paper. I had nothing to fear. Most of the contacts in my phone were karate trainers or karate students I had trained, and the rest were friends and relatives.

Then they told me that they needed to take my computer with them. I suggested that they instead put the data from the computer onto a hard disc, and then go back to their office and search the contents there. If they brought the computer out of my home, I insisted that I would no longer be responsible for it, because they would be able to modify the contents of it.

"We wouldn't do anything like that," one of the policemen promised.

"I don't know any of you," I responded. "I accept guarantees from myself only."

The police contacted their supervisor, who insisted that they take the computer with them.

Finally, around 2:00 a.m., they said they were finished. They took the computer and left. I thought it was over, but then one police officer in civilian clothes came back.

"Mustafa," he said, "can you come to the police station with us? We need to ask you a few questions."

"Fine," I sighed.

I wanted to take my own car, but the officer informed me that the police would take me and then bring me back. As I was leaving, my wife and son both started crying, my wife because she was scared and Mohamed because he was sick.

I tried to comfort them. "I am just going to go answer their questions and then they will bring me back," I said. "There is nothing to worry about."

I was not scared or nervous. I knew I had nothing to hide. But Mohamed started coughing and crying even harder.

"Daddy," he pleaded. "I'm sick."

That was when they took me away. I couldn't tend to my sick child. He was four years old, he was crying out for his father, and the next time he saw me he was eleven. I will never forget that. I will never forgive that.

They brought me to the police station in Sarajevo. There, a man took my fingerprints and my picture. I wondered why. I asked him, "Am I a criminal?" He told me that everyone the police find suspicious has to be fingerprinted and photographed. But I still did not know why they found me suspicious. They had not found anything at my home. I had not *done* anything.

Once they had gotten their prints and pictures, I was moved next door, to the Ministry of Interior. It was around 3:00 a.m. by this time. I wanted to get the whole thing over with, to return home to my wife and our sick son, so I encouraged the police to go ahead and ask their questions.

"We can't ask you any questions," they said, "until you have an attorney present."

"But I don't need an attorney," I told them. "Have I done anything wrong? What is the problem?"

"That is the law," they explained.

I had nothing to hide. I was not afraid of anything they might ask, so I tried again to advance the process.

"I don't have an attorney and I don't need one," I insisted. "You told me I had to come with you because you had to ask me some questions. Here I am. Please go ahead and ask me your questions. I am ready for your questions."

The officers did not budge. I had no choice but to sit there and wait, while four more hours slowly passed. It was around 7:00 a.m. when an officer entered the room, accompanied by a man in a suit and tie who introduced himself as my attorney. I told him that I did not need an attorney, but he told me that my wife had called him, and he sat down beside me.

"Now," one of the officers said, "I'm going to ask you some questions."

"Please, go ahead," I told him.

At first, the questions were very basic. Where was I born? When was my birthday? He asked about my work, my family, things like that. Then the questions changed. It began to feel like a real interrogation. He had a list of names, and he went down the list, asking me about each one. Did I know this man? Did I know that man? What did I know about him?

The names of five men who would later be imprisoned with me in Guantanamo were on the list. Three of them were good friends—Hadj Boudella, Mohamed Nechla, and Lakhdar Boumediene—and I answered all of the questions about them truthfully. Two other names, Saber Lahmar and Belkacem Bensayah, were unfamiliar. Another name on the list was Abu Zubaydah. I had never heard that name before in my life.

Once he was done with his questions, the interrogator told me that I was required to stay inside the Ministry of Interior for a period of at least twenty-four hours. My attorney left and I stayed there in the office, across from the interrogator, and waited.

Early the next morning, after a little over twenty-four hours in the Ministry of Interior, I was taken by car to the high-rise building that houses the Supreme Court of the Federation of Bosnia & Herzegovina. As I entered the courthouse, I was immediately handcuffed by an officer who told me that it was standard procedure. At that moment, I became certain the authorities viewed me as a criminal and planned to press charges.

They brought me before an investigative judge, and once my lawyer arrived, it was time for a new round of questions. The judge asked me the same questions the police had already asked, but she wanted more details. She was very courteous and her tone was even-keeled. But it was clear from the way she was wording things that she had received instructions from someone. She was not using her own words. She was not asking her own questions.

She wanted more information about the same people the police had asked me about earlier. In particular, she wanted to know about Abu Zubaydah. I had never heard of the man, so there was nothing I could tell her.

"Who is Abu Zubaydah?" I asked her. "Where does he live? Sarajevo? Maybe I know him by another name?"

"No," she said. "He does not live in Sarajevo. Abu Zubaydah is part of Al Qaeda. He is Al Qaeda's second-in-command. America is looking for him."

I told her again, "I don't know anyone by the name of Abu Zubaydah. I thought you were talking about somebody who lives in Sarajevo. The first time in my life that I heard that name was when the police asked me about him."

The judge asked me if I knew where the American Embassy was located. I told her that I did. I drove past it almost every day. It was located in between my home and downtown, so I would drive by it on my way to and from work, and to and from karate practice. Given its location, a lot of people drove past it regularly, but apparently my doing so was suspicious.

"Why," the judge asked, "didn't you take an alternate route to work? Why did you always take the route past the embassy?" She then proposed a specific route I could have taken that would not have brought me past the embassy.

"That route," I pointed out, "is more than thirty kilometers. The route I usually take is a little over ten. Why on earth would I drive an extra twenty kilometers for no good reason?"

"Fine," she said. "But why do you live there in the first place? Why not live somewhere else?"

"You could just as easily ask anyone else from my neighborhood that question," I pointed out. "Anyway, I lived in my home before the American Embassy was even there! When I moved into my home, that location was a park. So you should be asking the people at the American Embassy why they decided to build their embassy there, instead of asking me why I decided to live there."

It was all so ridiculous.

"Listen," I told the judge, "if there is anything with the Americans or the American Embassy, I am ready to answer anyone's questions. Bring people from the American army. Bring people from the American Embassy. They can interrogate me. And you can ask them if there is anybody there who ever received a call or a threat from me. Ask them if I ever talked to anybody there, or if I ever even stopped near the embassy while I was driving past."

"That will not be possible," the judge said. There were more questions, but I do not recall them. She was reading them off a paper, in a monotone, and it was clear that she was just asking questions that had been written for her by the Americans. She was a puppet.

When she was done asking questions, the judge drafted a report and asked me to sign it. My attorney requested that my handcuffs be removed so I could sign, but the judge refused.

"You need to remove the handcuffs," my attorney insisted, "if you want him to sign. For that matter, the handcuffs should be removed as soon as he enters this room. He should not sit in the courtroom handcuffed."

The judge would not relent. It took some contorting, but I somehow managed to sign the paper with handcuffs on. The judge informed me that I was going to be imprisoned for somewhere between a day and a month while a more thorough investigation was conducted.

My attorney protested. "Why does he have to stay in prison? There are no charges against him. There is nothing."

This was her response, verbatim: "This case is bigger than me."

It was around 4:30 or 5:00 a.m. when the police deposited me in a prison cell. There were eight other men in the cell, all of whom were asleep, and only eight bunks. Eventually, one of the men woke up and an officer told me to take his bunk. I lay down, but I was unable to fall asleep. My mind was racing. Would I actually be charged with terrorism? Was my family all right? I had never been in prison before. I wondered what it would be like.

Later that morning, my fellow prisoners woke up. One man walked over and greeted me.

"As-salaam alaykum, Coach Mustafa," he said. *Peace be upon you.*

"Wa-alaykum as-salaam," I replied. *And upon you peace.* "But how," I asked, "do you know me?"

"I used to receive karate training from you in Tuzla," he explained. I apologized for not recognizing him; I had trained so many students that I was not able to remember them all. I asked him why he was here. He told me that he had been working as a guard at a European embassy, and he had been accused of accepting bribes to help people skip to the front of the visa line. Years later, I learned that the charges against him were ultimately dropped.

Two of the other men in the cell had been charged with drug-related offenses. Another had been arrested for stealing computers. One was a businessman accused of money laundering. His case was very complex, with millions of marks involved, but all of their cases paled in comparison to mine.

When I turned on the television in our cell, I found out exactly how serious the accusations against me were. A news program was reporting that Mohamed Nechla and I had been arrested for plotting an attack on the American Embassy. *God Almighty*, I thought. *Now I am in trouble.*

My wife requested permission to visit me in prison, but the officials refused at first. After two weeks, they allowed a twenty-minute visit. The guards set up a large rectangular table with chairs on each side. They let several prisoners in from one side of the room, and then the visitors entered from the other side. The guards stood directly behind the prisoners while we talked. My wife brought our younger son, Hamza, but not Mohamed. Mohamed did not know that I was in prison, and we did not want him to.

Even though the superior court judge had informed me that I would be in prison for a period between one day and one month, a month passed and I was not released. Instead, I was told that I would be required to stay in prison for another two months because the authorities had not yet completed their investigation.

They claimed to need more time to look through the computer they had confiscated. Supposedly, they were also waiting for a report about my telephone calls. The government needed more than a month to get a list of my calls? An ordinary citizen like me can obtain such a list within a day or two; surely the government could do so in a matter of minutes.

Two more months passed slowly. There is nothing to do in prison, nothing at all. You just sit there, twenty-four hours a day. I did a lot of reading: my wife had brought me a Qur'an, plus there were some books and magazines available, as well as five Bosnian newspapers available for purchase each morning. I also sometimes played chess with other prisoners, and each day we were allowed a thirty-minute recreational walk for exercise.

More than anything else, we sat around watching the news on the television in our cell. We saw several reports about high-level meetings between Bosnian and American officials, including government ministers, military leaders, and diplomats. The meetings were secretive, and the press was not allowed to record them, but I remember telling my cellmates that they were probably talking about what to do with me and the other men arrested with me.

Throughout my time in prison, my cellmates treated me with deference and respect. They knew that I was a karate trainer and that I was on the Bosnian karate team, because of the fellow inmate who had recognized me, and I guess I simply did not seem like a criminal to them.

Food was not really a problem in prison. There was a cafeteria, but most of us preferred homemade cooking whenever we could get it. Sometimes my wife would bring rice, especially during Ramadan, which took place while I was in prison. My wife knew that my cellmates longed for a taste of home too, so she cooked large enough quantities that I could share.

After eating, prisoners were supposed to wash their dish, but I did not even have to do that. My cellmates would do it for me. Each time I got up to wash my dish, they would say, "No Mustafa, just sit down and relax." It was remarkable how respectful they were.

All they asked for in return was that I train them. They wanted to know what exercises they could do to become stronger. Honestly, I didn't feel up to being a trainer in prison, but after some pleading, I showed them what I could.

During Ramadan, I fasted observantly, as did a few of my cellmates. We fasted together and prayed together. Before we broke the fast after sundown each night, we warmed up our food on the radiator.

On Thursday, January 17th, ninety-one days after I had been arrested, the court ordered my release. I found this out from the evening news. As the happy news was sinking in, a police officer brought me a document written in Bosnian. It was the court's report, stating that I had not made or received any calls related to terrorism in the past six months, and that there was nothing suspicious in my CDs, DVDs, or computer except for the fact that I had visited some news websites featuring images of George Bush and Osama bin Laden. Of course, who hadn't read a news article with such pictures in the weeks following September 11th?

I don't remember the exact words of the court's report, but it was something to the effect of, "We find that these men have absolutely no connection with terrorism, and they are to be released at once."

Upon hearing the news, some of my cellmates began to cry. "We're happy that you're going back home," they told me, "but we are sad that you are leaving us here." Years later, after Guantanamo, one of my old Bosnian cellmates came to visit me. He told me that he had spent close to two years in prison for a crime he did not commit; he then went on to go to law school and now works as a lawyer.

While the other inmates were happy for me, I was a bit skeptical because of the timing of the court's report. I had received it around 9:00 p.m., and that just did not seem right. When a Bosnian court decides to release somebody from prison, the release tends to happen by 4:00 p.m. Bosnian courts usually stop their activity around 1:00 or 2:00 p.m., so when a judge decides to release a prisoner, the decision must be issued before 3:00 and the prisoner is usually released by 4:00. At the latest, 5:00. It was common knowledge in the prison that this was how things worked.

The news report on the television switched to a view of the prison. I saw crowds of protesters gathered around the building, and some of them were being interviewed by the press. Then there was an interview of Hadj's attorney. "I received official information," he declared, "that these men are going to be transferred to Guantanamo." How could this be? I had just been exonerated. I had the report in my hand.

I was escorted out of my cell and processed for release. I asked for the personal items that had been confiscated from me, and while they did return my money and some other personal effects, they would not give me back my Algerian passport. "No," they told me, "you will have to come back tomorrow or the next day to get it."

"What is happening?" I asked. "What is the story here?" I received no answer.

I was told to wait in the prison's lobby. Hadj and Lakhdar were there as well, along with some members of the Special Police. It was clear that this was not going to be an ordinary prison release. As we waited, we were joined by a judge named Salem Miso, who was holding some official-looking court documents.

And then a door opened. A police officer asked, "Who is Mustafa?"

"I am."

"You come first," he ordered.

I followed him out the door and into a nightmare.

I was ushered into the arms of men wearing Bosnian police uniforms, some of whom were definitely not Bosnian. One of them, a brusque man with a fresh cut over his eye, was issuing orders in Bosnian, and I could tell from his accent and his broken Bosnian that he was not a native speaker.

"You are American," I accused.

"No," he shot back. "I'm Bosnian."

"Even my Bosnian is better than yours," I scoffed.

The American consulted with Judge Miso, and I saw him hand over the official-looking documents that he had been carrying. That was when I knew this was an authorized handover. The Americans were taking us with Bosnia's permission.

I was handcuffed and something like an oversized hat was pulled down over my head, covering my eyes. I was forced into the backseat of a car. They tried to drive away from the prison, but the demonstrators outside prevented them from leaving. I heard the crowd chanting and felt the car rocking as people tried to topple it. They wanted the police to let us out.

I was having trouble breathing because of the "hat" they had put over my head. Luckily, I was able to push it up a bit, despite my handcuffs, and the police were too busy trying to control the situation to notice. Now that my eyes were uncovered, I could see a little of what was happening. Snow was falling on a large crowd of people, men and women from all walks of life, who had surrounded the prison to demand our freedom.

I saw beatings taking place. I saw young people lying down in front of our car to prevent the police from driving forward. I even saw an elderly woman sitting in the snow, steadfastly refusing to budge.

"If you want to take them," she declared, "you will need to run me over."

Through the din, I heard my wife. The last time we had spoken, she had asked if she should stop by the jail with clean clothes for me to wear on my way home. Now we were not sure if we would ever see each other again.

"Mustafa!" she shouted. "Mustafa!"

I was not able to see her in the crowd, but I knew it was her. I would recognize her voice anywhere. The police officer sitting next to me heard her too.

"She's calling you," he said.

"How do you know my name?" I asked. And then I realized that we had participated in karate training together.

The crowd was successful in blocking the car at the first exit, so they brought us back to the prison and attempted to exit via a different route. The protesters blocked them there too. They switched me into another car, and then another. At one point I shared a backseat with the man who I later learned was Belkacem Bensayah, and at another point I found myself next to Hadj.

The priority for the men in charge was to get us away from the prison. They were not concerned with our comfort. They pushed, prodded, shoved as they threw us into one car and then another. We were not able to sit upright; we simply lay where we had been tossed. Once, I looked down to see that I was practically lying on top of a firearm one of the officers had dropped.

Ultimately, the bedlam was not enough to prevent our extraction, and we were driven from the prison to a police station. At the station, the police had a physician examine Lakhdar, who had become quite sick en route. I heard the doctor tell the police that Lakhdar was frail, and that his body could not withstand so much trauma. They needed to bring him to a hospital.

The police were hesitant. Eventually, Lakhdar was loaded onto an ambulance. That was the last time I ever saw him on Bosnian soil.

WELCOME TO AMERICA

Lakhdar

MUSTAFA HAD TRIED TO WARN ME, but the guards pushed me out the prison door behind him. I saw uniformed soldiers and police officers and people with masks over their mouths. A bag was pulled over my head, my hands were cuffed behind my back, and I was shoved into a car.

I couldn't see, but I could hear the shouts of a crowd of protestors. I heard the driver mutter in Bosnian, "Get this trash out of my way." A group of protesters had thrown themselves in the car's path to try to block it. I'm grateful for their brave efforts, even though they were unsuccessful. Eventually, I felt the car roll forward and pick up speed.

I began to feel clammy and nauseous. I thought maybe it had something to do with the injection I'd been given earlier in the day. Or maybe it was shock. Either way, I felt miserable. And then I passed out.

I didn't know where I was when I came to. I heard people, I assumed the police officers who had seized me, speaking in Bosnian. They sounded scared. One of them called and requested an ambulance, and a short while later, a doctor and nurse arrived and started asking me questions. When I mentioned that I had gotten an injection earlier in the day and didn't know what it was, the doctor became agitated.

"He has to go to a hospital," he told the police officers.

They were reluctant. "You can't treat him here?"

"No," the doctor said. "And if he dies, you're responsible."

I was placed on a stretcher and into an ambulance, accompanied by the doctor, the nurse, and some officers. Someone took the bag off my head, but I couldn't see out of the ambulance, so I still wasn't sure where I was.

I heard us go through a tunnel and then, suddenly, the ambulance turned around and went back through the tunnel. Someone must have called the ambulance driver with new orders. We never did go to the hospital.

Thankfully, as time passed, I began to feel less ill. My worry about being sick gradually gave way to fear about where they were bringing me. Despite what my lawyer had said on the news, I was still hoping that I wasn't Guantanamo-bound.

But when I overheard the nurse say to the doctor, "My sister bought a house here in Butmir," my heart sank. The Butmir neighborhood, everyone knew, was home to the American military base in Sarajevo.

When the ambulance came to a stop, I was unloaded, still on a stretcher. It was dark out, but not quite pitch black—probably about 4:00 or 4:30 a.m. The Bosnian police handed me over to American soldiers. As I was carried through the front gate, I heard the soldiers tell the police and the doctor and nurse that none of them were allowed to enter.

The soldiers brought me to a large tent. There were rows of mats on the ground, spaced far apart, with iron chains next to each mat— it reminded me of an animal pen more than anything else. The soldiers put large headphones over my ears and goggles over my eyes, so I couldn't see or hear, and they placed me on a mat and chained my hands and legs to the ground. I was still in the clothes I'd been wearing in prison—no coat or hat or gloves—so I was freezing cold. I lay on the ground, shivering, and waited for morning to come.

A few hours later, I was unchained, the goggles and headphones were removed, and I was carried to a bathroom. One of the soldiers offered me breakfast. "Here," he said, speaking French—they knew Algerians speak French—"this doesn't have pig meat in it." I declined. Even if he were telling the truth, how could I eat at a time like this?

I was taken back to my mat for a while, and a group of soldiers came by. They were wearing masks, and one of them was videotaping. They ordered me to strip off my clothes, shouting that they would beat me if I didn't. So I did. I stood there, naked and humiliated in front of the soldiers and their video camera, while a doctor—at least, someone I assumed was a doctor—conducted a medical exam. He noticed that I still had my wedding ring and tried to remove it, but just like the Bosnian prison guards, he was unable to pry it off.

After the exam, the soldiers gave me a military camouflage flight suit to put on. They put a shackle around each of my ankles, with a chain coming up from each shackle and connecting at my waist. Over each shackle, they put a military boot that came up to my knee. They strapped the boots so tightly that I could feel the shackles digging into my ankle bone.

I was taken back to my mat, where I lay, shackled and sore, wondering what was going to happen next. I don't know if it was minutes later or hours later when the soldiers came back—between the pain, the fear, and the exhaustion, I was beginning to lose track of time. The soldiers put the headphones and goggles back on me and brought me to a vehicle.

We drove. When we finally stopped and the headphones and goggles were removed, I saw that we were at another military base, but I had no idea where. I found out, years later, that it was the American base in Tuzla, a Bosnian city about sixty-five miles north of Sarajevo. The soldiers went through the same procedure of forcing me to strip naked and conducting a medical exam, videotaping all the while.

They gave me water and offered me an egg and some bread, which I turned down. I was still unable to contemplate food. The soldiers put me back in chains, headphones, and goggles, and brought me to a new location. They chained my wrists and ankles tightly to a steel floor, so I was lying on my side, my face against the steel, unable to move my arms or legs like a lamb tied up for slaughter.

Using the floor, I was able to dislodge my goggles just enough that I could see a little bit around them. I was on the floor of a military airplane. There were at least a few others chained to the floor, like me, but I wasn't able to see well enough to tell how many there were or whether I knew any of them. Next to each of us, there was at least one armed soldier.

After takeoff, I fell asleep. I had never been so tired in my life. Still, between the biting chains and the cold steel floor, I woke up every few minutes.

At one point, I nudged my headphones against the floor enough to be able to hear. I heard a voice that sounded like Mustafa's. "My hand, my hand," he was screaming, in Arabic. He was never one to whine, so his shackles must have been far too tight. I was in pain too, but I was too exhausted to shout—and I figured the soldiers were more likely to beat me than to help me. I went back to sleep.

Another time when I woke up, I peeked around my goggles and saw a few soldiers standing nearby. Each one took a turn aiming his gun dramatically at one of the prisoners and making his best Rambo face while the other soldiers snapped photos. They were smiling and laughing the whole time.

I knew they had been told that we were terrorists, but still, I couldn't believe what I was seeing. What, I wondered, could possibly be manly about standing menacingly above a defenseless, chained man who can't see, hear, or move?

I have no idea how long we were airborne. I must have woken up and fallen back to sleep at least a few dozen times. I was relieved when the plane finally began its descent. At last, this horrible journey was almost over.

After landing, two soldiers unlocked my chains and stood me up. They led me, one at each armpit, off the plane and into a room. Once again, I was stripped, examined, and dressed in new clothes. I couldn't see—they had left the goggles on—but the clothes felt much lighter than the flight suit I'd had on before.

Then the soldiers led me outside. As they did, I shifted my head so that I could see around the goggles. I was crushed to see that I was being led toward a jet plane, surrounded by a large group of soldiers and dogs. We hadn't arrived yet after all.

I didn't see any snow on the ground, so I figured that if we were still in Europe, we were probably in Turkey. I knew from watching the news that the largest American bases in Europe were in Germany and Turkey—and since there was snow in Bosnia, I assumed I would have seen snow if we'd been in Germany.

The soldiers led me up a ramp at the back of the plane. This plane, unlike the last one, had a bench to sit on. The soldiers deposited me on the bench and connected the shackles on my wrists and ankles to each other and to a chain running the length of the plane.

I could see that other prisoners were seated on the plane, a soldier standing in front of each one. I think I counted six of us. Ten or fifteen minutes later, more prisoners were brought on the plane. I later learned that they were men who had been flown to Turkey from Afghanistan.

The last time I had been to Turkey, it was to meet my wife and our newborn daughter on their way home from Algeria. Now I was en route to Guantanamo.

This flight was even worse than the first one. I was chained to my seat, and if I so much as twitched or let my head droop to the side, I was slapped or punched by a soldier yelling, "Don't move!"

After several hours, an apple was placed in my hand. I couldn't see it—and with the soldier standing right next to me, beating me for even the slightest movements, I certainly wasn't going to try to adjust my goggles—so I had no idea if the apple was red or brown, fresh or rotten. I was so hungry, though, that I didn't care. It had been a day and a half since my last meal. I would eat the apple no matter how filthy it was.

But I couldn't reach my hand to my mouth. The chains were too tight. I leaned my head forward as far as I could while bringing my hand toward my mouth, and I got tantalizingly close to taking a bite, but my hand was in so much pain that I couldn't hold onto the apple. It dropped and rolled away. I'm sure the soldiers were watching the whole time.

I don't remember much else from the flight—just hunger, exhaustion, and pain. When the plane finally began its descent, I was relieved. *Whatever Guantanamo is like*, I thought, *it can't possibly be worse than this.*

Mustafa

AFTER LAKHDAR WAS WHISKED AWAY from the police station in an ambulance, the rest of us were brought to the American military base in Butmir, on the outskirts of Sarajevo. I noticed that the people transporting us took detours to make sure we traveled through Republika Srpska, a part of Bosnia that was under Serb control, instead of traversing Sarajevo proper.

When we arrived at the military base, the first person I saw was the American with the cut above his eye who had spoken in broken Bosnian outside the prison. He was furious that I could see my surroundings. He berated the officers who had been transporting me: "I told you! I gave you specific instructions, when he comes here, he should have his head covered!" He then walked up behind me and forcefully smacked the back of my neck.

I was led to a large metal hangar. Before I was brought in, soldiers handcuffed me, shackled my feet, and pulled a hood over my head so that I could not see my surroundings. Once inside, they secured my shackles to a metal ring in the floor and placed me atop a paper-thin mattress, which I later heard called an "isomat." It was impossible to sleep. I could not maneuver into a comfortable position because of the way I was shackled to the floor, and it was bone-chillingly, mind-numbingly cold. Outside the hangar, it was around −25 C°. Inside, they were running a large, noisy fan that somehow managed to make it even colder.

Eventually, two soldiers commanded me to stand up. They brought me into another room, removed the hood covering my eyes, and said that it was time to change my clothes. I was stripped naked, and they put me into a jumpsuit made of very light fabric. While the soldiers were bundled in warm coats and hats, I was essentially wearing nothing more than a bedsheet to protect me from the Bosnian winter. I shivered uncontrollably as the fan whirred overhead.

They kept me in the hangar until morning, at which point they brought me outside, sat me down on a chair, and put the hood back over my eyes. I could not see what was happening, but I could feel them fingerprinting me. Then they set a sandwich down in front of me and uncuffed one of my hands. It was difficult to eat blind, but I managed to take a few bites. When I was led back into the hangar, I still couldn't see, but I could hear the rattling of chains; it seemed as though I was being chained up along with several other people.

At one point, I told the soldiers I needed to use the restroom. They led me there and removed the hood from my head. The door to the restroom was open, and I could see an American general standing outside. I recognized him from the news reports I had watched in prison. The general had been a regular participant in the secretive meetings with American officials, the meetings I had suspected were about my future. And now here he was, in complete control of it.

They loaded us into what felt like a Hummer and drove for more than two hours to the city of Tuzla, home of the largest military base in Bosnia and a military airport. Upon our arrival, they removed our hoods, took our pictures, and again fingerprinted us. At one point, they gave me two or three eggs to eat. I also noticed that the air here was not as bitterly cold as it had been in the hangar back in Sarajevo, and I was grateful for that, at least.

They pulled the hood back over my eyes and brought me onto what sounded like a helicopter. Over the noise of the rotors, I heard soldiers swearing at us, laughing at us, mocking us. I remember a woman's voice in particular. Some of the soldiers also took turns hitting and kicking us. As we flew, I could feel my heart thumping in my chest.

When we landed, they led us off the helicopter. At the time, I thought we were on a military base in Germany, though I later found out that the base had been in Turkey. The soldiers forced us to sit directly on the cold, hard ground.

Though I did not know it at the time, we were waiting for a plane from Afghanistan with Afghan prisoners onboard. As we waited, I grew colder and colder. I tried to move around a bit to keep my blood flowing, but because of the shackles, I could barely shift my position on the ground. The soldiers refused to help. They left us there in the cold, on the ground, for hours. Parts of my body became numb and remained that way for a long time after they moved us.

Finally, the plane from Afghanistan arrived. A gray-haired American showed up to translate for us, or at least try to. His Arabic was extremely weak.

Through the interpreter, we were told to stand up. He said that they were going to remove the handcuffs and the shackles from our legs. If we made one wrong move, our interpreter told us, "we are going to shoot you down." Despite his poor Arabic, I was able to understand that clearly enough.

When they stood me up and removed my hood, I saw six or seven soldiers standing in front of me in a semicircle, their guns pointed directly at me. An older female physician came to examine me. When she was done, the soldiers used scissors to cut off the clothes I was wearing, and they put me into new, brown clothes. The hood went back over my head and I was ordered to sit down and wait.

They marched us onto a military plane, leading us onboard through a ramp in the rear of the plane. Once on the plane, we were seated on a long bench. Our feet were shackled and we were chained together with one long chain. I only know this because I saw it on television later. I could not see anything through the hood.

I could hear. I heard men screaming in pain and agony, some in Arabic and others in a language I had never heard before. I thought it might be Cuban, since I knew we were going to Guantanamo, but I later learned that it was Pashto, the native tongue of many people in Afghanistan.

The man seated next to me was one of the ones screaming. It was clear that he was wounded, and I heard him tell the soldiers he was hurt. I heard a soldier walk up to him and hit him. Any time someone tried to move even a little bit, a soldier would beat him. I almost never moved, and I was shackled in a way that made it almost impossible to move, but the people sitting next to me kept drawing the soldiers' attention, so I kept getting hit along with them.

We were given an apple and some bread. I ate a little bit, but it was very difficult because of how we were chained and because we were not allowed to raise our hands.

I do not know exactly how long we spent on that plane, chained together. I know that we landed in Guantanamo on Sunday, January 20th, three very long days after the Bosnian court had ordered that we be set free.

Lakhdar

ONCE THE PLANE ROLLED TO A STOP, the soldiers barked at me to stand up. They led me off the plane, still in chains, goggles, and headphones, and onto what felt like a boat. I later learned that the airport is on the west side of Guantanamo Bay and the prison is on the east. To get from one side to the other without going through Cuban territory, you have to cross the water.

After a twenty-minute boat ride, the soldiers carried me off the boat and sat me down on what felt like gravel. They put me in an uncomfortable position, sitting with my back straight and my legs extended, my right leg crossed over my left. If I got tired and shifted my weight, or if I tried to turn my face to avoid the hot sun, a blow would come from behind, accompanied by a shout of "Don't move!"

I had been sitting there for a while, trying to stay still, when I heard someone shouting in Arabic, loudly enough to be heard through my headphones. It was a military interpreter. He had a Lebanese accent, and he sounded young, like an adolescent whose voice had yet to deepen.

"We're doing intake procedures for each prisoner," he squeaked. I assumed that he was talking to everyone who had been on the plane with me. I was surrounded, I imagined, by dozens of others, all of us sitting there on the gravel, backs straight and legs extended, trying not to move. "Sit here," he continued, "and don't talk or move until it's your turn."

I sat for what must have been two or three hours. At a certain point, I realized that I needed a bathroom. I hadn't eaten anything in two days, but they had given me water in Bosnia and I hadn't gone to the bathroom since. But I knew if I said anything, they would just hit me. So I sat and waited. It had been a humiliating few days, but I had enough dignity left that I was determined not to urinate on myself.

When it was finally my turn to be processed, I asked about a bathroom.

"Not now," they told me. "After we finish our procedures."

They did yet another medical exam. Then they sat me in a chair, gave me a pen and paper, and told me to write my address and a short note to my family. I can't remember if they lifted the goggles so that I could write. I can't remember what I wrote, or even if I wrote anything at all. All I can remember is how much pain I was in and how badly I needed the bathroom.

The next step was a "shower"—the soldiers stripped me of everything but the goggles and headphones and hosed me down, as though I were an animal. Then they dressed me and, at long last, took me to a bathroom. It was a Porta-John, and the soldiers came in with me. Urinating as they stood there behind me was uncomfortable, but I had no choice.

The soldiers led me on a ten-minute walk, and then they removed my headphones and goggles. When the goggles came off, it was like something out of a cartoon: stars were spinning around my head and I was seeing double. I couldn't tell if there were two, three, or four soldiers standing in front of me. Through the blur, I saw, for the first time, that I was in orange clothes. I had a plastic hospital bracelet on my wrist with my name and some numbers. And I was in a cell.

My cell was like a cage at the zoo. I was outdoors, surrounded by four wire mesh walls, one of which had a door with a narrow slot in it. There was a corrugated metal roof maybe eighteen inches above my head. A two-inch thick isomat with an even thinner blanket lay atop a hard cement floor. The isomat took up most of the cell lengthwise, and a little less than half of it widthwise, so I think the cell was about 5' x 7'. There were two buckets in the cell—one with water for drinking and washing, and one for going to the bathroom. There was nothing else.

The soldiers left me in my cell. Later, as the sun was setting, another soldier came by with dinner: rice and beans in a Styrofoam cup. The food was rock-hard. As hungry as I was, I just couldn't bring myself to eat it. But I did drink a little water, and retched at the first sip. The water was hot, unsurprisingly—it had been sitting in a plastic bucket in the sun all day—and it was also dirty. (Days later, when I got toward the bottom of the bucket, I could see that it was caked with yellow mud. Some mornings I woke up to find a frog in the bucket.) I was thirsty enough, though, that I drank more, and kept down what I could.

When night fell, I tried to sleep, but it was hard. It got cold after the sun went down, and even with my blanket wrapped around me, I shivered through the night. And there were the soldiers—they talked with each other as they paced, and they made a point to walk within inches of the cells, kicking up stones and dirt as they walked past. A few of them would even grab the wire mesh and rattle it. Maybe they were following orders—or maybe they just hated their jobs, hated being up in the middle of the night, hated us even though they knew nothing of who we actually were.

After a night of fitful, dreamless sleep in what felt like fifteen-minute increments, I was woken up shortly after sunrise by the commotion of soldiers changing shifts. Around the same time, a group of brown-skinned men arrived, wearing yellow construction helmets and denim, and got to work. They were building a prison around us. Their loud equipment and even louder music remained a constant presence throughout the next several weeks.

Maybe an hour after I'd woken up, a soldier put breakfast—an egg, a slice of bread, and a cup of milk—on the ground outside my cell. He turned and walked away, kicking up dirt and dust that settled on my food. A little while later, another soldier opened my cell door and handed the dirt-sprinkled food to me. I ate. *This is your life now*, I told myself. *You have to get used to it.*

I spent the rest of the morning taking in my surroundings. I had a pounding headache and blurry vision—the wire mesh of my cell appeared to be in constant motion—but I could see a forest and a small mountain in the distance, and a variety of colorful, long-legged birds that I had never seen before.

As I gazed out at the trees and birds through the haze of dancing wire, I thought more about what I could possibly be doing here. I thought about the time I was arrested in Algeria, and about my recent involvement in helping Bensayah's wife find a lawyer, but it didn't add up. None of that made me a terrorist—and the Bosnian court agreed. So why was I here?

Later that morning, a soldier came by my cell, handed me a towel, and told me to remove my clothes. Once I had nothing on but the towel, the soldier shackled me. A group of soldiers, some male and some female, led me and several other toweled, shackled men into a small shower room. There were no curtains or walls for privacy—just a wide open room with a showerhead every few feet. The soldiers came by, collected our towels, and turned on the showers. I shut my eyes out of respect for my fellow prisoners, so I wouldn't see them naked, but I doubt the soldiers did the same. After the shower, I was given a towel and led back to my cell.

At lunchtime, they brought me, for the first of many times, a prepackaged military meal. The packages were numbered—for the first year or so, lunch was always number 1, 2, 3, or 4. They always gave us vegetarian meals, since the meat options weren't *halal*.* That first lunch, I think number 3, was lentils, which tasted like they had gone bad years ago. They were inedible. They came with a cookie, so my first Guantanamo lunch was a stale cookie dipped in hot, yellowing water.

---

* Translator's Note: *Halal* meat is meat considered permissible under Islamic dietary laws. Pork is not considered *halal*, nor is the meat of animals who were improperly slaughtered.

That afternoon, when there were no soldiers nearby, my neighbors and I started talking through the wire mesh. There was a Palestinian in the cell to my left and a Yemeni to my right. Each one was missing a leg—the Palestinian's was steel and the Yemeni's was simply gone, amputated at the knee. I thought about telling the Yemeni that I had lived in his country for a year, but since I didn't really know him yet, I just told him about living in Bosnia. Even though we didn't talk about anything of consequence, the small talk made me feel a little less alone.

Later that day, a soldier slid open the slot in my cage door and ordered me to put my hands through the slot. He cuffed my hands, placed a chain around my chest, and had me turn around so he could fasten the chain behind my back. Then he opened the door, shackled my legs, and led me out of the cell. As we walked, the chains dug into my skin, drawing blood.

The soldier forced me to walk with my head bowed, but I could still see dozens of cages as we walked past them. The men inside were all wearing orange, like me. Unlike me, they were all clean-shaven. I later learned that most of them had been at an American base called Bagram, in Afghanistan, before Guantanamo, and that they had been forcibly shaved there. Some of them thought I was a spy at first because I had been allowed to keep my beard.

After a fifteen-minute walk, we arrived at our destination: the clinic. It was a small, grimy room with a doctor, a nurse, and an interpreter. The interpreter spoke with a Syrian accent. Unlike the prepubescent who had barked at us in a Lebanese accent, this one seemed like a decent young man. I read his name, Ibrahim, off the nameplate on his uniform. (It wasn't until a few months later that all of the soldiers and interpreters stopped wearing nameplates.) Ibrahim translated as the doctor and nurse asked me some basic questions and drew some blood, and then I was walked back to my cell.

The next day, in addition to my still-throbbing headache and blurred vision, I noticed that the plastic bracelet around my wrist, which had been loose at first, was now taut—my wrists were swollen and oozing pus. The cuttingly tight cuffs must have caused an infection.

For the next week, I was in the clinic every day. First, they gave me some pills, but those didn't seem to stop the swelling. Then one of the nurses told me that he was going to inject me with a dose of penicillin.

"Wait," I objected, as he took out the needle. "I'm allergic to penicillin."

"Sure," he scoffed. "You're just afraid of the needle."

Shortly after the injection, I passed out. When I awoke, I had a bizarre feeling, as though I were outside of my body watching it. A doctor came in and injected me with something else, and after half an hour, I started to feel normal again.

On another clinic visit later that week, I saw my Yemeni cell-neighbor receiving treatment. When they removed the dressings from his amputated leg, the smell was overpowering. He appeared to be in tremendous pain—they didn't use an anesthetic—and I worried that what was left of his leg might get infected because the clinic seemed like such a dirty, germ-infested place.

After about a week of clinic visits, my wrists started to return to their normal size—but they bore scars that never healed.

As I got to know more of my neighbors, most of whom had been brought to Guantanamo from Afghanistan, I came to see that my injuries were much less severe than most. In addition to the amputated Yemeni and the Palestinian with the steel leg, there was a man missing a hand and another with only one eye. I began to think I might be the only person in my cellblock whose body parts were all intact.

There was one Afghan in a nearby cell who was downright insane. He ranted almost nonstop—I had even heard his shouts through my headphones on the flight from Turkey, followed by soldiers yelling "Shut up!" as they beat him. He spoke Pashto, so I couldn't understand him, but I recognized a few words here and there: "America," "Afghanistan," and his name, Abdurrezzaq.

At times, Abdurrezzaq stripped off all his clothes and stood naked in his cell. Once, he picked up his urine- and feces-filled waste bucket and flung its contents at a soldier walking by. More often, he would pour the bucket's contents over his own head. It was sad to watch. The Americans thought they were capturing terrorist masterminds, and in fact they were locking up mental patients. I later learned that after four months, Abdurrezzaq was diagnosed with schizophrenia and returned to Afghanistan.

I overheard some of my neighbors speculating about where we were. One was convinced we were in Korea. "No," another said. "We're in Oman. Oman has birds just like these." I, of course, knew better. There was my lawyer's statement, plus this place looked just like the footage I had seen on the news about the opening of Guantanamo. And I'd been a good geography student, so I knew that a tropical place like Cuba could certainly have these types of birds and this type of climate. But I didn't get involved in the discussion. I didn't want to wear out my brain with empty talk, and anyway, it didn't really matter. All I wanted to know was *why* I was here, wherever here was, and when I could go home.

Mustafa

WHEN I WAS FIRST DEPOSITED IN MY CAGE, I felt an overwhelming sense of relief. Finally, I was not being beaten. I had been kicked and punched so much on the way from Sarajevo to that cage.

After we landed in Guantanamo and took a short ferry ride, the soldiers had forced us to sit on a gravel drive with our legs straight out in front of us. I could not see, but I could hear soldiers cursing at us and prisoners crying out in pain. I also heard dogs barking and snarling nearby. It sounded like they were directly in front of my face.

The gravel was extremely uncomfortable, especially after the long plane flight, but we were instructed not to move at all. Whenever anyone adjusted their position even a tiny bit, to shake a leg that had fallen asleep or to shift themselves off of a sharp piece of gravel, they were beaten.

I was hit and kicked repeatedly. If my leg so much as twitched, they would beat me. It was especially difficult to remain perfectly still because I was so sleep-deprived. At one point, I slumped down a little, just from sheer exhaustion, and that was enough to catch the soldiers' attention. I was kicked in the face, in the body, everywhere.

That torture continued for hours. Finally, the soldiers stood me up. I was stripped, hosed down, and brought to a doctor for a medical examination. Then I was given a small piece of paper and instructed to write a letter to my family. I wrote a short note to my wife, telling her that I was being held in Cuba by the American military. I later found out that she never got the letter, and I doubt anyone ever mailed it. They were probably just using the letters as a ruse to gather information about us.

After that, they put us on a bus. There was a soldier sitting directly behind me. At one point, I lifted my head, and the soldier punched the back of it forcefully. "Lower your head," he ordered. I kept telling myself that I just needed to endure the beatings a little bit longer. I could not wait to get to my cell.

When I finally got there, battered and exhausted, the cell turned out to be a small outdoor cage, empty but for an isomat and a sheet. The soldiers put me in the cage, took the hood off my head, and removed the handcuffs from my wrists. I could see cuts where the steel had penetrated my skin, but I was lucky compared to some; I saw Lakhdar around that time and I could hardly believe how awful he looked. The cuffs had left one of his wrists a swollen, infected, misshapen mass.

After a short while, the soldiers brought me a little white bag with some very simple food inside. I had eaten next to nothing in almost four days, but I had not spent much time thinking about how hungry I was.

I had been thinking about my wife and children. I had been thinking about my son crying out for me as the police took me away from our home, and my wife in tears beside him. That image replaying over and over in my mind was the hardest part about the trip to Guantanamo. Not the hunger. Not the beatings. Those were nothing compared to the pain of hearing my son cry out for me, not understanding why his daddy was unable to go to him, to comfort him. To this day, that memory fills me with so much sadness and anger. Whenever I think back on that night, I think to myself, *May God curse President Bush and the Bosnian authorities like Lagumdžija and Limov for putting me in such a wretched situation.*

For my first few months in Guantanamo, I lived in what was called Camp X-Ray. The cells in X-Ray looked like they were meant for animals, not people. They were crude outdoor cages, completely exposed to the elements. In the mornings, it was beastly hot. We felt like our bodies were roasting underneath the hot Caribbean sun. We were never given sunscreen, and most of us left X-Ray with significantly darker skin than when we arrived.

At night, it grew bitterly cold. Our flimsy linen blankets provided little cover, and my thin isomat was not much warmer or more comfortable than the cold, hard concrete beneath it. During the first month, it also rained quite frequently. And in that part of the world, it does not drizzle. When it rains, it rains in sheets. A few of the cells had wooden boards laid across the top, but most offered no shelter at all. When it was hot, we burned. When it was cold, we shivered. And when it rained, we were drenched. Our clothes were soaked. Our blankets were soaked. The blankets were never replaced with dry ones, and we were only rarely given a dry change of clothes.

We all wore orange uniforms. Some of the uniforms were one-piece jumpsuits, while others were two-piece. The two-piece uniforms provided more ventilation, so they were cooler when it was blistering hot. The one-piece jumpsuits offered more insulation against the freezing cold. Neither was appropriate for the sweeping temperature changes we experienced out in those animal cages.

When the soldiers passed out the uniforms, they did not appear to be trying to match the size of the outfit to the size of its recipient. If anything, it was the opposite: the heavier detainees were given small uniforms, and the smaller ones received clothes that swallowed them up. Many of us had to make do with ill-fitting, uncomfortable clothes. Requests for better-fitting clothes were always denied, and when we tried to swap with each other, the soldiers would sometimes forbid us from doing so.

One Afghan inmate was a particularly large, heavyset man, so the soldiers gave him a particularly small uniform. It was the two-piece kind. He made a genuine effort to put it on, but he was unable to. The shirt was so small that he could not even fit it over his head. He told the soldiers he needed a larger size, but they told him to shut up and get dressed. Anyone could have seen it was an impossible task; that made no difference. When he failed to comply with the order, the soldiers beat him for disobedience. Then they stripped him naked and left.

"Since you don't want to wear your clothes," they said, "you can stay naked." For the next week, until new uniforms arrived, he had to cover himself, or at least try to, with nothing but his paper-thin blanket. It was all so arbitrary, so mean-spirited. It was a sign of what was to come.

Beatings were frequent, often without even an attempt at pretext or justification. Some of the soldiers would punish us merely for praying quietly in our cells. Seeing a prisoner knelt in prayer, the soldier would remove the man from his cell and force him down onto his knees, handcuffed and shackled. The ground around our cells was covered in sharp gravel, so kneeling there was intensely painful. The soldier would make his victim stay there, knees to gravel, sometimes for two, three, four hours.

When we were being punished this way, we were not allowed to make any movement at all. The slightest infraction would lead to a violent reprimand. Sometimes they would hit us square in the face. When a man was struck hard enough that it knocked him to the ground, his handcuffs prevented him from breaking his fall. He would simply have to lie, face down in the gravel, until the soldiers permitted him to move. Sometimes they would keep a man lying like that for hours on end. I saw men lose consciousness in that position. Once, I saw the soldiers pummel a man as he lay unconscious upon the gravel.

I did not talk much to my neighbors, because the soldiers would use that as yet another excuse to beat us. Also, the man in the cell just across from me had lost his mind. Lakhdar and I both witnessed this man stripping himself naked and flinging stones, gravel, feces, anything he could find, at the soldiers. I saw the soldiers routinely beat him, and I saw that it made no difference. Often a psychiatrist would sit on a chair in front of his cell and observe him. He was clearly crazy. Anyone who thought he could have planned *anything*, let alone a terrorist plot, was even crazier.

My other neighbors included a Tunisian, an elderly Pakistani, a Sudanese journalist, and a Saudi teenager. The teenager, Yasser al Zahrani, died in Guantanamo in 2006. Supposedly he committed suicide, but I have always wondered about that. Certainly he never struck me as suicidal. Like I said, though, I did not talk to him much; I did not talk to anyone much.

After a week or two in Guantanamo, I was interrogated for the first time. The man who came to interrogate me was a military officer. I remember that he wore glasses. He was accompanied by an officer who said he was originally from Croatia and knew the city of Split well. There was also an interpreter with them, who in theory spoke both English and Arabic. The only thing he knew how to say in Arabic was, "Do you speak Arabic?" He was incapable of competently translating my words, even with the help of an Arabic-English dictionary that he was constantly rifling through.

I began to notice that often when I said something in Arabic, the interpreter incorrectly translated it into English. I did not speak English well, but my English was better than his Arabic. During one interrogation, I looked at the interpreter and said, in English, "I speak English much better than you speak Arabic. So now you give me the dictionary and you go. I don't need you at all." But the interpreter did not leave, and the interrogators seemed utterly unconcerned about the fact that my words were being relayed to them by someone who did not know what they meant.

I was fortunate in that I spoke passable English, and had at least some sense of when the interpreter was mangling my words. Many other detainees did not speak English at all, and did not know that their words were being misrepresented. Later, many detainees were asked to explain statements that they had supposedly made, which were completely different from what they actually said. We were arguing our innocence to people who were incapable of listening to us even if they had wanted to.

Lakhdar

I WAS HAPPY WHEN INTERROGATIONS STARTED, midway through my second week at Guantanamo. I knew that America was a country that believed in democracy, freedom, and the rule of law. I was convinced that once I answered their questions, they would see that I was innocent, that this was all a terrible mistake. They would let me go.

Two soldiers led me, handcuffed and shackled, to my first interrogation. After a long, painful walk, we arrived at a ramshackle wooden building. The soldiers brought me into a room with nothing but a wooden table and wooden chairs. A third soldier, holding a rifle, stood there waiting for me. The first two soldiers left, and a short while later an interrogator walked in, accompanied by a young American interpreter.

The interrogator told me that he was of Croatian descent, and even said a few words to me in Bosnian, but for the most part the interrogation consisted of him asking questions in English and me answering in Arabic. That first day, he mostly asked me about my background—my childhood, my family, that sort of thing. After five or six hours of talking, he said, "Okay, we're done for today."

"We can keep talking if you want," I told him, eager to answer all his questions as quickly as possible. He seemed surprised.

"No," he answered. "We'll keep talking tomorrow." And with that, I was taken back to my cage for another night of broken sleep.

The interrogations continued over the next several weeks. There were a handful of different interrogators, with the man of Croatian descent and a young woman being the most frequent. The one constant presence was the young interpreter, who I came to realize was utterly incompetent. The interrogations often stalled as he flipped through his two dictionaries, searching for a word I had just said.

During one interrogation, after I said, in Arabic, "I worked for the Red Crescent," I heard the interpreter say, in English, "I bought the Red Crescent." I didn't know much English—just what I remembered from studying it for a few weeks in Yemen, plus what I'd picked up listening to the soldiers—but I knew the difference between "worked for" and "bought." I was furious. This was my one chance to convince my captors of my innocence, and this teenage idiot was ruining it. If he didn't know the difference between "worked for" and "bought," what else was he getting wrong?

I pointed at the interpreter. "You don't know how to translate," I snapped at him. "Get out of here. Get a different interpreter. I'm not saying another word until you do."

The interpreter and the interrogator had a conversation in English. The interpreter turned to me. "Look," he said, "if you don't talk, you're going to spend the rest of your life here. You'll die here."

"Threaten me all you want," I said. "I'm not talking until you get a translator who knows how to translate."

The next day, there was a new interpreter sitting alongside the first one. He had three dictionaries with him, which didn't inspire confidence. But the first thing he said was, "This other interpreter doesn't know what he's doing. I'm better than him," so I decided to give him a chance.

A week or two later, I was being questioned by two interrogators when one of them brought out my work license from Pakistan and put it on the table.

"You worked for this organization?" she asked.

"Yes," I told her. "I worked for the Hira Institute."

As I said this, the two interrogators looked at each other and smiled as though they had found buried treasure.

"So did you know this guy, Zahid Al-Sheikh?" the female interrogator asked, pointing at a signature on my work license.

"I recognize the name," I said. "He was the director of the institute when I worked there. But I never met him. Why?"

"He's the brother of Sheikh."

"Who do you mean?" I asked. "There are a lot of Sheikhs."

"Don't you know Khalid Sheikh Mohammed?"

"No," I answered. "I've never heard that name before. Who is he?"

She wouldn't tell me. I couldn't believe it. Was I here because a dozen years ago, one of my supervisors whom I'd never met was the brother of someone I'd never heard of?

"What about Osama bin Laden?" she asked. "Do you know him?"

"Sure," I answered. "The whole world knows him. He's on TV all the time. Even a child's heard of him."

"No," she said. "Do you know him personally?"

"Of course not," I answered, exasperated. "And even if I did, so what? I have nothing to do with what he did. Why am I here?" I pounded the table in frustration.

That was when the useless interpreter, who kept coming to all the interrogations while the other one translated, spoke up.

"Listen to me. Tomorrow, you're going to tell them the truth, or else!" he barked, gesturing threateningly at the gun-toting soldier standing behind him.

"What truth?" I snapped back. "What truth, you idiot?"

"That you're in Al Qaeda and that you know Osama bin Laden and Khalid Sheikh Mohammed. That's what you have to tell them!"

I'd had enough. I started swearing at the interpreter. I was still cursing as the soldiers picked me up to take me back to my cell.

The next day, everyone had calmed down and the interrogation continued. I told them a lot about my work for the Red Crescent, and then they asked me about two other relief organizations in Bosnia. I'd never worked for either one and I didn't know anything about them.

"Why," I said, "are you asking me about these organizations?"

"They teach children to use weapons and train them to be terrorists."

"But," I asked, "do you have any reason to think that the Red Crescent ever did anything like that?"

"No."

"I'll tell you what," I said. "I've got a good idea. Why don't you go pick up the directors of those organizations, bring them here, and question them?"

For the next several weeks, the interrogations continued along those lines. The interrogators asked me about people and organizations I didn't know anything about, and I suggested that they question those people instead of me.

One interrogation, though, stood out from the rest. When I was brought into the interrogation room, there was a man I'd never seen before. He sat and listened for fifteen minutes while the interrogator asked me some questions, and then he asked the interrogator to step out of the room. An armed soldier stayed.

"Listen," the stranger told me, speaking Arabic with a Jordanian accent. "You'd better start being honest. I'm from Jordan, and I'll bring you back there, where there are no rules against torture."

"I'm not Jordanian," I told him. "I'm Algerian. What right do you have to come here and threaten me?"

He started swearing. He picked up the pen in front of him and flung it at my face. "You want to fight?" he said, trying to sound menacing.

He was the classic schoolyard bully, picking on someone who couldn't fight back. "Take off these shackles, you sorry excuse for a man, and then let's see who wins," I shot back, throwing in a few curse words for good measure.

That set him off. He came toward me, swearing, and wrapped his thick hands around my neck as though to strangle me. The armed soldier stood there impassively and watched. I looked to see if there was a camera in the wall, like in some of the other interrogation rooms. There wasn't.

But I knew the Jordanian wasn't going to kill me. He was just trying to scare me. And I refused to let him.

"You want to kill me?" I asked.

"Yes."

"Then do it! If you're a real man, do it!"

As his hands tightened around my neck, I swore at him at the top of my lungs. He kept squeezing. I am a man of faith, I thought to myself. Only God has the power to end a life.

Fifteen or twenty seconds passed. Finally, the Jordanian loosened his grip and stormed out of the room. I gulped in air. A day later, I was taken to the clinic for a medical examination. I was bruised, and a bit hoarse, but otherwise fine. I hadn't let the bully get the better of me. The next day, the Jordanian was gone and the interrogations went back to normal.

Every time I was brought back to my cage from interrogation, I was overwhelmed by the stench of the cellblock. I don't know why they couldn't have given us lids for our waste buckets. The buckets would sit in the hot sun all day, and then at night we'd have to lay our heads on the ground just a few feet from them.

The soldiers would have appreciated lids too. They hated emptying the buckets. I once saw a soldier drop his set of keys into a bucket, and heard him unleash a torrent of curse words. I didn't recognize all of the words, but I heard both "bin Laden" and "Bush" a few times in his tirade. Another soldier, who was usually very polite and mild-mannered, swore at the top of her lungs when she was carrying a bucket and it splashed against her leg.

Eventually, the soldiers started making prisoners empty the waste buckets as a form of punishment. I watched as Saber Lahmar, whom I'd met on my last day in the Bosnian prison, carried a bucket several yards from a cell to the dumpsite, cuffed and chained the whole time. I could see blood dripping down him. I cringed at the thought of him having to do the same thing for another fifty-plus buckets.

As the weeks passed, the heat grew more and more oppressive. We were always exposed to the sun, roasting like chickens. Sometimes a prisoner would put a sheet or a towel up against the wire mesh of his cell to try to block the sun, but it never stayed up for more than a few minutes before a soldier ordered him to take it down. Many of us had arrived pale, and now we were dark.

We were also dirty. There was no timetable for when we could shower. A guard would simply show up, once every few weeks, and lead me to the shower room. In the three months that I spent in my outdoor cage, I showered maybe five times. Not once was I given soap or shampoo. They did give me toothpaste, which was twenty years old and smelled like it, and a toothbrush, but only the bristles. They removed the toothbrush handle because they thought someone might use it as a weapon.

And there were the animals. One morning, a prisoner was shaking out his isomat when I saw a scorpion fall to the ground and clatter away. It reminded me of my time on the border patrol in Algeria, except now I couldn't go inside and I didn't have a gun.

One night, my fitful sleep was interrupted by panicked screams. Apparently, a snake had started slithering through the mesh cages and then came within inches of a prisoner's face as he slept. The soldiers killed the snake before it bit anyone, but the thought of snakes crawling around while I tried to sleep at night was unsettling.

Despite the exhaustion, frustration, and pain, I was determined to stay optimistic. I just had to keep going to these interrogations, to keep telling the truth. In time, they would realize I was innocent, just like the Bosnian court had, and they would let me go home to Abassia and my girls. They had to.

Mustafa

IN APRIL OF 2002, after three months, I exited Camp X-Ray in much the same fashion as I had entered: bound, blind, and beaten.

The soldiers burst into my cell, ordered me to kneel, and cuffed my hands and shackled my feet. They threw a bag over my head, placed earmuffs over the bag, and led me onto a bus with other prisoners. They shackled me to the floor. For the entire bus ride, the soldiers hit me, over and over and over again. I could not see or hear. I could barely move. I was forced to sit there, in silence and darkness, waiting for the next blow to land. And then the next.

I could tell we were driving in circles. Maybe they were trying to disorient us, although I cannot fathom why, since none of us knew where we were to begin with. Maybe they just wanted more time to beat us. I spent at least forty-five minutes on that bus, slowly circling Guantanamo and enduring the soldiers' blows.

After the bus ride, the soldiers led me to a cell and removed my blindfold. One of the first things I noticed was that some familiar faces from Camp X-Ray were missing. I asked a soldier where they were, and he told me that they had been taken to the hospital because of the beatings.

My new cell, I learned, was in "Camp Delta." Camp Delta would grow over time to include several sub-camps and some concrete buildings, but at first it was nothing more than rows of converted trailers that had been partitioned into cells. Each cell measured six feet by six feet. The bed took up half of the cell by itself, and the toilet and sink took up space too, so there was very little room to move around. When I paced, I could take four steps before it was time to turn.

This was the space in which I spent six years of my life.

At least now I had a roof over my head to protect me from the elements. I had no privacy when I used the toilet in my cell, but at least I *had* a toilet. The water that came out of the faucet in my cell was often dark brown, especially after a storm, but at least I *had* running water. There were even two showers and a yard where I was sometimes allowed to take a walk.

There was a huge, powerful fan in the cell block. When they turned it on, it made the whole block shake. I felt like my head was going to explode. Sometimes they would run the fan at night, making it impossible to sleep. The fan was so loud that we could not even speak with one another when it was on. Not that that mattered much, since we weren't allowed to speak with each other in the first place.

Floor to ceiling, the entire cell block was made of metal. When it was cold out, our cells were freezing. When it was hot, we sweltered. There was no in-between. Sometimes the soldiers would punish us on hot days by covering all of the windows and vents with boards, making it so stifling that it was hard to breathe. Some of the inmates, especially the older ones, would faint and need to be hospitalized.

When our cells cooled at night, especially in the wintertime, our thin blankets were not enough. We requested heavier blankets, but the officers said no. Sometimes the soldiers would punish a detainee by taking away his mattress, his blanket, everything in his cell but his metal bedframe. Hot or cold, he would have to sleep on the bare metal or not at all.

There were few options to pass the time in Camp Delta. We had no books, other than the Qur'an, and no television. Sometimes, I would chat with the other detainees, but only when there were no soldiers nearby. If the soldiers heard us talking, they would punish us.

When we did talk, we usually kept the conversation light. We discussed our lives back home, our families, the jobs we had once held. We came from different countries, grew up in different circumstances, and in some cases spoke different languages. We did not know each other well enough for deeper conversation, and it was hard to become better acquainted when we could only speak in sporadic, stolen bursts.

What we *did* have in common, of course, was Guantanamo. Our most frequent topic of conversation soon became the inhumane living conditions and the brutality of the soldiers. We also talked about the interrogation sessions. What kinds of questions had the interrogators asked? What kinds of threats had they made?

The interrogations were not that bad at first. At least, they were no worse than every other aspect of life in Guantanamo. The interrogators asked basic, straightforward questions about my job, my family, my life back when it had still been my own. I had nothing to hide, so I gave truthful, complete answers. The interrogators did not prod or threaten, nor did they need to.

Then a switch flipped, and the interrogations and accompanying punishments suddenly became a hundred times harsher. It started with one particular interrogator. You might have seen the news reports, some years back, about the sexual harassment of detainees by a female interrogator at Guantanamo. I was one of her victims.

I still remember the first time it happened. I was sitting in the interrogation room, ankles shackled to the floor as usual, when she walked in. She sat a few feet from me and unbuttoned her shirt, exposing herself. She just sat there. She did not touch me. She did not say a word. She would just sit there and wait for me to react.

This happened many times. Often there were male soldiers in the room as well, watching her undress. Not once did she ask me a question, even though she was supposedly an interrogator. All she ever did was expose herself to me and to other Muslim detainees. I think she did this, or was instructed to, because it went against our religion. The goal was to make us feel like sinners, to make us feel humiliated and guilty, frustrated, weak and broken.

I do believe that it goes against both my religion and basic human decency for a man to stare at a naked woman he does not know. But I had lived in Europe for years. I had been bombarded with over-sexualized images, on billboards and magazine covers and the television, for years. They held no power over me. Certainly, I was not about to let this "interrogator" cow or intimidate me just because she was willing to disrobe in public. She could disrespect herself, disrespect me, disrespect my religion, but she would not break me.

"Listen to me," I said. "What you're doing is not acceptable. It's not good. But these sights you're showing me, compared to what I saw in Europe, it's nothing really. If you think this is going to have an impact on me, it's not going to happen. Absolutely not. Do what you please. You will not provoke me."

After that, everything got worse. I had been defiant. And as a result, I had to be punished. The soldiers started inventing reasons to harass me. I would be sitting quietly in my cell, and the soldiers would come in to conduct a "search." During the course of the so-called search, they would remove everything from the cell that was not bolted down. Days would pass before I saw my mattress, my blanket, or my Qur'an again.

"What am I being punished for?" I would ask.

Their answers varied. Maybe I had caused problems with a soldier. Maybe I had cursed at an interrogator. Maybe I had refused to follow an order. It was always something, and it was always false. I knew the soldiers were making things up, and I knew I wasn't the only one this was happening to. I think they targeted those they could not break.

Gradually, the punishments escalated. From time to time, guards would come to my cell, put me in handcuffs and shackles, and lead me to a pitch-black room with a single wooden chair in it. They would chain me to the chair and leave. Sometimes I spent more than twelve hours there, by myself, in the dark. I was not able to sleep or eat or drink or use the restroom. I could not pray properly, but still I prayed. And prayed.

Eventually, a soldier would come. He would remove my handcuffs and lead me back to my cell, where I could finally use the toilet. But it was not over. Fifteen minutes later, he would come back. He would again shackle me, take me to the dark room, chain me to the chair, and leave. Another twelve hours would pass, sometimes more. Some detainees, I heard, were left alone in the dark for more than twenty-four hours. One man was kept there for thirty-six hours. Thirty-six hours with no food, no water, no toilet. He soiled his pants.

We were no longer in outdoor cages, but somehow, we were now being treated even less like humans.

Lakhdar

WHEN I ARRIVED IN CAMP DELTA, my first thought was that it was a five-star hotel compared to Camp X-Ray. The three indoor-facing walls of my cell were wire mesh, but the wall to the outside was steel, with a small mesh window for ventilation, so I wasn't directly exposed to the sun. Better yet, each cell had its own sink and toilet. I no longer had to defecate into a bucket feet from where I slept.

Camp Delta could still be stifling and foul-smelling, especially on the days when the soldiers blocked all the ventilation to punish us. And animals could still sometimes find their way in—occasionally, for example, a crab would crawl out of the toilet bowl. One of the guards liked to catch the crabs and cook them. On the whole, though, Camp Delta was a significant improvement.

My cell was near one end of a row of about twenty cells, and there was another row of cells directly across from ours. I was able to talk with several of my neighbors when the guards couldn't hear us. There were men from Afghanistan, Saudi Arabia, and Yemen. I didn't recognize a single one of them from Camp X-Ray—either they had been in a different part of X-Ray or they were more recent arrivals to Guantanamo.

I'd been in Camp Delta for a short while, maybe three or four days, when there was a tremendous commotion. I heard the shouts and wails of what sounded like dozens of prisoners. The screams were coming from the cells at the far end of my row, so I couldn't tell what had caused them. Later on, once everything had calmed down, I asked my neighbors what had happened.

"I heard," one of them told me, "that a soldier went into some-one's cell and flushed his Qur'an down the toilet."

"Unbelievable," I said.

It was a few days later that I got into trouble. I had been taken out of my cell to interrogation, and I was being questioned by a female interrogator. She was trying to be intimidating, getting in my face and shouting "Look at me!" whenever I looked away, even if it was just to look at the interpreter. I was tired, sore, and growing increas-ingly frustrated with this interrogator, who seemed more intent on browbeating me than on listening to me. After one "Look at me!" too many, I'd had enough. I lashed out.

"Why would I look at you?" I demanded. "You aren't my wife. You aren't my friend. In fact, you're the ugliest woman I've ever seen in my life."

That ended the interrogation. But instead of being sent back to my cell, I was put in an isolation cell. It had four steel walls, so I couldn't see or hear anything outside it. There was a small opening in one wall, covered by mesh, from which ice cold air poured forth at all times.

It was almost impossible to sleep in isolation. There were two powerful lights—like the headlights of a Jeep—positioned in such a way that no matter where I faced, they shone in my eyes. They were protected by mesh, so I couldn't smash them. And there was the cold. I slept on an isomat, and I had a thin blanket that the guards brought at 10:00 every night and took away around 4:00 every morning. The blanket was small, so I had to contort myself to try to keep warm. I spent most of my time in that cell exhausted but awake.

The only human contact I had was when the nurses came to check on me. On one visit, they noticed my wedding ring and told me I wasn't allowed to have it in Guantanamo. "You'll have to cut my finger off," I laughed, remembering the last two times people had tried to remove the ring. But one of the nurses applied some creams and yanked on the ring until it came off. As it did, I could see blood dripping down my ring finger. The cut eventually healed, but I never saw my ring again.

In isolation, I was so deprived of sleep and human connection that I became hypersensitive to even the littlest things—my hair, for example. It had been months since I'd shaved or gotten a haircut. And I had no way to wash my hair: there was no shampoo and the soap smelled too disgusting to even wash my hands in. So I had smelly, clumpy, shoulder-length hair and a long, scratchy beard—and nothing to distract me from the thought of how much I itched.

I'm not sure exactly how long I was in that room, itchy, tired, and alone. I tried to count the days based on when meals were brought to me, but I eventually lost track. After what felt like about three weeks, I was taken out of isolation and brought back to a normal cell.

The next time I was interrogated, it was by two men.

"We want you to take a lie detector test," one of them said.

I was happy to take the test—I had nothing to hide—but I didn't want them to think they could just throw me into an isolation cell whenever they wanted to get me to do what they asked.

"I'll take the test," I told them. "I know I'm innocent. But there's one condition."

"What's that?"

"I get a haircut first."

They hemmed and hawed. "We'll ask our supervisor," they said, and I was taken back to my cell.

A week passed before I was taken back to the interrogation room. This time, there were two men I'd never seen before, and an interpreter. I was shackled to a chair, and the two men started attaching wires to me.

"These men are specialists," the interpreter told me. "They're going to administer the lie detector test."

"No," I protested. "I told them. I won't take the test until I get a haircut."

"Who are you to be setting conditions?" the interpreter demanded.

I was so tired of these interpreters doing everything but translating. "Who are you, you dog, to talk to me that way?" I shot back. "Your job is to translate. You say my words to the Americans. That's it."

He seemed cowed. After a conversation in English with the lie detector experts, he told me, "Look, they don't know anything about this haircut business. They were just told to give you the test. Why don't you take it, and afterwards, we'll do what we can to get you a haircut."

I didn't believe that for a second. "No," I told him. "You bring a barber here and cut my hair, and then I'll answer all the questions you want. Until then, I'm not going to say a word."

That was the moment I stopped being scared. I knew I was innocent, and I knew there was no prison worse than this that they could throw me into—so what was there to be afraid of? From then on, I determined, I would speak from a position of strength. I would answer their questions, but I would demand to be treated like a man.

They didn't get a barber, so I didn't take their test. They returned me to my cell, where days passed. I was taken to the interrogation room a few more times, but I made it clear that I wouldn't answer any of their questions until I got a haircut. Eventually, they put me back in an isolation cell, but I was determined not to budge. I had made a decision and I was going to stick to it.

After a few days in isolation, a soldier stopped by and asked if I wanted a haircut. "Yes," I said, but I was sure it was just a ruse. There was no way they were actually going to cut my hair.

Ten minutes later, the soldier came back, bound my hands, and led me out of my cell. With an electric razor, he cut my hair and trimmed my beard. When he finished, there was hair everywhere, including all over my clothes. He led me back to my cell, where I doused myself with water from the sink and ran my hands through my newly cropped hair. For the first time in months, I felt fresh and clean. It was a little thing, but it made me feel like a new man.

. . .

The next day, there was a different interrogator. "Hi," he said, in a friendly voice. "I'm not like the other guys. I'll treat you well. I'll co-operate with you." *Okay*, I figured. *This must be the good cop.*

"What do you want?" I asked him.

"Just to talk with you," he replied. "Let me take you out of isolation, put you back in a normal cell, and we'll just talk."

"Sure," I said. I knew his kindness was just an act, but I was happy to talk with him. I still thought that if I kept telling the truth, eventually someone might believe me. At least I had gotten a haircut.

True to the interrogator's word, I was taken from isolation to a new cell, in a ward called "Mike." There was a familiar face in the cell diagonally across from mine. Saber Lahmar, the member of the "Algerian Six" whom I'd met on my last day in Bosnia, was now my neighbor.

"As-salaam alaykum," I greeted him. *Peace be upon you.*

"Wa-alaykum as-salaam," he replied. *And upon you peace.* And then Saber asked me the same question I'd been asking myself for months.

"Do you have any idea what's going on?"

"I don't, Saber," I answered. "By God, I don't."

Over the next few months, I remained in the same cell, near Saber. Once a day, a soldier was supposed to take me outside for a short walk. Sometimes, he would make up a reason not to. "Detainee refused rec walk," he might write. The process of taking me out of my cell—I held out my hands, he cuffed them, chained me down, entered the cell, shackled my legs together, unchained me, and off we went—required a lot of effort on his part. It was easier for him just to lie.

I wanted to do something worthwhile with all the time I was spending in my cell, so I started to memorize *suras* (chapters) of the Qur'an. It was difficult to concentrate—my eyes would be on the Qur'an, but my mind would wander. *How are Abassia and the kids doing without me? Do they have enough food? Is there a roof over their heads?* Still, it was good to have a concrete task to try to focus on.

The first *sura* I memorized was "Youssef," about a prophet who was unjustly imprisoned for years before he was found innocent and set free (see page 235 in "Additional Material"). I would repeat to myself over and over lines from "Youssef" about God's mercy and "His subtle ways," about Youssef's dogged patience, his steadfast faith, his eventual victory over injustice, and his reunification with his family. They were a powerful source of inspiration and hope for me, and I was proud to know all 111 verses by heart, including the one containing the phrase "Witnesses of the Unseen." I also memorized "Maryam," a beautiful *sura* of 98 verses, and I worked on Al-Baqara ("The Calf"), but it was 286 verses long and I could never quite master it.

In November of 2002, I observed my first Ramadan in Guantanamo. Some of the guards wanted to make it especially difficult to keep the fast from sunup to sundown. In the mornings, they delayed bringing *suhoor*—the pre-dawn meal—until after sunrise, so we couldn't eat it. In the evenings, they wouldn't bring *iftar* (the post-sunset meal) until several hours after sunset, and they made a point to bring tiny portions. You could literally count the grains of rice.

I lost so much weight during Ramadan that the doctors instructed me to drink two cans of Ensure each night. Two nights in a row, a nurse came by my cell at 3:00 a.m. with the cans and I drank them. But then the Ensures stopped coming, and I didn't know why. Maybe I was being punished? (Months later, after I had been transferred to another cellblock, one of my neighbors mentioned that he had unexpectedly started receiving two cans of Ensure a night during Ramadan. It turned out that his detainee number, 0005, was similar to mine: 10005. What I had assumed was yet another intentional cruelty was probably just incompetence.)

In early December, Ramadan ended and I was able to regain some weight. Throughout all of this, my interrogations with the "good cop" continued. He asked the same questions as the other interrogators, and I gave the same answers. I didn't tell him about a time Bill Clinton had visited Sarajevo and I saw him from a distance—I was nervous the interrogator might suspect me of plotting to attack the president—but otherwise, all of my answers were honest and complete.

They were not, however, what the people in charge were looking for. In February of 2003, after I had been in Guantanamo for a year, they switched back to "bad cop."

It was midnight, and I was asleep, when a soldier walked into my cell.

"Move!" he barked.

"Where are we going?" I asked groggily, as I stood up.

"To interrogation."

"At this hour?"

"Those are the orders. Shut up and move."

When we got to the interrogation room, a man whom I'd never seen before was waiting for us. His teeth were black. He strode up to me, his face inches from mine, and started firing questions at me. His breath was a memorably bad combination of foul-smelling food, cigar smoke, and bad hygiene.

This, I thought, *is no way to talk to a man.* If it had been a reasonable hour, if he'd treated me respectfully, if he'd brushed his teeth sometime in the past month, I probably would have answered his questions, just like I had answered everyone else's. But I wasn't going to talk to him now. Not like this. I simply stared straight back at him, silent and calm.

"Do you hear me?" the interpreter asked. I didn't even glance at him. I kept my gaze fixed on the interrogator and my mouth shut.

As I stayed quiet, the interrogator became more and more agitated. He yelled. He paced. He threw a notebook on the floor. And then, after all that, he said something that truly startled me.

"Look, Lakhdar," he sighed. "We know you're innocent. But there are two others in the Algerian Six, and we need you to testify against them. Just tell us the truth about them and then you can go home."

I was stunned. I had spent a year answering all of my interroga-tors' questions, even offering to keep going after a full day of ques-tions, all so that they would realize I was innocent—and they knew I was innocent all along?

I realized then that nothing I said would get me home any sooner. Convincing them of my innocence clearly didn't matter, and I could hardly testify against people who, as far as I knew, had never com-mitted a crime. So what was the point of talking? I kept my mouth shut while the interrogator kept up his drivel. After several hours, I was taken back to my cell.

A few hours later, when the soldiers brought me breakfast, I de-cided not to eat it. They were holding me here even though they knew I was innocent. This wasn't a misunderstanding, it was a kidnapping—and I was going to protest it. I wouldn't speak or eat until my treatment improved.

An hour or two later, I was taken back to an interrogation room. There was a new interrogator.

"Still not talking?" he asked. "Do you really want to spend the rest of your life here? Don't you have a wife and children?"

He kept threatening me, and I kept quiet. After half an hour or so, he turned to the soldier and said, "Take his chair."

The soldier stood me up, took the chair, and left me standing there. I guess the goal was to wear me out. The interrogator and the interpreter played cards while I stood. Every few minutes, the inter-rogator asked me if I wanted the chair back, or some water, to try to get me to speak. I stayed silent. *I'll show you*, I thought. *As long as you keep treating me like this, by God, you will know who Lakhdar Boumediene is.*

After a few hours, I was taken out of the interrogation room and back to my cell. That afternoon, they moved me to an isolation cell with nothing in it but an isomat. Like the last isolation cell, it was bitterly cold. They brought me lunch and dinner, but I didn't touch either one. I only paid attention to when they brought meals so I could pray at roughly the right times.

I was getting hungry, but I'd fasted before, and my mind was made up. I wasn't going to back down.

Neither were they. That night, I was taken back to an interrogation room. The foul-breathed interrogator from the night before and a few armed soldiers were waiting for me.

The interrogator talked at me for an hour or two, and when he'd had enough of my silence, he turned to the soldiers and muttered a few words that I wasn't able to catch. The soldiers left the room, and a few minutes later, a new group of soldiers walked in.

"Take him outside," the interrogator told them. They led me up a flight of eight or nine concrete steps to a long gravel drive. It was pitch black out, and completely quiet. There was no one around. One of the soldiers grabbed my left arm, and another took my right. And then they started running.

I tried to keep up, but my legs were shackled together. First, my flip-flops fell off, and after a few barefoot strides, my legs fell out from under me. The soldiers didn't even slow down. They kept a firm grip on my arms while my legs bounced and scraped along the ground, gravel biting into them. When the run finally ended, the soldiers brought me back to the interrogation room, bloody and bedraggled.

"Now," the interrogator asked, "do you want to talk?"

What they had done only made me more determined. *They'll never get what they want*, I resolved, *by treating me like this*. I kept my mouth shut, and eventually the soldiers brought me back to my isolation cell.

The next day was a repeat: I skipped my meals during the day, stayed silent through the morning and evening interrogations, and at night, did my best to keep pace with the soldiers until I fell and was dragged across the gravel.

On the third day, I was taken to the clinic in the morning, where I was examined and given fluid through an IV. That night consisted of more interrogation and gravel. And that's how things went for the next ten days. In the mornings, the nurses gave me IV fluids to keep me alive, and at night, the soldiers literally ran me into the ground.

Some nights were worse than others. One night, as we approached the concrete steps leading up to the gravel drive, a soldier decided that I wasn't moving fast enough. He yanked on my arm, throwing me off balance, and dragged me up the concrete stairs, my left knee slamming into each step. My knee took years to heal.

During one interrogation, the interrogator decided to make some especially vivid threats. "Unless you talk," he said, "we're going to put you in lipstick and blush and send you to an American prison. Do you know what they'll do to you there?" He took out a post-it note and a pen, drew an image of one man raping another, and affixed it to my shoulder. He kept talking about prison showers and sodomy, and at one point he reached out and touched my thigh.

For the first time, I opened my mouth—not to say anything, but to spit on the interrogator. When I did, he reared his hand back as though to strike me, but at the last second he stopped himself. Maybe he thought his supervisors were watching from behind the glass? Instead, he grabbed a fistful of my shirt, shook me, turned, and stormed out.

Another night, when I was brought into the interrogation room, there was a circle of photographs on the ground in front of my chair. There were photos of me, the other prisoners from Bosnia, and an assortment of refugee children. As the soldier forced me into my chair, I had no choice but to step on the photos. The interrogator was watching, and I refused to give him the satisfaction of trying to avoid the photos or appearing upset about stepping on them.

As I calmly stepped on the photos, the interrogator started shouting. "Have you no mercy?" he screamed. "You're a criminal. How can you put your feet on these innocent children?" His indignation was so transparently fake, and his ruse so juvenile, that even as exhausted and hungry as I was, I found it hard not to laugh. But I kept a straight face, determined not to show emotion, while he carried on with his skit.

The next morning, my visit to the clinic was especially unpleasant. While I was receiving fluid through an IV, a nurse handed me a vial, said he needed a urine sample, and walked out. I wasn't able to urinate at that point, so when the nurse came back fifteen minutes later, the vial was still empty. The nurse got a doctor, who said, "Enough. You take it." A group of nurses, some male and some female, pulled down my pants and inserted a catheter. It was both embarrassing and extremely painful. I really wanted to speak at that point, to ask them to please stop, to tell them that I would urinate as soon as I could—but I had made a decision.

After almost two weeks of silence, my captors began to wonder if there was a medical explanation for it. For the first time, a doctor attended one of my nighttime interrogations. The doctor acted like he was important, and he had an eagle insignia on his shoulder, so I figured he was a colonel. The colonel held a bag of smelling salts in front of my nose, which made me reflexively sniff; he shone a flashlight in my eyes, which made me blink; and he unexpectedly clapped his hands directly behind my ears, which made me start.

"Okay," the colonel said. "You can continue with the interrogation."

Later, the colonel threatened me himself. "Listen," he said. "If you don't stop your strike, the next time you have an IV put in, it won't be the nurse who does it. It will be one of the soldiers."

I thought it was an empty threat, but the colonel was true to his word. The next day, he was waiting for me in the clinic, and he said to the soldier who had brought me, "Do the IV for him." The colonel then walked out of the room. The soldier didn't seem excited about the prospect, but he'd been given an order. He started poking me with a needle, repeatedly missing my vein, while a nurse stood and watched. Eventually, once my arm had become a bloody, sodden mess, the nurse intervened.

"Enough," she said. "I'll do it."

Painful as that had been, it only hardened my resolve. As long as they kept treating me like this, they wouldn't get a word from me. I went to the interrogations and sat there, silently eyeing the interrogator's wristwatch and counting down the time until I could go back to my cell. Sometimes I was so exhausted that I fell out of my chair, collapsing into a heap on the ground—at which point the guards would simply pick me up and sit me back in the chair.

After several days, the people in charge decided to try "good cop" again. Instead of an interrogator, they sent a tall, blonde interpreter to speak with me. She said her name was Alia, and she spoke with sympathy in her voice.

"I just want to talk with you," she said. "I don't care about the soldiers and the interrogators. I know they're disrespectful and mean. They're rude to me too. But look, I've read about hunger strikes, and they aren't good. Your kidneys and pancreas can be permanently damaged. You really need to eat."

I was glad that someone was speaking to me politely—kindly, even—but I kept my mouth shut. *If I talk to Alia now,* I figured, *the foul-breathed interrogator will be back in no time.* Alia spent a little while telling me about a recent prank that a troublemaking prisoner named Hamza had pulled, and then she left.

The next evening, when I was taken to the interrogation room, I was greeted by a black soldier I had never seen before and an interpreter. The soldier had a carton of hamburgers, maybe a dozen of them, and he offered one to me. I thought it was funny that the delectable feast he was trying to tempt me with consisted of *hamburgers.* "Come try Abassia's chicken and olives," I wanted to say to him, "and then talk to me about your hamburgers." But I kept my mouth shut.

The soldier unwrapped one of the hamburgers and inhaled. "Smell that," he said. I didn't. He thrust the hamburger toward my mouth, and I jerked my face away to avoid it. "Fine," he shrugged, and then he and the interpreter started eating hamburgers in front of me.

The evening after that, there was a new "good cop" with a new approach to try to get me to talk. He told me that when he was younger, he had traveled from Morocco to Syria by train, and the train had passed through Algeria.

"I don't want to ask you any questions," he said. "I just want to talk to you about the Algerian countryside."

I liked "good cop" better than "bad cop," but I was still determined not to speak. They knew I was innocent and didn't care, so I had nothing to say to them. I sat there silently until I was returned to my isolation cell.

The next day, as late afternoon turned into evening, I waited to be taken to yet another interrogation. But the guards never appeared. The night came and went and I was left alone. I thought that maybe the interrogators had given up. Maybe they realized they couldn't break my will. When a guard brought breakfast, I thought about eating—I had outlasted the interrogators, and I was starving—but it was too soon. I decided that I would eat if two more days passed without anyone interrogating me.

They left me alone, and on the third day, I ate. The food was as bad as always, but I was glad to have it. And once the guards saw me eating, they took me out of isolation and returned me to my old cell, next to Saber. For the next several months, no one tried to interrogate me. I stayed in my cell, save for the occasional rec walk or trip to the clinic. I talked with my neighbors, ate my meals, read the Qur'an, and wondered about how my family was doing and whether I would ever see them again. Things had gone back to normal.

Mustafa

IN SOME WAYS, the quiet, everyday hardships of life in Guantanamo were the worst part, worse even than the physical abuse. I had endured physical pain prior to Guantanamo as an athlete, though certainly not so much of it. Never before had I felt like I was losing hold of everything that made me human.

The inability to be there for my family, to even know what was going on in the lives of my wife and children, was indescribably painful. When I had been arrested, my wife was pregnant with our third son, Abdullah. He was born on July 1, 2002, but I did not find out until months later, when I received a letter from my wife with some pictures of our adorable baby boy. In the meantime, all I could do was worry, hope, and pray that everything was all right.

Although we were occasionally permitted to exchange letters with our families, they were always heavily redacted. The authorities used a computer and scanner, rather than a marker, and they were liberal with their redactions. Basic pleasantries like *As-salaam alaykum* were allowed to survive, but very little else made it past the overzealous censors. One of my fellow inmates received a letter where every single word was blacked out but two: "your mother." The man was terrified. Was his mother sick? Had she died? Was she simply saying hello?

The censors not only made our mail indecipherable, they also delayed it by months, sometimes years. Toward the end of my captivity, as an experiment, I wrote a letter to myself, addressed to my house in Sarajevo. The letter was delivered to me two-and-a-half years later.

Sometimes, the delays could be heartbreaking. Tragically, my friend Hadj's daughter passed away while he was in Guantanamo, something he learned about not from his family but in a meeting with his attorneys. Then, precisely one year to the day that his daughter died, the authorities delivered Hadj a letter that his daughter had written to him when she was still alive. I do not know if they purposely picked that day to deliver the letter; I do know that I will never forget the sight of Hadj weeping as he read his daughter's words from beyond the grave.

All of us lived in a constant state of concern about our families. If something happened to them, how would we find out? I knew nothing about what was going on in my family's lives. Everything was on a time delay; everything was redacted. This sense of isolation, of being removed from the regular flow of time and events, left me feeling disoriented and alone.

I thought about my family often. I thought about my wife. I thought about our sons. I thought about their financial situation, and I worried about them. One of my wife's letters said that she had gone back to being a schoolteacher, and I wondered how she could possibly work and take care of the children and run the household all by herself. Life is often hard enough for a young family, even when the husband and wife can take on the challenges together; my wife was forced to confront those challenges on her own for seven years.

It was reassuring to know that my wife had a job, and that my sons had a roof over their heads and a wonderful woman raising them. Still, every boy needs his father. When my sons went skiing with their classmates, for example, my wife's brother would take them, while all of the other boys went with their dads. I should have been there. My absence weighed on me often, as I am sure it must have weighed on them. Knowing that my children were growing up without their father was more painful than any physical trauma the soldiers might inflict.

Guantanamo also robbed me of my identity as an athlete. Before prison, I had exercised every single day, practicing karate and playing soccer for hours on end. Now, I was allowed an occasional "rec walk." There was nothing recreational about it.

Initially, in Camp X-Ray, the rec walk yard had been some six hundred feet from our cells. As the soldiers marched us from our cages to the yard, shackled and handcuffed, they beat us. Not until we were in the yard, bruised and bleeding, did they remove our shackles. The handcuffs never came off. After five minutes, the shackles went back on and we were marched, step by step, blow by blow, back to our cages. This was what qualified as "recreation" in Guantanamo. Many detainees started declining the rec walks. Once we were placed in Camp Delta and our cells were closer to a rec yard, several people still felt that the pain of being marched to the rec yard outweighed the benefit of being there.

I never turned down a rec walk. I was an athlete, and it went against my nature to sit still. I would have liked to do exercises in my cell too, but the soldiers would not let me. They knew about my karate background, and they were afraid that I would somehow train my fellow detainees. I tried limiting my exercise to movements wholly unrelated to martial arts, but to no avail. The soldiers told me that I was not allowed to do so much as a single push-up.

It was ludicrous. Other detainees were going to see me do push-ups and suddenly know karate? I was tired of the nonsense, tired of atrophying, tired of being bossed around by people who lacked all logic. I started doing push-ups.

A group of soldiers came by and threatened to punish me if I did not stop.

"Go ahead and do it," I said, continuing to raise and lower myself in rhythm above the cell floor, finally feeling like an athlete, like a man, once more.

That was how I wound up in solitary confinement.

The soldiers brought me from my cell to a smaller one, one that was completely dark save for a small, powerful light, like a movie projector, that poured into the room from outside. I tried to position myself so the light was not shining directly in my eyes, but I was told that this was not allowed, supposedly because then a soldier outside the cell would not be able to see what I was doing. I tried to cover my eyes with my hands, but they told me that was forbidden too. They claimed that they wanted to make sure I was not going to harm myself; I am certain that in truth, the only thing they were trying to "protect" me from was falling asleep.

They kept that damned light on for twenty-four hours a day. When the light went out, they brought me to a different cell with a working light rather than let me have even a brief period of relative darkness to sleep. I somehow managed to catch some sleep despite the harsh glare, but it was difficult. I spent days there, staring into a bright light, all because I had the audacity to do some push-ups.

Because of the sleep deprivation, the physical stress, and the squalor all around us in Guantanamo, illness was a constant presence in our lives. I started experiencing a sharp, shooting pain in my lower back, and my distress must have been visible to the soldiers. During one interrogation session, my interrogator said that he had heard I was in pain.

"Do you want some medication?" he asked.

"No, thank you," I responded. I had heard some grim stories about the medical "treatment" on offer at Guantanamo, and I was determined to avoid the prison hospital if I could help it.

"But you're sick," the interrogator protested.

I told him that was my problem, not his. I did not want treatment.

"If you change your mind, we can let the hospital know."

Again, I politely refused.

Eventually, though, the pain became overwhelming, and I told a soldier that I needed to go to the hospital. The soldier would not take me. A short while later, I collapsed. Apparently, that was what it took in Guantanamo to actually see the inside of a hospital, despite my interrogator's earlier offer. By the time a doctor finally saw me, I was gasping in pain.

The doctor told me I had a kidney stone and a bladder infection. He gave me a painkiller, but he said that he could not treat the underlying condition. He had been instructed not to provide further treatment unless I would provide more information to my interrogators.

"All we can do," he said, "is prevent you from dying. We can only bring you back to your previous state, even if that means you remain in pain. Anything more than preventing your death requires permission."

It was entirely up to the interrogators, not the doctors, whether I received medical treatment or not. That was the kind of power they wielded over us. That was the insanity of Guantanamo. Had I been a terrorist, I could have traded information for medical treatment. Because I was innocent, there was nothing I could tell them. I was not a terrorist. I did not know terrorists. I had no information that would interest them. So they let me suffer.

UNTIL PROVEN INNOCENT

Lakhdar

IN EARLY 2004, the powers that be decided to start holding what they called CSRTs, short for "Combatant Status Review Tribunals." These were panels of three military officers who would review the government's evidence against a prisoner, hear arguments from the prisoner's legal representative, and then determine whether the prisoner was actually an enemy combatant.

It quickly became clear that, whatever their actual purpose, the tribunals were never meant to give us a real chance to prove our innocence.

My first meeting with my "legal representative" was in one of the rooms where I had been interrogated. He was a soldier, not a lawyer, and he told me that his job was not to defend me—it was simply to deliver any messages I wanted to convey to the officers on the tribunal. Nothing I told him would be in confidence, and I would not have a chance to see any of the government's evidence against me.

I refused to speak with my representative or to attend my tribunal. The tribunal wasn't a real trial—it was a charade, a play, and everyone already knew how it was going to end.

Since I had declined to participate in my tribunal, I was surprised when, one day, the guards took me out of my cell and brought me into a hearing room. It looked like the interrogation rooms, but it was newer and bigger. There was a large table with an American flag on it and an officer seated behind it, flanked by two other soldiers, an interpreter, and a stenographer. Across from them, shackled to a chair, was my old friend Hadj Boudella, who three years earlier had walked into the Sarajevo police station at my request.

I was afraid they wanted me to testify against Hadj.

"Why," I asked, "am I here? These tribunals are plays—shams—and I told you, I don't want any part of them."

The officer told me that it was actually Hadj who had requested my presence, because he wanted me to testify as a character witness for him. I didn't trust the officer, so I asked Hadj if this was true. He nodded.

"Okay," I said. "If you want me to participate, then for you, my brother, I will."

After being sworn in, I told the officer that Hadj was a good man, an honest man, someone who would never be violent to anyone. The officer asked me if I had any idea why anyone might accuse Hadj of being a terrorist.

"No, I don't," I answered, exasperated. This was the same question I had been asking for the past two-and-a-half years. The officer asked me a few more questions about Hadj and my friendship with him, and then he asked me if there was anything else I could tell him to convince him of Hadj's innocence.

"Well," I asked, "if you know you are a terrorist and you know people are looking for you, are you going to escape or not?"

The officer seemed reluctant to answer, but eventually he did. "You would have . . . thought that a person would try to flee, yes."*

So I told him the story of how I had called Hadj and he had willingly come into the police station. Then the tribunal ended, and of course, none of it mattered. Hadj was still deemed a terrorist.

The same thing happened with my friend Mohamed Nechla, whom I had known in Albania and Bosnia. He requested me as a character witness; I told the tribunal that I knew Mohamed like a brother and knew him to be a peace-loving man—and it didn't matter one bit. The only difference was that this time, four hours before the hearing started, the guards left me by myself, chained, in a stiflingly hot room

---

* This quote is taken from page 23 of the transcript of Hadj Boudella's CSRT, which is available online at www.WitnessesBook.com.

next to the hearing room. There was an AC unit, with the switch in the "off" position, just out of my reach. I grew even more uncomfortable after the first hour, when I started to badly need a bathroom. But no one came to check on me. It was as though they were punishing me for testifying on my brother's behalf.

Mustafa

WHEN I FIRST HEARD about the CSRTs, I had no interest. I was not naive enough to believe that this was a legitimate opportunity to win my freedom. After considering it, though, I decided to participate. I did not want to give anyone a reason to think I had anything to hide.

On October 11th, 2004, in the early afternoon, soldiers brought me from my cell to a hearing room. The room was designed to intimidate, with the "jury" of three military officers looking down on me from a raised platform, but I felt completely calm. I was ready to speak my piece.

The officer in charge invited me to make an opening statement. I described everything that I had been through, from being arrested in Bosnia to being interrogated in Guantanamo. Another officer began reading the list of allegations against me, supposedly so that I would have an opportunity to respond. However, they refused to tell me *why* they suspected me of these things in the first place, which made it impossible to counter the allegations. How could I refute evidence I had never seen? This excerpt from the CSRT transcript best illustrates the absurd, show trial nature of the whole process:

> Recorder [reading Allegation 3.a.4]: While living in Bosnia, the Detainee associated with a known Al Qaida operative.
> Detainee: Give me his name.
> Tribunal President: I do not know.
> Detainee: How can I respond to this?
> Tribunal President: Did you know of anybody that was a member of Al Qaida?

Detainee: No, no.

Tribunal President: I'm sorry, what was your response?

Detainee: No.

Tribunal President: No?

Detainee: No. This is something the interrogators told me a long while ago. I asked the interrogators to tell me who this person was. Then I could tell you if I might have known this person, but not if the person is a terrorist. Maybe I knew this person as a friend. Maybe it was a person that worked with me. Maybe it was a person that was on my team. But I do not know if this person is Bosnian, Indian, or whatever. If you tell me the name, then I can respond and defend myself against this accusation.

Tribunal President: We are asking you the questions and we need you to respond. . . .*

The rest of the allegations were equally far-fetched, and the factual support for them equally nonexistent. When we reached the end of the list, I told the officer in charge what I thought of the allegations:

Tribunal President: Mustafa, does that conclude your statement?

Detainee: This is it, but I was hoping you had evidence that you can give me. If I was in your place—and I apologize in advance for these words—but if a supervisor came to me and showed me accusations like these, I would take these accusations and I would hit him in the face with them. Sorry about that. [Everyone in the Tribunal room laughs.]

Tribunal President: We had to laugh, but it is okay.

Detainee: Why? Because these are accusations that I can't even answer. I am not able to answer them. You tell me I am from Al Qaida, but I am not. . . . I don't have any proof to give you except to ask you to catch Bin Laden and ask him. . . . What should be done is you should give me evidence regarding these accusations because I am not able to give you any evidence. I can just tell you no, and that is it.†

* This quote is taken from page 13 of the transcript of Mustafa's CSRT, which is available online at www.WitnessesBook.com.

† This quote is taken from pages 14–15 of the transcript of Mustafa's CSRT.

After I gave my opening statement and tried to refute the allegations against me, the three military officers asked me some questions. They asked about Lakhdar, Mohamed, and Hadj, and I responded:

> Detainee: If one of those three [is] a terrorist, then I am a terrorist. If one of them is from Al Qaida, then I am from Al Qaida. If you imprison one of them for a terrorist act, then I am prepared to go to prison with him. I say these things because I know them as well as I know my wife and kids."*

Finally, as the hearing drew to a close, I tried to appeal to whatever still remained of the soldiers' basic human decency:

> Tribunal President: I don't have any other questions. Mustafa, do you have anything else you would like to present to us?
>
> Detainee: I just want to say a small thing. I hope that this is real. I am not berating you with these words, but this is something I don't want to keep inside. I hope this Tribunal is really real. I hope that a person who has made a mistake would admit to making a mistake. . . . [M]y wife and children are suffering . . . because some idiots acted stupidly and do not want to right their wrongs. They do not want to say that we made a mistake. . . . Today is the 11th of October, I think. In seven more days, I will have been [imprisoned] for three years. . . . I hope that the mistake that you made; not you personally, you did not make this mistake, but those who are responsible, will fix this mistake. That is all I have.†

All I had was not enough, not for the CSRT. The three soldiers determined that I was an enemy combatant. In this, I was hardly unique. As far as I know, no CSRT ever found anyone innocent. If you had been standing before them, or rather below them, you would have been deemed an enemy combatant too.

---

* This quote is taken from pages 14–15 of the transcript of Mustafa's CSRT.
† This quote is taken from pages 22–23 of the transcript of Mustafa's CSRT.

Lakhdar

IN LATE 2004, one of my neighbors, a man from Bahrain, was taken out of his cell in the morning. When he returned that evening, he shared an interesting story with those of us in earshot. He told us he had been taken to another facility, Camp Echo, where he had met with a group of civilian lawyers who offered to represent him and help him win his freedom.

We were all skeptical. Why believe these people? I had heard stories about interrogators pretending to be lawyers. I had even heard about one Kuwaiti detainee whose lawyer—at least, someone claiming to be his lawyer—encouraged him to confess that he was a member of Al Qaeda, even though he wasn't, in order to get credit for cooperating with the government. There was no one we could trust.

A few weeks later, the guards brought me to Camp Echo. As usual, they didn't tell me where we were going—they just appeared outside my cell and barked "Move!" They led me into a windowless room. The room was partitioned in two by a mesh grate, with a shower and cot on the far side of the grate and a table and chairs on my side. The guards sat me in a chair and locked the chain connecting my shackles to a metal loop in the floor. A short while later, two men walked in.

The first man certainly looked like a lawyer. He appeared to be in his sixties, with silver hair and a distinguished air about him. He carried himself with a sense of seriousness and, at the same time, warmth. I might have been inclined to trust him if it weren't for the man accompanying him.

"Boutros Farid," the second man said, introducing himself to me. "The lawyers hired me to translate for them." He clearly didn't recog-

nize me, but I recognized him: two years earlier, he had been one of
the interpreters during my interrogation sessions. Why would a real
lawyer have hired a military interpreter?

I thought about confronting Boutros, but I decided to see what
the "lawyer" had to say first. He told me his name, Steve Oleskey, and
he said that he was a partner at a law firm in Boston. He slid some
documents across the table. There was a letter from Abassia, along
with pictures of her and the kids. Raja and Rahma looked older than
I remembered them, but it was wonderful to see their faces. In her
letter, Abassia told me that she had talked to Steve and other lawyers
at his firm, and trusted them. "Please work with them," she wrote.
"They're going to help you." The letter sounded like Abassia, but I
couldn't be sure.

Steve told me about his childhood and why he became a lawyer.
He had grown up in the 1950s, during a time when many Americans
were being falsely accused of being Soviet sympathizers. His mother
had been an activist who worked with lawyers to try to protect innocent people from unjust persecution. Steve admired her greatly, so
he decided to become a lawyer. My case, he said, was an opportunity
to follow in his mother's footsteps and fight injustice.

When Steve finished speaking, tears were welling in his eyes. If he
was a liar, he was a very good one. But I still had doubts.

"Who," I asked, "is paying you to represent me?" After all, I knew
that my family didn't have enough money to afford a lawyer.

Steve told me that his law firm dedicated 5 percent of the money
it made to represent people who couldn't afford a lawyer—people
like me. That seemed plausible, and I told Steve I was grateful for his
firm's help.

But I still wanted to know why Steve was using a military
interpreter.

"Tell me," I said to Steve, with Boutros translating my words into
English, "Did you bring this interpreter along from America, or was
he provided to you by the army?"

"He came with me from America," Steve replied. "Why do you ask?"

"Because," I told him, "I know this man. He used to work here. He was an interpreter in the cellblocks and during interrogations. So what are you doing with him as your interpreter?"

Steve was at a loss for words. He seemed surprised. So surprised that I thought he might be telling the truth. Maybe his law firm had hired Boutros without realizing that he used to work in Guantanamo.

The next time I saw Steve, he had a different interpreter with him. I never saw Boutros again.

In the following months, I had several meetings with Steve, and he gradually earned my trust. He introduced me to several other lawyers from his firm, including another partner, Rob Kirsch, and two young associates, Melissa Coffey and Lynne Soutter. Lynne was pregnant, and it meant a great deal to me that she still took the time and energy to travel to Guantanamo to work on my case.

When the lawyers visited, they did their best to make Guantanamo a little bit less miserable. They brought me letters from Abassia and good food from Boston: Middle Eastern pastries, usually, and a thermos or two of coffee. After a few months, though, the people running Guantanamo put strict restrictions on what lawyers could bring in—so instead of pastries and thermoses, they brought me sandwiches and cups of coffee from the Subway and McDonald's on base. And instead of being able to hand me a letter from Abassia, they would have to give the letter to soldiers to be screened. I wouldn't see the letter until a month later; sometimes I never saw them.

During our meetings, the lawyers would ask me questions about my life and I would answer them. It was a lot like the interrogations, except the people asking the questions were friendlier. And sometimes Steve would tell me specific details about my journey that I hadn't been aware of—for example, that the military base where we stopped en route to Guantanamo was in Turkey (my guess had been right), or that the flight from Turkey to Guantanamo had taken roughly thirty hours. Also, unlike the interrogations, there were microphones and a video camera in the room so that the military could record every single second.

Steve told me that his law firm was planning to file something called a writ of *habeas corpus* with a federal judge in Washington, D.C. Under the U.S. Constitution, Steve explained, people have the right to claim that they've been unjustly imprisoned and to insist that a federal judge review the evidence against them. But Steve warned me that there was a catch: only American citizens and people imprisoned on American soil have that right, and the American government was going to argue that Guantanamo wasn't technically American soil.

I didn't have high hopes, especially after Steve told me that the federal judge, Judge Leon, had been appointed by President Bush. I knew my case had more to do with politics than with the law. After all, one of my interrogators had told me that he knew I was innocent, and it didn't matter. And Judge Leon was George Bush's appointee—of course he wouldn't set me free. Still, I had no other options. It was worth trying.

When Steve told me that his law firm was going to file writs of *habeas corpus* for all six members of the so-called "Algerian Six," and that the case would bear my name—it would be called *Boumediene v. Bush*—I was a bit nervous. Would Bush hold a grudge against me? And who was I to take on a president?

"Listen," I said to Steve. "I'm an ordinary man. I can't go up against a president."

Steve reassured me. He reminded me that the Algerian president from 1965 to 1978 had also been named Boumediene. "It will be a president against a president," Steve joked. "And we'll see who wins."

Mustafa

WHEN I FIRST RECEIVED A LETTER from Rob Kirsch and Steve Oleskey, claiming that my wife had hired them to be my attorneys, I was suspicious. Like every other detainee, I had been robbed of my capacity to trust. But I also had nothing to lose. I had already told my interrogators everything, and I had been completely forthright with them. If this were some sort of ruse, they would learn nothing new.

My initial meeting with Rob and Steve took place in a room not much larger than my cell. There were cameras in the room, and I am certain that soldiers were monitoring our conversation. Rob and Steve asked me several questions about my background and what had happened to me, and then they told me a bit about how the legal process would work. Honestly, I was not especially interested in the minute details. This was about politics, not the law. I was certain that even if we did win, the government would just appeal, keeping our case tied up in court forever.

Rob and Steve sent me a letter every time there was a development in my case, and they met with me in person whenever they could, every three to four months. They needed authorization from the U.S. Department of Defense for every visit, so sometimes one of their visits was pushed back because of bureaucratic delays.

When the attorneys came to Guantanamo, I usually met with at least two or three of them at once. Either Rob or Steve was almost always present, and I also became familiar with three of their associates: Lynne Soutter, Melissa Coffey, and Doug Curtis. During our meetings, the attorneys would update me on the case and the goings-on in the world, and then ask me questions to get information that they needed for the case. Sometimes they would read me statements that the government claimed I had made to make sure they were accurate. Often, they were not.

Meeting with the attorneys was a rare and welcome respite from everyday life in Guantanamo. It was refreshing to be treated like a human being, to be talked to like a man. And the soldiers would sometimes treat me better in the days leading up to the attorneys' arrival, although they often made up for it by being especially harsh after the attorneys left.

I will never be able to thank Rob, Steve, and their co-workers enough. They fought for me tirelessly, and for free. It is staggering to think about the time, effort, and expense required to win an innocent man's freedom, and more staggering still to think about what would have happened if these men and women had not poured so many hours and dollars into my case.

Lakhdar

WHILE OUR LAWYERS DID THEIR BEST to win our freedom, I did my best to survive the daily trials of life in Guantanamo.

Once each day, a nurse would order me to stick my arm out of the slot in my cell so he could give me an injection. At first, I complied. But I began to wonder what the injections were for (a medical issue? If so, what? Were they using me as a guinea pig?), so one time, when an interpreter was present, I asked the nurse what he was injecting into me. He refused to answer, so I refused to give him my arm. And that's when he called for an "IRF" team.* A group of men wearing helmets and body armor stormed into my cell and held me down while the nurse injected me. That was the first of many times that I was IRFed.

I continued to pass time in my cell by memorizing the Qur'an. I read the letters that I received from Abassia and the children—long letters with large portions blacked out by the soldiers. Sometimes I wrote replies, but I always kept them short, just two or three lines. "I'm doing all right. All I want is to see you. I'll see you soon, God willing." I knew that if I wrote more, if I mentioned anything specific about Guantanamo, the soldiers who checked the mail would either black it out or just throw out the whole letter. Plus, I didn't *want* to tell my family what Guantanamo was like. I wanted them to stay hopeful.

. . .

* Translator's Note: "IRF" stands for Initial Reaction Force. Detainees would sometimes refer to it as the "Extreme Repression Force," or ERF.

Sometime in mid-2004, my interrogations resumed. My new interrogator was a beefy giant of a man. He introduced himself as James, but I always thought of him as "The Elephant."

The Elephant's approach was completely different from my earlier interrogators, maybe because they had been such a failure. He didn't try to physically intimidate me. He didn't strut or shout or strike me. I could curse him out and he would just sit there calmly and listen. He was no brute. And yet, in some ways, The Elephant was the meanest person I've ever met.

For two years, The Elephant exercised complete control over my life. Where the other interrogators had tried to break my body, he went after my mind. He put in place a program designed to drive me mad. Some of his tactics involved the smallest details: having the guards mix uncooked rice into my meal, for instance, so that I would bite down on rock-hard grains. Other aspects of his psychological torture program were more significant, like instructing the guards to put me in an isolation cell for weeks or months at a time.

Through it all, The Elephant pretended that he was on my side. After I had been in an isolation cell for several weeks, the guards brought me to an interrogation room where The Elephant sat waiting for me. Feigning surprise, he asked me why I was in isolation, as though it hadn't been part of his program to put me there in the first place. I didn't answer.

"Ah," he said, glancing at a report in front of him. "It says here that you threw milk at a soldier."

That was a lie—I had never thrown milk at anyone—but I suppose they couldn't just throw me in an isolation cell without inventing a reason.

"Well," The Elephant said, keeping up his act of friendliness, "I could get you out of there and back to a normal cell if you want." By then, I knew him well enough to know he was playing mind games with me. He wanted me to ask him for something, so he could withhold it until I answered his questions.

"Actually," I told him, "I like it there. I don't have to worry about other prisoners bothering me. I'm a solitary person and I like the peace and quiet."

"What about the cold?" he asked.

"It's great. I used to love the winters in Bosnia."

The next day, the guards took me out of isolation and back to a normal cell.

Another time, I was sitting in an interrogation room when The Elephant burst in, dripping with sweat, a stack of letters in hand. "Whew," he said, putting on his best nice guy voice. "I've just come from the mailroom. I was looking for your letters. Someone misplaced them, but I was able to track them down."

I had been wondering why I hadn't gotten a letter from Abassia in the past few months. Now I had my answer. Not that the letters had been misplaced—I knew better than to trust The Elephant. He had been withholding them. If I showed any interest, he would have leverage. He could have my mail "misplaced" anytime he wanted. I knew other people who had been told that they'd get their mail as soon as they confessed.

I refused to give The Elephant that kind of control.

"Letters from who?" I asked. "No one sends me letters."

He seemed surprised. "What do you mean? They're from your wife and kids."

"I'm not married," I replied. "And I don't have kids."

"Of course you are. Your wife is Abassia. Your kids are Raja and Rahma."

"I don't recognize those names. That's the first time I've heard them."

He approached my chair and put the letters in my lap.

"Look," he pointed. "Your name is right there. This is your mail."

I could see my wife's handwriting, and a picture of Raja standing with some of her friends. *They look so grown up*, I thought. My emotions were about to overtake me. The Elephant was about to win. And I couldn't let him.

I picked up the mail and flung it at The Elephant's face. "These aren't my letters," I said, as the photo of Raja fluttered away. "That isn't my family."

The Elephant never thought I was a terrorist. At least, that's what he told me. "Your case is political," he said. It had nothing to do with guilt or innocence. I would get out as soon as President Bush agreed to let me go and Algeria's President Bouteflika agreed to take me. And that, The Elephant promised, would happen much sooner if I cooperated with him.

"Look," he said. "I don't care if you talk to me or not. But it'll be better for you if you do. Your friend Mohamed Nechla, he cooperates with me, so I make sure that he gets good food and coffee. And soon he's going to go to Algeria, because he talked—and you aren't cooperative, so you'll stay here."

I didn't believe him for a second.

"I'll tell you what," I said. "After Mohamed gets to Algeria, put me on the phone with him. Once I confirm that he's a free man, I'll cooperate with you all you want. All right?"

The Elephant had no response.

During one interrogation, The Elephant told me that a delegation of Bosnian officials was planning to visit Guantanamo and wanted to meet with me. The Elephant wanted me to refuse.

"You used to work in a charitable organization in Bosnia," he sneered. "You gave Bosnian children food and clothing. And look how they repaid you. They handed you over so you could be taken to Guantanamo. They sold you. Look what they did to you. If I were in your shoes, I wouldn't talk to them."

Sure, I thought. *Look what* they *did to me*. What a hypocrite.

"So," he asked, "Do you want to meet with them?"

I knew better than to give him a definite answer. If I said "No," he would report that I refused to meet with the delegation. If I said "Yes," he would have something he could hold over me as leverage. So I shrugged.

"I don't know," I told him. "When they get here, I'll decide."

When the delegation arrived, I decided to meet with them. I was furious with the Bosnian government, but I was willing to hear them out, if for no other reason than that The Elephant didn't want me to.

The meeting took place in an interrogation room. When I got there, three men were waiting for me: a man who introduced himself as Amir Pilav, from the Bosnian Ministry of Justice; Amir's translator, a Serb who spoke Bosnian and English; and an American I'd never seen before. Unlike the interrogators, who usually wore jeans and button-down shirts, these men were dressed in suits and ties.

"Do you speak Bosnian?" Amir asked.

I was determined not to speak to Amir in Bosnian. Not after Bosnia had sold me to the Americans. I shook my head.

"How about English?" asked the translator.

I shook my head again. My English was getting better, but I was nowhere near fluent, and I was in no mood to accommodate. The American made a phone call and requested an Arabic translator.

While we were waiting, Amir and the American talked to each other, with the Serb translating from Bosnian to English. I understood almost all of the Bosnian, although they assumed I couldn't. They talked about their plans for the following day—what they would have for breakfast and where they would go to buy a computer. It was bizarre to hear such an ordinary, everyday conversation.

When the American mentioned the name of the translator we were waiting for, John Shimon, I was intrigued. I knew "Shimon" was a Jewish name, and I didn't think any of my translators had been Jewish. To my surprise, though, when John arrived, I recognized him—he was a skinny young man who had interpreted in some of my interrogations. He was one of the few competent, kind interpreters I'd had. He didn't argue with me and he didn't play Rambo. He simply translated what I said. And every time I saw him, he greeted me with "As-salaam alaykum." Based on his greeting and his accent, I had assumed he was a Muslim from Syria.

Amir's first question, which was translated from Bosnian to English by Amir's interpreter and then from English to Arabic by John, was a simple one.

"Could you please state your name?"

"My name is Osama bin Laden," I answered. It was an absurd thing to say, I know, but the Bosnian government had treated me as though that's who I was.

John Shimon looked confused. "I think maybe I translated the question wrong," he said.

"No," I told him, "I understood the question. Translate what I said. My name is Osama bin Laden."

"My name is Osama bin Laden," John said, in English.

"My name is Osama bin Laden," Amir's translator said, in Bosnian.

Amir's face clouded. He asked his question again.

"Osama bin Laden," I answered again.

We repeated that exchange for a few minutes. Eventually, Amir said, calmly, "Look. You have every right to be angry. But I've traveled a long way to talk with you. I just want to find out what's going on here and try to help."

There was friendliness and sympathy in Amir's voice. My anger toward his government wasn't going to dissipate, but I decided to stop directing it at him. I told him my name and then we talked about Guantanamo and what the last few years of my life had been like. When he left, Amir said he would relay our conversation to his bosses, who would do what they could to help.

I had seen the Bosnian government in action before. I didn't have high hopes.

.   .   .   .

In January of 2005, I heard from my lawyers. Judge Leon had ruled against me. He agreed with the government that I wasn't on American soil, so the American Constitution didn't protect me. I didn't have the right to try to prove my innocence in a real court of law.

I wasn't surprised—I had expected Judge Leon to rule in favor of the man who had appointed him—but I was frustrated. My lawyers told me that they would appeal to the U.S. Circuit Court for Washington, D.C., but they cautioned me that it could be a lengthy process. I had to stay patient.

I was determined not to let Guantanamo break me. Every time The Elephant interrogated me, he started with the same question: "How are you?"

I always gave him the same answer: "Better than you."

And I was. The Elephant could put me in isolation. He could withhold my mail and make me deny my own family's very existence. He could force me to pretend that I was cold and heartless, that I cared about nothing, because anything I cared about would be ammunition he could use against me. But I would always be pretending. Nothing he did would ever turn me into the kind of person he already was.

Camp Delta, by now, had been split into several different sub-camps. Camp Four was for detainees who "behaved." Each cell in Camp Four had a bed, a locker, and a shower. When I was in Camp Four, I was given white clothes instead of orange ones, I could take more frequent rec walks, and I was allowed to eat meals with other people instead of alone in my cell.

But I was almost never in Camp Four. The Elephant had other plans. If he didn't make up an excuse to have me thrown into isolation, he would make up an excuse to have me sent to Romeo Block.

Romeo was for the "troublemakers." When I was there, I was allowed to have three items in my cell: an orange pair of shorts, an orange shirt, and an isomat. Otherwise, the cell was empty except for a toilet and a water faucet. There was no toothbrush or toothpaste. No pants or flip-flops. And no Qur'an.

Romeo was indoors, but the mesh of our cells had a hard, plastic-like sheeting, which meant that during the day my cell felt like a brick oven. At night, it was an icebox.

To stay cool during the day, I took several "showers." The faucet was not far from the floor, so I couldn't fit under it, and they wouldn't give me a cup to pour water over my head. Instead, I would place my leg over the drain in the floor and wait until enough water pooled there for me to splash some onto myself.

Sometimes, the guards would punish one person's behavior by using the outdoor shut-off valve to turn off the water in all of the cells. On those days, I just sat there sweating until nightfall.

At night, I huddled in the fetal position, flipping from my left side to my right and back to try to stay warm. I rarely stayed asleep for more than twenty minutes at a time. In the early mornings, the metal floor was still too cold to stand on barefoot, so I would stand on the isomat and shuffle over to the toilet, careful to keep the isomat between my feet and the floor the whole time.

I got a bad respiratory infection while I was in Romeo. My coughing fits were so frequent and so forceful that I felt sorry for my neighbors. It was hard enough for them to fall asleep as it was, and now they had to listen to me.

I had heard stories of other prisoners, ones who had good relationships with their interrogators, getting medicine and coffee when they were sick, and sometimes even a magazine about cars or sports. Obviously, I didn't have that kind of a relationship with The Elephant. I didn't tell him what he wanted to hear, and I didn't get any medicine. My cough lingered for months.

Mustafa

I DON'T REMEMBER what the official "reason" for putting me in Romeo Block was. The real reason, I am certain, is that it was part of the interrogators' plan. They wanted to make my life even harder, so that I would crack.

When I was transferred to Romeo, I was not allowed to bring anything with me but a bag containing my legal documents. The soldiers deposited me in a cell and then placed the documents on top of it. Inside the cell itself, there was nothing at all but a thin isomat atop a bed even smaller than what I had slept on before. This, the soldiers told me, was a different kind of cellblock.

"We call this the punishment block," one of them said.

The conditions in Romeo were even worse than those in solitary confinement. Nothing was allowed in the cell but an isomat. The cell walls were covered with plexiglass, so there was no ventilation whatsoever. Never before in my life, not during soccer games or karate training, had I sweated so much.

I soon learned that the differences between Romeo and other blocks did not stop with the cells themselves. Almost immediately, we were ordered to remove our prison-issue flip-flops. All detainees in Romeo were required to go barefoot. I did not protest; I handed my flip-flops over without complaint. The others did not seem to mind either.

The soldiers' next demand, however, was unacceptable. They told us to remove our slacks and hand them over. We were unwilling to do that. Men are supposed to cover their 'awrah, the area from the navel to the knees, during prayers. If the soldiers took our slacks and did not return them, we would not be able to pray as our religion instructs us to.

"I am not going to give you my slacks," I told the soldier standing outside my cell. "It is impossible. It is not going to happen. How do you expect me to perform my prayers without my slacks?"

"These are the regulations," he insisted. He told me that his authority came directly from the men in charge of Guantanamo.

"I don't care if President Bush himself said to come take my slacks," I said. "There is no way that it's going to happen."

The soldier I was speaking with left and returned with a higher-ranking officer.

"Are you going to give me the slacks or not?" the officer asked.

"I am not going to give you anything," I vowed.

"Then we're going to take them by force."

"Go ahead," I told him. "If you want to take them by force, go ahead and do it. But I am not going to give them to you."

"Fine," the officer shrugged. He and the first soldier walked away. Minutes later, a mass of soldiers swarmed Romeo Block. They had sent in the IRF teams. A group of soldiers went to each prisoner and demanded his slacks. One man complied; he was sickly and knew that his body could not endure whatever punishment the rest of us were about to suffer. The rest of us refused.

The IRF soldiers started going into one cell after another, beating detainees and forcefully removing their pants. The sounds of violence grew louder as they worked their way across the block, growing closer and closer. When they reached my cell, one of the soldiers demanded my slacks. I knew it would earn me a beating, but I simply could not bring myself to hand them over. Some things are just too much.

"If you don't hand them over," the soldier threatened, "we're going to come in and take them."

"Go ahead," I replied.

"We have six guys here, and we're all coming in."

"I hope you'll be first," I said, anger coursing through me. I am not a violent man. For me, karate has always been about competition and physical fitness, not blood-sport. But every man has his limit. As

I stood there in my cell, barefoot, listening to the screams and cries of my fellow detainees being savaged, disrobed, and humiliated, I had reached mine. I wanted to hit this man. I wanted to hurt him. I was ready for a fight.

I took off my slacks and ripped them into pieces. I would rather destroy them than let these bullies seize them from me. I threw the shreds into the corner of my cell, behind me. To get what was left of the slacks, they would have to come through me. I stood on the tiny bed in my cell and waited, in my boxers, silently challenging these six armed, armored soldiers.

The soldier again demanded that I hand over the shreds. I again told him that I would not.

"Why?" he asked. Obviously, they were of no use to me now.

"Because I want you to come in and get them."

An order was given, and the soldiers started piling through the narrow door to my cell, trying to rush me. When the first soldier came within range, I struck him. Hard. He tumbled backward into the rest of his team before most of them had even cleared the door, and they all scrambled back out. I suppose they had not been expecting a barefoot prisoner in his underwear to put up quite so much of a fight.

A short while later, another IRF team arrived outside my cell. I could tell from the emblems on one man's uniform that he was a high-ranking officer.

"Are you gonna give us your slacks?" he asked.

"There is no way I will give them to you myself," I told him. "If you want them, come in and get them."

The officer started talking to the other soldiers. They spent a long time in conversation, trying to figure out what to do. Eventually they settled on a tactic. First, they hit me with pepper spray, or something like it. I tried to turn my head, to shield my eyes, but it was no use. Soon I could hardly see, and there was a terrible stinging pain in my eyes.

Four of them rushed me. That was when my training took over. I kicked the first soldier to enter my cell, drawing blood and knocking him to the ground. The next one reached out and tried to grab me. I was still standing on top of the bed, so he ended up grabbing hold of my foot. Another soldier came at me from the other side and wrapped his arms around my waist. I used his momentum against him, pulling him further in toward me and then hitting him very hard, knocking him into the hard sheeting that lined the wall behind me. The impact dislodged a section of the sheeting, which fell to the ground with a crash.

Somehow, the soldier did not let go. He started pulling me toward the ground, forcefully, while I kept punching him. The rest of the soldiers soon jumped into the fray, hitting and kicking me. There were too many of them to fend off at once. When I could no longer stay upright, I purposefully fell forward, facedown, so that they could not hit my face. I was worried they would fracture my skull. As I lay there on my stomach, protecting the back of my head with my arms, they pummeled me, hitting and kicking every single inch of me.

Then they pinned my hands behind my waist, so I could no longer protect my head. They flipped me over onto my back, still beating me. Even then, I refused to give in to these brutes.

I managed to wrest my hands free and grab hold of a soldier's arm with one hand. I pulled him toward me, trying to tear at his face with my other hand, but he grabbed my hand and started twisting. I pulled my hand away from him, back behind me where he could not reach it, but another soldier was there to grab hold of it. He started bending my little finger backward, as though he were trying to touch my fingernail to the top of my wrist, until the bone snapped. I was in horrendous pain. I had already taken a tremendous beating, but until right then, I had hardly felt any of it. This I felt.

Once they had beaten all of the resistance out of me, the IRF team filed out. They left the shredded slacks behind, in the corner of the cell. Some time later, a soldier came in, warily, and took the slacks as I lay there bloodied and broken. He did not offer to get me medical attention, nor did anyone else, even though my body was covered in bruises and my hand was so swollen that I could not move my fingers.

Though they did not treat my wounds, they did transfer me to another cell, right next to Lakhdar, shortly after the beating. Perhaps they wanted to hear what we had to say to each other; perhaps they just wanted to intimidate Lakhdar by showing him what they had done to his friend.

"As-salaam alaykum," Lakhdar greeted me.

"Wa-alaykum as-salaam," I replied.

We were a long way from the soccer fields and coffee shops of Sarajevo. I was glad to see that Lakhdar was surviving, and it was nice to be able to have a real conversation with someone I knew. I wish, though, that Lakhdar had not had to witness what happened to me next.

I was sitting in my cell when an IRF team arrived outside the door. One of the soldiers told me that they were going to search my cell. He said it in a rude, harsh tone, and I could tell that he was trying to provoke a reaction.

"Why do you need to search my cell?" I asked. I had no possessions in the cell; it was literally just me and my underwear. There was nothing to search.

The soldier offered an explanation, but it was obviously a pretext. The IRF team was hoping I would say "no," hoping I would start another fight. They wanted revenge for what I had done the other day. Breaking my finger was not enough. I'd had the audacity to fight back, and for that, they wanted to teach me a lesson.

"Fine," I told the soldier. "Go ahead and search." I did not want to give them any excuse to hurt me any more.

Unfortunately, they did not need an excuse. They opened the slot in my cell door and immediately started pepper-spraying me. I turned my head, but another soldier was waiting just outside the window, where I could not see him. He opened the window and started spraying my eyes from that direction.

They sprayed and sprayed me. They must have used two full bottles of that awful stuff. They kept spraying from both directions until I collapsed on the floor, my eyes burning. It was an ambush, not a precaution. I had not threatened them, or behaved menacingly. I had acquiesced to their search and was sitting peacefully on the bed when they attacked.

One of the soldiers ordered me to lie down and remain prone on the floor while they entered the cell. Even though I did exactly as he said, the first soldier through the door jumped into the air and landed on my back with his knees, nearly breaking my back. The pain was intense. The rest of the IRF team followed after him, piling on top of me. Then they used plastic wire to tie my hands and feet.

The soldiers dragged me out of my cell, across the cellblock, and onto the gravel driveway outside the cellblock. They threw me down onto the sharp gravel, and then they proceeded to beat me, punching and kicking with all their might. Someone without my years of karate training could easily have died from such an assault. Praise God, I knew how to take a punch. I knew how to move so that my attackers would do as little damage as possible. I knew my body's most vulnerable spots and how to protect them.

While the soldiers were laying into me, an officer approached. For a moment, I was hopeful. Surely, the officer would be upset to see soldiers beating a defenseless man. Instead, though, she was only upset about the soldiers' lack of creativity. She took a high-pressure firehose off the wall nearby and forced the nozzle into my mouth. As the soldiers held my head in place, one of them turned on the water. The pressure was so strong that water started spilling from my nose.

They held me down on the sharp stones, choking on the water from the firehose, for a long time. I twisted my head to the side and gasped for air whenever I could; the few times I managed it, the water sprayed painfully into my ear before they forced my mouth back over the nozzle.

Finally, they were done with the hose. But not with me. One of the soldiers grabbed hold of my fractured finger and started twisting. I cried out that it was broken, but they did not care. They just kept shouting curse words and torturing me.

The soldiers forced my face down against the gravel and held me there. One of the soldiers leapt into the air and slammed down onto me, knees first, with all the force he could muster. For the second time that afternoon, my back was almost broken. The attack also drove my body forcefully into the gravel beneath me. I felt the jagged stones pierce the skin of my face. I am grateful I did not lose an eye.

In desperation, I tried a ruse. I pretended to faint, hoping that even these brutes would draw the line at hitting an unconscious man. They dragged my limp body, still bound hand and foot, back indoors and into a cell, where they threw me to the floor. I was hopeful that my ruse had worked.

They began kicking me again. One of the soldiers grabbed me by the hair and repeatedly slammed my head against the bottom edge of the toilet until I lost consciousness. This time, it was not a ruse.

When I came to, the left side of my face was bloody, swollen, and completely numb. Even my left eye was blood-red. And the damage lingered. For four or five months after that, I could not even drink water without some dribbling from the left side of my mouth. When eating, I had to be careful that I did not chew on the numb parts of my cheek; sometimes, I would taste blood and know that I had bitten myself. I suffered severe headaches, and I had only limited control of my left eye. I could not close the eyelid at all. Even when I slept, the eye remained open.

I requested medical attention, but the soldiers refused to do anything to help me. They would not even bring a nurse. Instead, they mocked me. They made fun of the way my injured face looked. They laughed at the trouble I had eating and drinking. They took pride in my disfigurement.

Lakhdar

I WILL NEVER FORGET the guards attacking my friend. One minute Mustafa was talking with a handful of guards, and the next minute one of them was pulling out his pepper spray canister and spraying Mustafa in the face. The guards rushed into his cell, attacked him, and dragged him out of the cellblock.

By pressing my face against the wall of my cell, I was able to see outside. I watched the guards carry Mustafa onto a gravel road. They threw him to the ground, face down, two guards pinning his arms to his side, and they beat him. I heard Mustafa cry out, which was truly jarring. He is one of the strongest, most stoic people I've ever met. For him to show pain, he must have been in agony.

The guards picked Mustafa up again and carried him out of my line of sight. When I saw him next, he was bruised and battered. He pointed to his cheek, just below one eye, and told me that it was extremely painful.

"Can you see what's going on?" he asked. Mustafa, of course, didn't have a mirror to examine himself with.

It was hard to see past the bruises and scrapes. "I can't tell," I said. "It looks like maybe a piece of gravel is lodged in there?"

It wasn't until weeks later that Mustafa was taken to a doctor.

For the next few weeks, I mostly sat in my cell. A couple of times each week, a guard would come by and ask if I wanted to go for a rec walk. Most of the prisoners in Romeo were too exhausted, but I always went for my walk—if nothing else, I wanted to make the guards do the work of chaining and unchaining me, shackling and unshackling me, and walking with me in the hot sun. Why should they get to relax?

After a month or so, I was brought to an interrogation room for another round with The Elephant. On the way out of my cell, the guards offered me a pair of long pants—instead of the shorts I was forced to wear in Romeo—but I declined. I was determined not to let The Elephant think Romeo was getting the better of me.

"How are you?" he asked.

"Better than you. Always better than you."

"Why are you in shorts? Didn't the guards offer you pants?"

"I like the shorts," I told him. "It's great. In the other camps, I'm always too hot, but I'd be embarrassed to take off my pants. Now I get to wear shorts all the time. It's like I'm at the beach."

"So you like Romeo?"

"It's excellent."

"All right," The Elephant shrugged, and he sent me back to my cell in Romeo right next to Mustafa.

A week or two later, I was brought back to The Elephant.

"Well," he told me, "your time in Romeo is almost up." I forget what excuse he'd manufactured for sending me there in the first place—maybe spitting on someone? Maybe throwing milk at a soldier again?—but apparently, I had served the punishment for the offense I had supposedly committed.

"But," The Elephant said, "I know you like Mustafa. And since he attacked a guard, he's going to be in Romeo for several more months. So tell me—do you want to go back to a better camp, or do you want to stay next to Mustafa?"

That was an easy choice. I hated everything about Camp Romeo—the extreme heat and cold, the exhaustion, the infrequent rec walks, the constant IRFing of other prisoners, the lack of pants and showers and a Qur'an—and watching one of my best friends suffer was very difficult for me. I had no desire to spend another minute there. So, of course, I told The Elephant the opposite.

"I'll stay with Mustafa," I told The Elephant.

"You're sure?"

"I'm sure."

"Okay," he said, and the guards brought me back to Romeo.

When I told Mustafa that I'd asked The Elephant to let me stay in Camp Romeo, he was baffled.

"Why would you do that?" he asked. "Why wouldn't you want to go to a camp with pants and blankets and showers? That's what anyone would choose."

"You don't understand how these people work," I said. "Whatever you ask for, they'll do the opposite."

He seemed skeptical. Maybe forty-five minutes later, as we were eating dinner, two guards appeared at my cell.

"Hurry up and finish eating," one of them said. "We're taking you to another cell."

I looked at Mustafa and laughed.

"You see? You see how these people are?"

Mustafa

IT HAD BEEN ABOUT TWO WEEKS since the soldiers battered me past the point of losing consciousness, and despite my repeated requests, I still had not received any medical treatment.

Finally, during one night shift, a friendly guard happened to walk past my cell and saw my condition.

"What happened to you, 10k4?" he asked.

Like most of the soldiers, he addressed me by my serial number, 10004, rather than my name. Unlike most of the soldiers, though, he had always treated me like a human being. One time, when he had seen me looking at pictures of my children, he showed me photos of his own children and talked about how much he missed them. He was a good man, one of the few who had not let Guantanamo rob him of his capacity to be kind. And now he could tell that I was in bad shape.

"The soldiers hit me," I told him.

"When?" he asked.

"About two weeks ago."

"Are you taking medication?"

"No," I said. "They're not giving me any medication."

"Did you see the nurse?"

"No, they did not let me see anybody."

Even though it had been two weeks, my face was still swollen and bruised. My little finger was still visibly out of place. Anyone could see that I desperately needed medical attention; this was the first person to care.

"I'm going to make sure you see a doctor," he said, and then he got in touch with his commanding officer.

When his commanding officer came to my cell and saw the condition I was in, these were her exact words: "Shit! They didn't take you to the doctor?!"

"No," I told her. "They didn't."

"When did this happen?" she asked.

"Two weeks ago."

"Two weeks ago," she repeated, incredulous, "and no one came? No nurse, no doctor, nothing?"

"Nobody," I said.

She called the clinic and told them to send someone over right away.

When the nurse arrived, instead of treating me, he mocked me.

"Are you sick?" he asked, sarcasm in his voice.

"Don't you see what I look like?"

The nurse wanted to have me handcuffed and chained before entering my cell, but the officer who had summoned him shook her head.

"He doesn't need to be handcuffed," the officer said. "Just open the door and get into the cell."

The nurse hesitated, even after the officer promised to take responsibility if anything happened.

"It's not a problem," the friendly guard told him. "I'll come in with you."

The guard asked me to sit down on my bed, and I did as he asked. Once I was seated, the guard and nurse entered my cell together, and the nurse told me to lift my head so he could get a better look at my face. Once I did, he looked me in the eye and asked a truly ridiculous question.

"Do you have AIDS?"

This nurse knew the answer to that. He had examined me before. Praise God, I had lived a clean life. I never used drugs or anything like that.

"I have been in jail for years and years," I answered, "and you're asking me if I have AIDS? If I have AIDS, then I got it here, from your needles."

He continued to ask me questions that clearly had nothing to do with my injuries. Did I have typhoid? The plague? He ran down a list of fanciful diseases, and it quickly became clear that he was making fun of me.

"Where," I asked him, "would I have gotten these diseases from? I am not suffering from a disease. I am suffering from having been beaten."

I showed the nurse where the IRF team had hit me. I showed him the fractured bone in my still-swollen hand.

"When I eat food," I told him, "I can't taste it. With my eyes closed, I cannot tell the difference between juice and water. Give me an apple and a piece of bread, I can't tell you which is which."

The nurse gave me pain medication and then left the cell without offering any further treatment. The officer, thankfully, realized that more needed to be done. She told me that she would make an appointment for me at the hospital, so I would be seen by an actual doctor.

Sure enough, soldiers came to escort me to the prison hospital the very next day. The doctor there gave me a cursory examination. She rang a bell right next to my ear, and I could not hear it. After she finished looking me over, she told me that I had cerebral palsy.

I knew, as I am sure the doctor did, that this was absurd. I was not suffering from a lifelong illness that only suddenly revealed itself after my head had been pressed into gravel and then slammed into a toilet. Still, I wanted the doctor to do what she could to treat my wounds.

"Call it what you want," I said. "Is there anything you can do about it?"

She prescribed some medications. That evening, the nurse brought me pills and watched as I swallowed them. He also gave me a plaster for my left eye, which I still was not able to close. After I held my eyelid shut with my finger and applied the plaster, the eyelid actually stayed shut, which made it much easier to sleep.

While the plaster helped, the pills did nothing. When a soldier told me that the doctor had scheduled another appointment for me at the prison hospital, I was hopeful that she was planning to prescribe some new medications that might be more effective. However, she had other ideas.

"You are not here for treatment," she told me, when I started to ask about my medications. "We asked you to come here today because we have new interns and they want to learn about your condition."

The doctor escorted a group of five or six young, white-robed interns into the room and started lecturing them on cerebral palsy. She had them each examine my face while she clinically discussed the finer points of nerve damage, pointing out my damaged eyelid, where the left side of my mouth drooped, and so on. When she finally finished, the interns filed out and she brought another group in for the same lecture.

It was too much. "I am not a lab rat for you to study," I insisted. "Are you going to treat me?"

"No," she replied. "I brought you here so that the interns can learn about your condition."

"Then I want to go back to my cell," I told her.

The soldiers returned me to my cell, and that evening the nurse came with the same useless pills, watching carefully as I swallowed them. I took them for weeks and weeks, and nothing improved.

By the grace of God, I was moved to a new cell with two new neighbors: a Yemeni physician and an Afghan pharmacist. Before Guantanamo, the physician had worked in the prestigious Saudi German Hospital in Riyadh. When I told him about my medical problems, he asked me what kind of medicine I was taking.

"I don't know," I answered. I was just swallowing the pills the nurse handed me.

"The next time they bring your medicine," the doctor said, "don't take it. I want to have a look at it."

When the nurse brought the next round of pills, I pretended to swallow them while he watched. Once he left, I showed them to the doctor. He told me that most of the pills were fine to take, but there was one that troubled him.

"Mustafa," he warned, "don't you ever take this pill again."

"Why not?"

"This is an anti-psychotic. They give it to people when they're acting crazy."

I wanted to be sure, so I passed the pill to the pharmacist on the other side of my cell. He did not speak Arabic, but he spoke enough English for us to be able to carry on a conversation with each other.

"Don't take this," he said.

The next time the nurse brought me my pills, I refused to take the anti-psychotic. The nurse left and returned with an officer.

"Why," the officer demanded, "are you refusing to take your medicine?"

The Yemeni doctor answered for me.

"This is not the right medication for him. This is for psychotics, and this man is not psychotic. You are criminals! How can you do this? You were the ones who beat him. You know what his injuries are. This man does not need anti-psychotics, he needs a series of injections to bring down the swelling in his face, and he will need physical therapy as well."

As the doctor spoke, the nurse's face started to redden. Apparently he was capable of feeling shame, after all. That was the last time anyone tried to treat my injuries with an anti-psychotic.

Over the next several months, my condition improved. In addition to taking the medicines they gave me, I routinely splashed water on my face; one of the detainees near me blessed the water by reciting the Qur'an over it. I gradually began to regain the ability to taste, and the swelling in my face gradually subsided. My doctor expressed surprise at my speedy recovery.

Some of the injuries I suffered, though, are permanent. I will never be able to straighten the little finger that the soldier snapped; I recently saw a doctor who told me that if the finger had been set in a cast right away, it might have healed, but it is far too late to repair it now. I still have trouble with my left eye sometimes, and I still have to be careful when I chew because of the numbness in my face. After my release, I consulted a neurologist in Sarajevo who told me that I have permanent nerve damage because of the blows to my head.

Considering what they did to me, though, I thank God that I did not die. Some detainees were less fortunate. One Saudi man had a bone dislocated by an IRF team, and I saw a nurse come to his cell accompanied by soldiers. I thought the nurse was there to administer medication, but instead, the soldiers pepper-sprayed the detainee, dragged him out of the cell, held him down, and kicked and hit him as he lay there, helpless. The nurse instructed the soldiers on where to hit so they would not leave any marks, pointing and saying, "Hit him here, hit him here, hit him here." The poor man did not survive. I often wonder whether, had it not been for my years of training, I would have lost my life in Camp Romeo too.

Lakhdar

AFTER I TRICKED THE ELEPHANT into switching me out of Camp Romeo, I spent the rest of 2005 and most of 2006 in "normal" cells rather than in isolation or Camp Romeo. At a certain point, I stopped being interrogated by The Elephant—I lasted longer than he did in Guantanamo—and I was cycled through a handful of different interrogators. What I remember most from that time period, though, isn't the interrogators. It's the guards, and the disrespect that they showed toward me, my fellow prisoners, my religion, and even one another.

More than once, I heard a group of white soldiers talk about "that nigger" as soon as the one black soldier in the group left the room. And the Hispanic soldiers were treated the worst of all—they were belittled by black and white soldiers alike, and they were forced to do most of the grunt work.

One time, a Hispanic soldier was distributing food to prisoners when a white soldier called out to him.

"Hey, come over here!"

"Just a second. I'm almost done here."

This response annoyed the white soldier so much that he picked up a bright green, rock-hard pear—typical for the food we were given—and angrily hurled it at the Hispanic soldier's head.

Another time, I was sitting in my cell when two soldiers got into a heated discussion with each other. I couldn't tell what they were arguing about, but eventually, they started punching each other in the face. They kept trading blows until more soldiers arrived and pried them apart.

I like to think that in their regular lives, the guards are neither as violent nor as racist as they acted in Guantanamo. Guantanamo is the kind of place that brings out the worst in everyone.

It seemed like the guards had been ordered to make life especially difficult for my fellow prisoners and me.

Once, when the guards gave me new, clean clothes and took away my old ones, I put on the slacks to discover that the inside of them had been sprayed with Mace. I wore the slacks by themselves—I wasn't given underwear with them—so the Mace caused painful burning in sensitive areas. After this happened multiple times to multiple prisoners, we got in the habit of repeatedly soaking our pants in soapy water before putting them on. That meant standing half-naked in our cells for hours, but it was better than the alternative.

The guards also invented excuses to IRF us. Sometimes, when they gave me my meal, they withheld an item from the food pouch—plastic silverware, for example—and then, when they collected the pouch after mealtime, they would demand to know where the missing item was.

"We're going to have to search your cell for it."

"But you never gave it to me," I would protest.

And then they would call the IRF team.

In the early days of Guantanamo, back when everyone still wore nameplates, there was one guard, Phillips, who liked to take advantage of the rule that prisoners weren't allowed to make eye contact with guards. Phillips would sit outside a prisoner's cell and stare at him intently for several minutes. If the prisoner so much as glanced up, Phillips would pounce.

"Hey! Stop looking at me!"

The prisoner would quickly snap his gaze back to the ground, but it was too late. Phillips would summon another soldier, and the two of them would administer the punishment for making eye contact: entering the prisoner's cell and stripping him of all his belongings. The prisoner would spend the next several days sitting on bare concrete with no isomat, no blanket, and no Qur'an.

That basic attitude persisted the whole time I was at Guantanamo. Some guards leaped at any excuse to inflict hardship on us.

And the guards disrespected Islam.

In each cellblock, one prisoner would sing the call to prayer. The guards often imitated him in a mocking, sing-song voice, laughing as they did. When the rest of us started praying, the guards did everything they could to disturb us. Sometimes they walked as loudly as they could, each footstep clanging against the metal floor. Sometimes they turned on noisy, rattling fans. Sometimes they blared American music. Sometimes they had detailed conversations with each other about who they wanted to have sex with and how.

Some of the guards would wait until we were mid-prayer to talk to us, knowing that we could not interrupt our prayers to respond. Once, for example, I was praying when a guard interjected.

"I need to search your cell."

I didn't look up. The guard wasn't more important than God.

And since I didn't respond, I was IRFed.

Another time, a fellow prisoner greeted me with the traditional Muslim greeting, "As-salaam alaykum"—peace be upon you. Halfway through my response to him, "Waalaykum as-salaam"—and upon you peace—a guard barked at me.

"Shut up!"

As a devout Muslim, that wasn't an option. Clearly and calmly, I finished saying "as-salaam." The guard threatened to put me in isolation, but I didn't care. I had been to isolation before. I had never failed to return the peace.

One of my neighbors returned to his cell one day and opened his Qur'an to find that the word "Fuck" had been scrawled inside. After that, many people started requesting to have their Qur'an removed from their cell so that the guards wouldn't be able to desecrate it.

Often, the guards would humiliate us by shaving our beards against our will. Sometimes they went a step further: they would shave a prisoner's head and his beard, but leave patches of hair in certain spots to make him look ridiculous. The guards gave one prisoner a Hitler mustache. With another prisoner, they shaved most of the hair off his head. All they left was a patch in the shape of a cross.

There was also sexual humiliation. One of my neighbors told me that during an interrogation, he had been forced to wear women's underwear. I also heard about a time when a Yemeni prisoner was held down on his back, stripped, and then humiliated by a female soldier who took off her pants and sat on top of him. One of my greatest fears was that this would happen to me, or that I would be sodomized by a male guard. My interrogators frequently threatened both.

I am afraid some people will hear about these affronts to Islam and to basic human decency and think that violence is the appropriate response. I hope they won't. I think the guards acted the way they did precisely because they didn't know what a peaceful, beautiful religion Islam is. They hardly knew anything about Islam at all. (I remember one prisoner telling me about an interrogation session in which he had mentioned the famous Islamic scholar Ibn Taymiyah—who lived from 1263 to 1328—and his interrogator, not recognizing the name, demanded to know Ibn Taymiyah's current address and the names of his associates.) Of course, ignorance is no excuse. What the guards did is unforgivable, and their ignorance is no one's fault but their own and their supervisors'. But ignorance is only strengthened by violence. Education and example will defeat ignorance more powerfully than explosives ever could.

I will always remember the handful of guards whose basic humanity won out over the ignorance and cruelty that surrounded them. There was one man who never swore or talked down to the prisoners.

One night, he walked up to a Yemeni prisoner during his rec walk and gave him an Eskimo ice cream bar. The prisoner tried to express his gratitude, but he didn't speak English, and the guard mistook his gestures as asking for more—so the guard went and got a second ice cream bar for him.

Later, that same guard sat down outside my cell and had a conversation with me.

"Are you Muslim?" I asked him. He was dark-skinned, and I had assumed he was being kind and respectful because he shared our religion.

"No," he said, to my surprise. "I'm Christian." He was dark-skinned because he was Hispanic.

"Why," I asked him, "are you so nice to the prisoners?"

"When I was a young boy," he said, "my mother taught me to be a good person, and not to hurt people but to help people. That's what my mother always told me."

"Thank you," I said. "Your mother is a good woman."

Mustafa

I WITNESSED several affronts to Islam. There were so many religious insults that I am convinced it had to have been part of a concerted effort, not simply a few soldiers acting of their own accord. I know of at least one instance when a respectful soldier was hesitant to search a detainee's Qur'an and his commander ordered him to do so anyway.

They often picked up our Qur'ans and rifled through them. I asked one soldier why they were always doing this.

"You hide weapons inside," he replied.

This was preposterous. If he had said that they were looking for secret messages or documents, I might have believed him, but weapons? In a book? Clearly this was just an excuse to give them an opportunity to degrade us and our Holy Book, which they found multiple ways to do. They were creative in their desecration.

One soldier searched a Qur'an while standing next to the toilet in a cell neighboring my own. When he finished flipping through the pages, he threw the Qur'an onto the toilet seat. I think he meant for the book to land in the toilet water, but the seat was too small. How vile and sacrilegious this was, tossing God's words in the toilet. Acts like this were commonplace.

I witnessed a soldier enter a detainee's cell to conduct a search. The detainee had carefully placed his Qur'an on top of his isomat, keeping the Holy Book off the dirty floor. The soldier grabbed the isomat and began shaking it vigorously, unceremoniously dumping the Qur'an onto the floor, where she left it. She seemed pleased with herself as she exited the cell.

I saw a soldier place a stack of Qur'ans on a chair and then sit down on top of them. What possible reason could he have had to do that, except to demonstrate his contempt for us, his contempt for our religion, and our utter powerlessness in this place?

Those were the kinds of abuses that I witnessed myself. I often heard shouts of indignation when the soldiers were searching cells outside my line of vision. It reached a point where I decided that I would prefer not to have a Qur'an at all. Many other detainees had used their time in prison to memorize the Qur'an; I would rely on them to help me do the same, and I would no longer have to worry about the soldiers defiling my sacred book.

Ironically, at a certain point, the soldiers started forcing us to keep Qur'ans in our cells whether we wanted to or not. If you said that you did not want a Qur'an, the soldiers would remove you from your cell, deposit a Qur'an in the cell, and then put you back in. After that, it was just a matter of time until they treated the Qur'an in a way they never, ever would have treated the Christian Bible or an American flag.

The handful of Muslim soldiers in Guantanamo were often treated with disrespect too. I remember speaking with one military chaplain, a hulking Air Force officer named Hamza, who had been posted to Guantanamo to serve as our imam. He was standing just outside my cell when another soldier walked right up to us and hovered over our conversation. Hamza asked him why he was standing there.

"I was given instructions not to let anybody talk to a prisoner without one of us listening."

"I am not just anybody," Hamza replied. "My rank is higher than yours."

The soldier insisted that orders were orders. He did not move. Apparently, Hamza could not be trusted to speak with me alone. It did not matter that he was American or that he was an officer in the U.S. Air Force. He had converted to Islam, and his beliefs made him suspect. Hamza left Guantanamo after just a few months.

.   .   .

There were other, subtler ways in which the soldiers insulted our religion. A detainee would be interrupted, distracted, or worse while praying. If a detainee did manage to pray five times in a day, he would be far more likely to have his cell searched and his Qur'an mistreated the next day. We were occasionally given hard candies that came in wrappers with Christian messages on them. "Jesus is the son of God," one wrapper read. The candies themselves had little crucifixes imprinted on them. I might have believed this was just a result of well-meaning naiveté, had it not been for all of the other attacks on our faith.

Everything they did was designed to provoke, to make us feel enraged and impotent, to break our spirits and grind us down. And it worked.

I saw a soldier searching a nearby cell after its occupant, a double amputee, was taken to the hospital. A pair of underwear was lying on the floor. The underwear they issued was tight and uncomfortable to wear, so most of us just used it as a rag to clean our cells. The soldier picked up the underwear, essentially a dirty rag, and placed it directly on top of the detainee's Qur'an.

I could not contain myself. I started banging on the wall of my cell to get the soldier's attention.

"Why are you doing this?" I cried. "Remove the underwear from the Qur'an!"

"It's none of your business," the soldier replied.

Even though I knew that everything they were doing was an attempt to get under our skin, what he had done was so vile, so blasphemous, that I let it get under mine. I looked the soldier directly in the eye and spat in his direction. I knew I would surely be punished for this, but the worst punishment was how I felt in that moment. There was nothing I could do to protect anyone or anything I cared about.

Lakhdar

IN 2006, I was moved to a cell neighboring a man I had met before Guantanamo: Belkacem Bensayah, the man whose wife had called me in tears and begged for my help after his arrest. If it weren't for him—if he hadn't walked into my office, if I hadn't given him diapers for his kids, if he hadn't taken my card, if I hadn't paid for his lawyer—maybe my friends and I wouldn't have been arrested. Maybe Mustafa and Mohamed and Hadj and I would have had the chance to be fathers to our young children.

I was sure the interrogators had arranged to have Belkacem in the neighboring cell so they could listen to our conversation. But I couldn't help it.

"All of this," I told him, "is because of you."

Belkacem sighed. "I swear to God, I didn't do a thing. I don't know why I'm here. But I heard that they brought you here because of me—because you got me a lawyer. And I feel terrible about that."

He could have been lying, but he seemed earnest. And it wasn't hard to believe that the authorities had arrested an innocent man. If so, what had happened to him was horrible enough without him shouldering the blame for my arrest too.

"Let it be," I told him. "I'm not angry at you. I was just trying to do a good deed in the name of God. I didn't know you, and you didn't know me. It was just fate."

Throughout 2006, my lawyers continued to visit me every few months, but there were no developments in my case. The lawyers told me that the U.S. Circuit Court for Washington, D.C., still hadn't ruled on my appeal of Judge Leon's decision. As time passed, it grew more and more difficult to stay hopeful.

One morning in mid-June, when I was in Camp Two, I heard a loud commotion from Camp One. Hours later, a group of soldiers stormed into Camp Two and went from cell to cell, removing all of our belongings. They took my toothpaste, my blanket, my Qur'an—everything but my isomat. They offered no explanation.

A couple of days later, we found out what had happened. "Three prisoners," a soldier told us, "committed suicide by hanging themselves." I found that hard to believe. How could they have hanged themselves without a single guard noticing?

Whether the deaths were self-inflicted or not, in their aftermath, the climate at Guantanamo became even more strict. Not only did the guards seize our belongings, but they would harshly punish us for even the slightest infraction.

It was December of 2006, just before dinnertime, when that happened to me. My cell was at the end of the corridor and the window shutters were open, so I was able to see outside as a group of guards approached with our food. I saw one of the guards open a few MRE packets, pull out some pieces of fruit and some packages of cookies, and carefully set them down. He was stealing our food.

When he entered the cellblock, I confronted him.

"I saw you—why did you take our food?"

"Shut up," he said. "That's none of your business."

"How is it not my business? That food belongs to my brothers."

I raised my voice loud enough for my fellow prisoners to hear. "Your food," I said, "is right outside that door. This man is stealing from you."

A second guard walked over and barked at me to quiet down. As I responded, heatedly, a fleck or two of spittle flew out of my mouth.

"Did you see that?" the second guard said to the first. "He just spat at me."

I know what it is to spit at someone. I spat at interrogators and guards more than once during my time in Guantanamo. But not this time. This was no different than what happens to a student who sits in the front row of a class with an animated teacher.

"I didn't spit," I protested.

It didn't matter.

The guards carried me out of my cell, held me down, and used an electric razor to shave all the hair off my head and face. For the first time in my adult life, I was completely shorn. When the guards brought me back to my cell, my toothpaste, blanket, and Qur'an—which had finally been returned—were again gone. All I had were my isomat and my scratchy clothes. There was more hair on my clothes than on me.

And there was one additional punishment. The guards started bringing me especially disgusting food. They took all of their cooking scraps, like vegetable peels, mixed them together, and cooked them into something that looked like chicken fingers and smelled like rotting waste. The guards served them—in a wrapper, not on a plate—for breakfast, lunch, and dinner.

I decided, looking at the putrid food, that I would show them. I didn't have to eat this garbage. I didn't have to eat anything at all.

As it happened, the holy month of *Dhu al-Hijjah* had begun just four days earlier. The tenth day of the month is the holiday of *Eid al-Adha*, "The Feast of the Sacrifice." During the first nine days of the month, some Muslims fast—it isn't morally required like it is during Ramadan, but it is considered to be an especially good deed. So I decided not to eat for the next five days and nights, until *Eid al-Adha*. It would be a way to demonstrate my faith in God and to protest my unfair punishment at the same time.

During the day, I didn't eat or drink. When night fell, I would "break the fast" by drinking several handfuls of water from the faucet in my cell. But I still wasn't going to eat the trash that they were feeding me as punishment.

It was difficult at first, but as the days passed, my anger intensified and my resolve hardened. Not only were they keeping me in this island prison even though they *knew* I was innocent, now they were punishing me for spitting on a guard even though it was obvious I hadn't. I had to do something to express my indignation—so I decided that even after *Eid al-Adha*, I would continue my hunger strike for as long as I could. It would be difficult, but I would get my strength from God.

Eventually, the guards started offering me regular MREs again instead of kitchen scraps, but it was too little, too late. I had made up my mind.

"You punished me for something you know I didn't do," I told them. "The next time I eat, it will be in my home, from the hand of my wife."

I kept going on my rec walks at first, but as the days passed, I grew weaker and weaker. My body was feeding on itself: first the fat, then the muscle. As I wasted away, my fellow prisoners—including Mustafa and Hadj, whose cells were within earshot—encouraged me to eat. It pained me to upset my friends, but I was determined not to back down.

I had been on strike for two-and-a-half weeks when, as the guards were walking me toward the showers, my legs gave out underneath me and I fell. The guards carried me back to my cell. When they set me down, standing upright, I was still too weak. I felt a rush of dizziness and collapsed to the floor.

I was still huddled on the floor, dazed and completely spent, when a guard stopped by my cell.

"Listen," she said. "We need to take you to the clinic. Are you willing to come voluntarily or do you want to be IRFed?"

"I'm willing to go," I said. After all, I didn't want to die. I just wanted to protest the unfairness of my treatment. "But," I told her, "I'm not able to walk." I barely had the strength to speak.

"No problem," she said. "We'll get a stretcher."

At the clinic, they gave me IV fluids, which made me feel much better. I was able to walk back to my cell without falling once.

Five days later, though, I was again so weak that I could barely stand or speak. The guards brought me back to the clinic. This time, the doctor decided that the IV fluids wouldn't be enough.

"That's it," he said. "We're going to have to force-feed you."

I didn't know what to expect. A soldier brought me into another room and sat me down. Weeks later, I was introduced to a special force-feeding chair—the other prisoners and I referred to it as the "torture chair"—but that first time I was just cuffed and chained to a regular chair.

The soldier brought out an apparatus with a long yellow tube and started measuring out the length of tube he needed. He stopped when he got to a marking somewhere between 45 and 50 inches. That was the amount of tube he was going to insert through my nostril.

"When this goes in," he said, "make sure you swallow."

And then he started feeding the tube into my left nostril.

He made it a few inches before he met resistance. The doctors later determined that my left nostril is impassable—there's a small bone fragment blocking it, most likely due to a broken nose I had suffered earlier. But we didn't know that then.

The soldier pounded on the tube, trying to force it in further. It was excruciating, but he got nowhere. After several tries, each one more painful than the last, he gave up and switched to the right nostril.

Again, he met some resistance. Again, he pounded on the tube a few times. And this time, he was successful. I could feel the tube begin to snake down my throat.

"Swallow," he commanded, as though I had a choice in the matter.

Reflexively, I swallowed, and the tube proceeded into my stomach.

It's almost impossible to explain what a feeding tube feels like to someone who hasn't experienced it. I felt like I was choking, and being strangled, and yet somehow still able to breathe, all at the same time.

The soldier taped the tube in place. I could see Ensure trickling through the tube, one droplet at a time. It felt cold as it reached my stomach. I later learned that a full feeding normally takes fifteen to twenty minutes, but that first time they went exceptionally slowly. I sat in the clinic, chained to the chair, a tube protruding down my throat, for the rest of the afternoon and all through the night. I was exhausted, but I couldn't sleep.

At one point, a nurse asked me how I was doing, but the tube made it too difficult for me to respond. Even if I'd been able to speak, I never could have found the words to describe how miserable I felt.

Finally, mid-morning on the day after the tube had been inserted, the soldier removed it. Then a doctor came into the room and spoke with me. There was kindness and sympathy in his voice.

"I advise you," the doctor said, "to stop your strike. Your kidneys could fail. Your pancreas could be destroyed. And the feeding tube is horrible."

I agreed that the feeding tube was horrible. But I had made a decision.

"Why did they punish me for something I didn't do?" I demanded. "I never spat on the soldier, and they started feeding me garbage."

"Listen," the doctor said. "Stop your strike. They won't feed you that garbage again. They'll bring you regular meals. And I'll give you some cans of Ensure to drink, so you can put some weight back on."

As the doctor spoke, I thought of a way that I could keep up my protest and avoid the feeding tube at the same time.

"I'll tell you what," I said. "I said that I would never eat the food here again, and I meant it. But I'll drink the cans of Ensure if you give them to me. And then I won't have to be fed through a tube."

The doctor was satisfied with that arrangement. I spent the next five days in the clinic drinking Ensure and regaining my health, and then I was returned to my cell with instructions to keep drinking two cans of Ensure for breakfast, two cans for lunch, and two cans for dinner.

And that would have worked, if it weren't for the guards.

I had seen the guards steal other prisoners' Ensure before. One nurse had an agreement with a guard where she would give him a can and then write down that the prisoner had drunk it. If the prisoner complained, who would believe him? He might even get punished for lying.

Still, I didn't expect the guards to steal my Ensure. Not when they knew I wasn't eating anything else.

I was wrong.

"Here you go," a guard said, handing me one can of Ensure.

"Where's the other?"

"It says here you only get one can."

I knew he was lying. I had seen the doctor write the prescription. And the last guard had brought me two cans.

"It says two," I insisted. "One, two."

The guard just smirked.

I'd had enough. I had tried to be reasonable. And still they were acting like this. They could all go to hell.

"Keep both cans," I said. "I'm not going to drink them anymore."

Once it became clear that I was back on a full-fledged strike, I was moved to a special ward for hunger strikers. One of my new neighbors was a man named Sami al-Hajj. Before Guantanamo, he had been a journalist for Al Jazeera.

"I'm nervous about the feeding tube," I told Sami and my other neighbors. "It was extremely painful last time."

"Don't worry," they reassured me. "The first time is the worst."

They told me about two Saudi men who were on strike and had endured force-feeding for over a year. I had gotten to know one of them, Ahmed Zaid, before he had started his strike. His wife was Bosnian, so we had talked about Bosnia and even exchanged a few words in Bosnian. He was a laid-back, good-humored man who loved to tell jokes. The fact that a man like him was on strike made me even more convinced that it was the right thing to do and that I could do it.

Still, a few days later, when the guards brought me from my cell to a small room in which the feeding apparatus was set up, I was afraid. I shuddered at the sight of the yellow tube. And this time there was a special chair, with thick straps for my ankles, wrists, shoulders, and head.

The guards sat me down in the chair, my legs still cuffed together. They wrapped chains around my torso and fastened them behind the chair to bind me to it. They put the ankle straps over the cuffs on my ankles and tightened. Next came the shoulders and wrists. They turned my head to the left and used the strap to secure it in place against the chair back. I was completely immobilized.

A nurse inserted the yellow tube in my nostril—the right one this time—and pushed it into place. Thankfully, Sami al-Hajj was right. It was less painful than the first time had been. Faster, too: they poured the whole can of Ensure into me in about twenty minutes. There was still a cold sensation in my stomach, and the bizarre feeling of becoming full without tasting any food, and the claustrophobia of being unable to move while a tube was snaked down my throat. But I could handle it. *I passed the test*, I told myself. *The next time I eat, it will be as a free man.*

The guards in the hunger strike ward used several tactics to try to break our will and convince us to eat. The only items we were allowed to have in our cells were our clothes, an isomat, and a thin blanket that the guards removed from 4:00 a.m. to 10:00 p.m. every day even though they kept the AC on full blast. If we wanted anything else, they told us, it was very simple.

"You want a blanket all day, not just at night? End the strike."

"You want soap? End the strike."

"You want a toothbrush and toothpaste? End the strike."

"You want a Qur'an? End the strike."

There was also an interrogator who tried to tempt me with different foods. Once, he offered me a jar of jam that his mother had made on their family farm. Another time, he brought in cooked chicken and vegetables. As he unwrapped it, a delightful aroma wafted into the air. Imagine your favorite meal, and now imagine smelling it after not having eaten anything for more than a month.

"Bring it closer," I said.

He pushed the steaming food toward me.

"Mmmm," I inhaled. "It smells delicious."

"Tell me about it," he said. "I cooked it just for you."

"Well," I told him, "it would be a shame to let it go to waste. You should share it with your friends tonight. But I won't eat it."

There was one soldier who viewed it as his personal mission to make my force-feeding so miserable that I would have no choice but to give up. When he tightened the straps around my shoulders, wrists, and ankles, he went out of his way to pull them as tight as he possibly could. When I gasped, he just smirked. I could feel the straps biting into my skin the whole time I was being fed.

I didn't think it would make a difference, but I wanted to complain to one of the soldier's supervisors. After all, I had sat still in the chair while he strapped me in. I hadn't resisted him or even cursed at him. I had done exactly what he had asked. And still he had gone out of his way to make an always-uncomfortable procedure even more painful.

When the guards came to bring me back to my cell, I told them that I wanted to speak to their supervising officer.

"No," the soldier who had tightened the straps snorted. "Go back to your cell. You can talk to the officer there."

"No," I replied. "I want to show him something here."

"What's that?"

"I can't tell you. I want him to see with his own eyes."

"No."

"Don't be stupid," I told him. I started to say it a second time, but he wasn't interested. He was ready for the guards to take me back to my cell.

The soldier leaned forward and started to loosen the strap around my right wrist. His face was just inches from my hand. And I couldn't help myself. I've never been a violent man, but I was so tired of being injured and ignored. So as he undid the strap, I struck him in the nose as hard as I could.

He staggered backward and fell on his backside. The guards rushed to his side and pulled him to his feet. One of the guards pointed at me and shouted, "Don't move!" Maybe he forgot that I was still chained to the chair.

I was worried that the soldier might retaliate, but the guards brought me back to my cell without incident. A few hours later, the officer came to speak with me.

"What happened?" he asked.

I laughed. "I politely asked to talk to you, and nothing. Then I caused a problem, and now here you are."

"Why did you want to talk to me?"

"Look," I said, pointing to my shoulders. There were deep blue patches where the tight straps had caused the blood to congeal.

The officer left and came back minutes later with a camera, which he used to photograph my injuries. *Maybe*, I thought, *they'll actually punish the soldier who did this to me.* A day or two later, though, I saw the soldier back on the cellblock going about his normal routine as though nothing had changed. As far as I could tell, he hadn't been disciplined for what he'd done.

But they didn't punish me for hitting him, either. Maybe they thought that the punch was fair payback for how he'd treated me. More likely, though, they just realized that there was nothing left for them to take away from me.

In February of 2007, after two months of my being force-fed by American soldiers, the U.S. Circuit Court for Washington, D.C., upheld Judge Leon's ruling that I wasn't being held on U.S. soil and therefore wasn't protected by the U.S. Constitution.

My lawyers said they would appeal to the Supreme Court. In the meantime, I was more determined than ever to continue my hunger strike. It was the only way to protest a system that was designed to make sure I would never have a chance to prove my innocence.

It was difficult, though, when I read a letter that my lawyers brought me from Abassia. She was begging me to eat.

"If you die," Abassia wrote, "we will have no one but God. Who will care for us? What would our family be without you?"

It was a heart-wrenching letter. But I couldn't back down. I couldn't just accept the way I was being treated. I would continue my protest, and with God's help, I would survive long enough to eat once again at a table with my family beside me.

During my hunger strike, I generally felt weak, fatigued, and despondent. I knew that I was being unjustly imprisoned, and I had no idea when it would end. Still, even in a place like Guantanamo, there are moments that remind you what it is to smile.

There was the time I caught an iguana.

I was on a rec walk with Adnan, a prisoner from Yemen. Our guard had brought us to a fenced-in enclosure about the size of a tennis court. The guard opened the door to the enclosure, ushered us in, shut the door behind us, and reached in through a small slat in the fence to unshackle our legs.

After I was unshackled, I looked up to see a large iguana gazing at me from several feet away. He must have come into the enclosure at some point when the door was ajar. Now that it was shut, he had no way out.

Iguanas were hardly an unusual sight in Guantanamo. One of the guards had told me that in Cuba people ate iguanas, but on the military base they were protected: if a soldier killed one, he had to pay a $10,000 fine. And the iguanas often came right up to the fence during my rec walks. In fact, back when I had still received meals, I sometimes snuck small portions to them. (Banana was their favorite.) But they had always been on the other side of the fence.

I turned to Adnan. "Let's catch him."

We each picked up an isomat—they were scattered about the rec yard, I guess because people had been using them either to pray or to exercise—and advanced on the iguana, holding the isomats in front of ourselves to protect against his sharp teeth. He started to run, but eventually we cornered him. I grabbed the scruff of his neck with my left hand, his tail with my right, and scooped him up into the air.

"Let's give this guy to the guard," I said, grinning for the first time in a long time. We were in the opposite corner from the entrance to the rec yard, so I crossed the yard, iguana in hand. As we approached the guard, who was sitting just outside the entrance, he glanced up from his magazine and started. He shot out of his chair, sprinted away, and returned moments later with a few more soldiers.

"Let him go!" they commanded.

"Sure," I said. "Just open the door and I'll hand him to you."

But the guards wanted no part of him. I don't know if it was his sharp teeth or the $10,000 fine, but he terrified them. I extended my arms, bringing him nearer to them, and even with the fence between us they scurried back.

"Let's give him some water," I said. "Then I'll let him go."

One of the guards brought us a small bottle of water, which Adnan gently poured into the iguana's mouth. He drank for a little bit and then sneezed.

After a few more minutes of playing with our new friend, I gently set him down on the ground. The guards opened the door and he scampered off to freedom.

One prisoner, a Saudi man named Abdulhakim, was given an Arabic-language copy of *The Da Vinci Code* as a reward for cooperating with his interrogators. Abdulhakim got punished—I'm not sure why—and all of his belongings, including his book, were taken from him and placed in a small plastic bin on top of his cell that he could only access when a guard handed it to him.

Abdulhakim kindly agreed to share *The Da Vinci Code* with the rest of us. Sami al-Hajj, the Al Jazeera journalist a couple of cells down from me, convinced a friendly guard to bring him the book from Abdulhakim's bin. Then Sami hid it. And every day, for half an hour between sunset and evening prayers, he would read to the rest of us in the cellblock. He got through fifteen or twenty pages a day.

Sami was a natural storyteller. His voice quickened during the exciting sections. He was a master of the dramatic pause. And he loved to leave us with cliffhangers. Right before a key detail was about to be revealed, he would stop reading and say, "You'll have to come back tomorrow for the next episode."

What Sami did was nothing short of magical. For half an hour a day, he made us feel like we were almost human.

Once Sami finished reading the book to us, I asked if I could borrow it.

"No problem," Sami said. He snuck the book to me, and I hid it in a folder with letters from my lawyer. I spent hours in my cell with *The Da Vinci Code* in my lap, reading it while pretending to pore over my legal mail.

Even though I already knew the plot, it was a joy to read it for myself, to let the writing transport me from my island prison to a world full of excitement and possibility.

Mustafa

FOR MUCH OF MY TIME IN GUANTANAMO, I took refuge in my memories. My body was confined in a cramped, solitary cell, but in my mind, I was reliving happier times with my family. I was watching my son take his first steps. I was playing soccer in the park and chatting with friends over coffee. When I closed my eyes, I could hear my children laugh. I could see my wife smile.

These sweet memories sustained me, and saddened me too. They made me think about the new memories I was missing, there in my tiny cell. Instead of all the milestones in my children's young lives, my mind was being filled with memories that I wish I could erase.

Some men think about the day their son learned to ride a bike, to read a book, to drive a car. I think about the day Mohamed learned I was in Guantanamo. My wife had tried to shield him from this knowledge, because she did not want him to worry, and for the first five years she was successful. He thought I was away on a lengthy business trip. One day, he came home from school in tears. His classmates had been teasing him about his father being held in Guantanamo.

"The soldiers are beating him," they told him. "They are breaking his bones."

He was ten years old. My heart breaks every time I think about that day. What could my wife have possibly said, in that moment, to comfort our son? She must have felt utterly helpless. What his classmates had said was true: I was being beaten, my bones were being broken. No child should have to feel the kind of desperate worry that my son must have felt for me after that day. No father should have to feel the kind of desperate worry that I felt for my family every day for seven years.

In late 2007, I had the opportunity to speak with my family on the phone. It was the first time I ever heard my youngest son's voice. He was five. The first words Abdullah spoke to me were, "Peace be upon you, Daddy. How are you doing? Are you doing well?" His voice was tentative; I was a stranger to my five-year-old son. After we spoke for a while, Abdullah began to cry. He did not understand why I could not be at home with him.

I have not forgotten what my wife said during that same call. "Mustafa," she told me, "the boys have everything they need. They have a house. I have a job. The only thing they still need is their father."

I hope the men responsible for me being in Guantanamo will think about what my sons went through. Some of those men, like Bosnian foreign minister Zlatko Lagumdžija, claim that they had no choice: the Americans ordered him to hand me over, and disobeying them would be too risky. But I want Lagumdžija to imagine his own son crying out as his daddy is ripped away from him. I want him to imagine his own son learning from his classmates that his father is being beaten in a prison halfway around the world. I want him to imagine meeting his own son for the first time over the phone. If it had been him, if it had been his family, would he still have kowtowed to the Americans?

FREEDOM

Lakhdar

IN EARLY JULY OF 2007, my lawyers told me that the Supreme Court had agreed to hear my appeal. It would review the U.S. Circuit Court's ruling that my fellow Algerians and I couldn't file *habeas* petitions because the American Constitution didn't apply to us. The Supreme Court grouped our case with another case, *al Odah*, involving sixteen other prisoners' *habeas* petitions. But the case still bore my name. It was still me against President Bush.

Five months later, in December of 2007, my legal team and the government presented oral arguments to the Supreme Court. And then we waited. My lawyers told me that it would probably be several months. They encouraged me to stay positive—Steve and Lynn even brought a rice dish to one of our meetings and begged me to eat—but it was hard to believe that this court would be any different than the last two.

In the spring of 2008, one of the prisoners in my cellblock, a man named Najm al-Din, told me that he'd had a dream about me. In his dream, he had been sitting in the back of a bus as it bounced along a bumpy, winding, tortuous mountain pass. Finally, the bus had reached a highway and the ride smoothed out.

"You," Najm al-Din said, "were the bus driver."

We told Sami al-Hajj about the dream. He had studied the interpretation of dreams and liked to tell people what their dreams meant.

"Maybe," Sami said, "it means that Lakhdar will do something that will result in some prisoners here being released."

"What can I do to get anyone released?" I asked. "Who am I?"

But then I thought of my court case. *Maybe*, I hoped, *that's what Najm al-Din's dream is about.*

It was a few months later, on June 12th, 2008, when the Supreme Court ruled in my favor. "In every practical sense," Justice Kennedy wrote, "Guantanamo is not abroad." It was under complete American control, so the American Constitution applied. The government could not simply "switch the Constitution on or off at will." My fellow prisoners and I all had the right to file *habeas* petitions and try to prove our innocence in federal court.

It made me proud to have my name in law books and to know *Boumediene* stood for the principle that all people, even people in Guantanamo, have a right to a fair trial. But I didn't think it would do me much good. After all, my case was now going back to Judge Leon—the judge who hadn't wanted to hear my case in the first place, and who was still one of George Bush's cronies. Why would this time be any different? He would just come up with some other excuse to rule against me.

Still, it was nice to have a glimmer of hope.

In the summer and fall of 2008, there was a lot of talk about the presidential election. I learned about the two candidates, Barack Obama and John McCain, from my lawyers, the guards, and other prisoners. I was skeptical about Obama's promise to close Guantanamo—after six years, I had come to distrust all American politicians—but I liked him better than McCain, who said that he was going to expand Guantanamo even though he himself had been tortured in a prison in Vietnam.

Many of us, guards and prisoners alike, scoffed when McCain selected Sarah Palin, an Alaskan beauty queen who didn't seem like a serious person, as his running mate. That was when I began to think that Obama was going to win.

On the afternoon of November 4th, the day of the election, I was talking with a black guard.

"Will you be here tomorrow?" I asked.

"Yes."

"Will you tell me who won?"

"Sure."

The next morning, as the guard approached, I could tell from the bounce in his step that Obama had won. All of the black guards, in fact, were carrying themselves with a quiet pride. And while I didn't share their optimism about Obama, I was relieved that McCain had lost.

Around that time, my lawyers told me that my trial was going to start soon. Judge Leon had announced that he intended to resolve all of his Guantanamo cases by the end of December. I figured that he must want to decide the case while his friend Bush was still in office. More than ever, I was convinced my case was about politics, not the law. There was no way Judge Leon was going to decide the case in my favor.

On Thursday, November 6th, 2008, my trial began.

I was huddled at a small table with Mustafa, Mohamed, Hadj, and Belkacem Bensayah, in a room where I had once been interrogated. One of our lawyers, a man named Paul Winke, and his interpreter were also there. The sixth member of the so-called "Algerian Six," Saber Lahmar, wasn't allowed in the room. He was being punished for something, I don't know what.

A speakerphone had been set up on the table so we could listen to the proceedings in Judge Leon's courtroom in Washington, D.C., where our trial was getting underway. We were sitting on hard chairs with our feet chained to the floor.

Our lawyers had told us, in the days leading up to our trial, about a recent bizarre development in our case: the government had dropped its allegation that we had plotted to blow up the U.S. Embassy in Sarajevo. Just like in Bosnia seven years before, authorities were eager to toss around bomb-plot allegations right up until a court required them to provide evidence.

Instead, our lawyers told us, the government now said that the reason it considered us "enemy combatants" was that it had evidence—

classified evidence that I wasn't allowed to see—that we had made a plan to fly to Afghanistan and join Al Qaeda's fight against American forces there. This was the first time I had ever heard this allegation. No one—no police officer, no Bosnian official, no American interrogator—had ever asked me a single question about it.

And it was a ludicrous allegation. I had a travel plan but no plane ticket? I was going to leave my job without telling my employer? I was going to abandon my family without making arrangements for their care? But the government was determined. They didn't have any proof to support the first reason they had given for locking me up—so they had to come up with another reason.

We had been told that each side's lawyers would present a public opening statement while we listened over the speakerphone. Then, the court would go into closed-door sessions—which we wouldn't be allowed to listen to—where the government would present classified evidence and our lawyers would respond. Finally, a few days after the end of the trial, Judge Leon would announce his verdict in open court while we listened over the speakerphone.

That first day, though, no sound came forth from the speakerphone. We sat there for four hours, chained, in total silence.

That evening, Paul told us that there had been some sort of "technical difficulty"—I wasn't sure whether to believe that—and that Judge Leon had been furious when he found out about it, so furious that he had a courier fly an audiotape of the court session to Guantanamo that night. We gathered in the same room the next day and listened to it.

My lawyer, Steve Oleskey, made an eloquent opening statement. He explained that my co-defendants and I had been charitable workers and family men in Bosnia at the time of our arrest, that we had been locked up for no reason and with no evidence, and that the court had the power to make things right.

"While it lies outside your power to restore to these men their lost seven years, you can restore to them their liberty," Steve said. "This is a moment when you can reaffirm by what you do here the extent to which we are a nation of laws and justice."

We'll see, I thought.

Over the next week, our trial proceeded behind closed doors. Each evening, Paul met with us in the same conference room to share updates from the lawyers in Washington. Of course, Paul couldn't tell us anything about the classified evidence, but he tried to give us a general sense of how things stood. He grew more optimistic as the days passed. Judge Leon was asking the government's lawyer probing questions, and the lawyer was struggling to answer them.

While we were together in the conference room, Mustafa, Mohamed, and Hadj urged me to eat some of the food that Paul had brought us. They had high hopes. I wasn't going to break my strike just because a judge had asked some fair questions—but I also didn't want to dampen their spirits.

"I will eat," I promised them, "if we win."

My neighbors in the hunger strike ward were hopeful when I told them about my trial. They laughed that my cell must be the lucky one. Sami al-Hajj had been living in the same cell earlier in the year when he found out that he was going to be released, and I'd been transferred into the cell after Sami left. But I refused to raise my hopes only to have them dashed again. I feared that politics, not luck or the law, would dictate the outcome of my case.

On Friday, November 14th, after six days of closed hearings, the trial ended. Paul told us that Judge Leon had scheduled a public court session for the following Thursday to announce his verdict.

Again we were gathered around the conference table. Again our feet were chained to the floor. This time, there were no "technical difficulties." We could all hear Judge Leon's voice, and his interpreter's, crackling over the speakerphone. We gazed at the phone and at each other, none of us saying a word.

"Welcome," the judge said. The lawyers for both sides introduced themselves, and Judge Leon thanked them for all their hard work on the case. Then he began to summarize the background of the case. As he did, I listened carefully to try to glean some clue as to how he might rule. But I couldn't tell.

Minutes passed. Despite my best efforts not to let hope creep in, a small part of me started to believe we had a chance.

And then I heard Judge Leon say this:

> The Government alleges that all six Petitioners planned to travel to Afghanistan to take up arms against U.S. and allied forces. . . . For the following reasons, the Court finds that the Government has failed to show by a preponderance of the evidence that any of the Petitioners, other than Mr. Bensayah, either had or committed to such a plan.

I couldn't believe it. I looked at Mustafa and Mohamed and Hadj to make sure they had heard the same thing I had. The quiet elation on their faces confirmed it. Judge Leon had found us innocent. Belkacem Bensayah's expression was more stoic, and I felt bad for him, but I also didn't really know him. My thoughts quickly turned to my wife and daughters. For the first time in a long time, I allowed myself to imagine getting to see them again.

The rest of Judge Leon's words washed over me. At one point, I heard him talk about the weakness of the government's evidence. He said that the government's case relied exclusively on a document from an unnamed, uncorroborated source. "To allow enemy combatancy to rest on so thin a reed," Judge Leon said, "would be inconsistent with this Court's obligation."

And the last thing Judge Leon said was truly remarkable:

> One last point I would like to make. The Court appreciates fully that the Government has a right to appeal its decision as to these five detainees whose petitions I have granted. I have a right, too, to appeal to the seniormost leadership at the Department of Justice, Department of Defense, and

the CIA and other intelligence agencies. My appeal to them is to strongly urge them to take a hard look at the evidence, both presented and lacking, as to these five detainees. Seven years of waiting for our legal system to give them an answer to a question so important, in my judgment, is more than plenty. The appellate process for these five detainees would, at a minimum, constitute another 18 months to two years of their lives. It seems to me that there comes a time when the desire to resolve novel, legal questions . . . pales in comparison to effecting a just result. . . .*

I was impressed. Once the Supreme Court had required Judge Leon to consider the evidence, he had done so fairly and seriously. He had put justice ahead of politics, and he had come to see us as actual human beings. Maybe there was something to this notion of "the rule of law" after all. It was slow, far too slow. But it was real.

* The full transcript of Judge Leon's remarks is available online at www.WitnessesBook.com.

Mustafa

UNLIKE LAKHDAR, I was not at all surprised by Judge Leon's ruling. Honestly, before the hearing even started, I had predicted to Rob
Kirsch that Judge Leon would set most of us free but keep at least
one of us in prison.

"If Judge Leon decides that we are all innocent," I said to Rob,
"this will mean that George Bush was wrong. His friend was wrong.
By the same token, if he says that we are all criminals, he will have to
explain how this can be so when there is no evidence against us. So,
he will release some of us, but for some he will say, 'It is at least possible that they did something wrong, and we have to know for sure.'"

In Algeria we have a saying, "Don't let the shepherd cry and don't
let the wolf get hungry," to highlight how difficult it is to please
everyone. I thought Judge Leon would sacrifice one of us to the wolf,
and as it turned out, he did.

I had told Rob that I was willing to be the one who stayed behind, if it meant that my friends would get to return home to their
families. Rob, however, was confident that the case against me was
particularly weak.

"If anyone is going to be released," he said, "you will be first
among them."

In the weeks leading up to the hearing, one of my interrogators accused me of being an Al Qaeda member. I told him, "Just wait until
I appear before a judge. See if he thinks I was in Al Qaeda."

The interrogator said, "You're not going to appear in court."

"Why not?"

"Because," he replied, "if you appear in court, you will go home."

"So you know that I'm innocent."

"No," he said, "as far as we're concerned, you're not innocent."

The facts and evidence were irrelevant to the interrogator. I was in Guantanamo. How could I possibly be innocent?

"There's no such thing as an innocent Muslim, right?" I scoffed.

In early November of 2008, my court hearing began. The soldiers led me from my cell to a cramped room and seated me at a crowded conference table along with Lakhdar, Mustafa, Hadj, Belkacem, an interpreter, a government attorney, and one of my attorneys. There was a large satellite dish and a lot of other electronic equipment; it was quite a production. It took them more than a day to get everything working. Once they finally did, the teleconference screen on the wall was occupied by Judge Leon, a large man who wore a massive ring that he occasionally tapped against his desk.

The government's attorney was the first to speak at length. He stated the allegations against us. The government had dropped the allegation of planning to bomb the American Embassy, acknowledging that there was zero evidence to back up the sole accusation that had put us in prison in the first place. Instead, the attorney argued, we needed to stay locked up because the government had a suspicion that we had been plotting to travel to Afghanistan for terrorist training. I will never understand why anyone would suspect me of that.

As the government's attorney laid out its case, I got the impression that Judge Leon was taken aback by how flimsy the evidence was. I saw him shake his head more than once.

A few days later, on November 12th, it was time for me to have my day in court. Our attorneys had recommended that I testify, since I spoke English relatively well, even though it is not my first language. As I sat in front of the teleconference screen, testifying before a judge in a courtroom hundreds of miles away, I felt completely at ease. I had nothing to hide, and therefore no cause to be nervous.

My attorney asked me about my background before I was arrested, and I talked about the peaceful, hard-working family man I had been. He asked about Lakhdar, Mohamed, and Hadj, and I described my friendship with them. Finally, he asked me some questions about my thoughts on terrorism and violence in general:

Q. What was your reaction to the news of the September 11 attacks?

A. . . . I did not believe that there [are] people who can do the attacks like that . . . people who can attack with the airplanes . . . and kill the people in that way.

Q. But you understand that was done in the name of Islam.

A. I know, but my belief in Islam, I don't consider that [to be] Islam, because Islam does not allow us to do . . . things like that. . . . [T]he people who did it are Muslims, but [their actions] have nothing to do with Islam. Islam is against those things.

Q. Have you ever been affiliated with al-Qaeda?

A. Never.

Q. How about the Taliban?

A. Never.

Q. Were you aware of the U.S. military's plan to strike in Afghanistan after 9/11?

A. Yes.

Q. Now, prior to October of 2001, had you had any weapons training?

A. Never.

Q. Had you ever engaged in any combat?

A. Never.

Q. Had you ever held a firearm?

A. Never.

Q. In October of 2001, did you have any plans to travel to Afghanistan to
fight against U.S. or allied forces?

A. Not at all.*

My entire testimony lasted twenty or thirty minutes. I had been
fighting for almost seven years for the opportunity to have a judge
hear my case, and when it finally came, it was over in the blink of an
eye. When I finished answering the attorneys' questions, Judge Leon
said, "Thank you, sir." From the look in his eyes, I got the impression
that he was genuinely upset about what had happened to me. In that
moment, I was certain he would find me innocent.

Eight days later, on November 20th, 2008, he did. We had all
gathered in a room to hear Judge Leon announce his decision. He
called each one of us by name and declared the man innocent, until
he got to the last name. Five of us would go free, but Belkacem Bensayah would remain, because of classified evidence the government
claimed to have. I believe the whole thing was a political matter; the
supposed "classified evidence" was simply an excuse to allow George
Bush to save face.

We tried to comfort Belkacem. "Be patient," we told him. "God
willing, you will be released soon too." Of course, he was upset, as was
I. Thrilled though I was to be able to go home, I could not celebrate
as long as an innocent man had to remain behind. As the soldiers
brought me back to my cell, I cried, both for Belkacem and because
I was simply overwhelmed by what it had taken, and what I had lost,
to get to this point.

* The full transcript of Mustafa's testimony is available online at www.WitnessesBook.com.

Lakhdar

AFTER JUDGE LEON ORDERED MY RELEASE, the guards who escorted me back to my cell could see the joy on my face.

"What are you smiling about?" one of them asked. This particular guard had always been a jerk.

"I get to go home," I told him, "and I'm going to leave you behind in this furnace. I'm going home and you're going to hell."

It was exhilarating to swear in triumph rather than in a desperate rage.

The guard simply shrugged and deposited me in my cell. I shared my news with the prisoners in earshot, and as word traveled, the cellblock began to fill with applause, songs, and shouts of encouragement.

"I knew it," one of my neighbors told me. "From the beginning, you never belonged here."

At dinnertime, I told the guards that they didn't need to bring me to my force-feeding. I had made a promise to my friends.

"Tonight," I said, "I'm going to have a real meal."

The guards took me out to the rec yard and brought me food. I took a few bites. It might sound strange, since I hadn't eaten a meal in two years, but I don't remember what they fed me. All I could think about was the fact that after more than seven years, I might actually get to go home.

The next morning, when the guards offered me breakfast, I declined. I had told my friends that I would eat a meal, so I did. But I wasn't going to end my hunger strike. Not until I was actually a free man. After all, this wasn't the first time a court had ordered my release. When Abassia and my daughters were in my arms, and only then, would I believe it was real.

Later that day, an officer came by my cell to speak with me.

"Listen," he said. "You've been found innocent. You're close to leaving. Why don't you start eating again, and we'll move you to Camp Four with Mustafa and Mohamed and Hadj?"

"No," I told him. "Never. I'm going to stay in this cell, and I'm not going to eat until I get home. The only reason I ate yesterday was to express my joy when I heard the court's decision. I won't eat here again. Your food is bad, your treatment is bad, and you are bad."

"Okay," the officer shrugged, turning to the guards. "Leave him here."

Since I was still in the hunger strike ward, I wasn't allowed any possessions beyond my clothes and an isomat. I thought about complaining—maybe requesting a few basics, like a toothbrush, now that I had been found innocent—but I decided not to. I was optimistic that I would be released soon, and I didn't want to provoke any trouble in the meantime.

Some of the prisoners in the hunger strike ward, upset about their mistreatment and unable to do anything else to protest it, had started throwing their feces at guards, officers, nurses, and doctors as they walked past, giving the whole ward an awful odor. I didn't participate in the protest. It just seemed too filthy, and again, I didn't want to cause trouble.

I can survive this, I told myself. *Just a little bit longer.*

Mustafa

EVEN AFTER I WAS FOUND INNOCENT, I was treated like a guilty man in Guantanamo. It was just a few brief moments after Judge Leon ordered my release that I was shackled and handcuffed. Soldiers placed me in an armored car with tinted windows, so I could not see the sky, and drove me back to my cell.

I had to spend almost a full month in Guantanamo after I was found innocent. Nothing changed at all in those last days. I still had to wear a detainee jumpsuit. I ate the same disgusting food, slept on the same sorry excuse for a bed, lived in the exact same prison cell as before. The guards still treated me the same. In their eyes, I was not an innocent man. I was Detainee 10004, still and always.

Even the interrogations continued. When I refused to talk to the interrogators, they punished me by having all the items removed from my cell. The interrogations continued through December 13th, my second-to-last day in that cell.

When I needed to speak with my attorneys, the guards escorted me to the phone in handcuffs and shackles. My attorneys told me that although Judge Leon had ordered my release, he had not specified what country I was to be released to. It seemed likely that I would be able to return to Bosnia, but there were still some details to sort out, some red tape to cut through.

On the morning of December 14th, I still did not know when I would be released, or to where. Soldiers showed up outside my cell that morning and announced, "Okay, you're coming with us." They escorted me to a room where I was photographed and fingerprinted, and they gave me a shirt, a pair of slacks, and some cheap blue shoes. I still have the outfit they gave me.

Then one of the soldiers said, "Okay, now you're going to go home."

"What do you mean?" I asked. "Which home?"

"Bosnia," he said.

They gave me some papers to sign, and then they put me back in a cell for the last time, next to the four other men who had been found innocent with me. We were all excited to be going home.

Hours later, they separated me, Mohammed, and Hadj from the rest of the group. I did not know why Lakhdar and Saber were not with us. After night fell, they loaded the three of us onto a bus, chained together and chaperoned by dozens of soldiers. I felt the bus drive onto a ferry, most likely the same one that had carried us from the plane to the prison years before. The windows of the bus were covered, so we could not see out.

After crossing the water and driving a bit further, we were escorted off the bus and led onto a military plane. We sat there on the plane for somewhere between thirty minutes and an hour, waiting to take off, before we were told that the weather was not suitable for flying. A group of soldiers led us off the plane and back onto the bus.

They brought us to the part of Camp Delta where we had first been imprisoned after the animal cages of Camp X-Ray. They were no longer keeping detainees there, so we had the area to ourselves. A soldier would come by once every hour or so, but otherwise there was nobody in that part of Camp Delta but the three of us. It was eerily quiet. We could have screamed at the top of our lungs and no one would have heard us.

At some point, a soldier brought us dinner. I hoped that it would be my last taste of prison food, but they kept us there in that ghost-block for two more days. Finally, they brought us back to the airport and back onto an airplane. This time, praise God, the plane took off.

Lakhdar

WHEN MUSTAFA LEFT GUANTANAMO, in mid-December, I did not. Hours before the flight to Bosnia, a Red Cross official told me that I was not going to be on board. "You were supposed to be on the plane," he said, "but your name got removed from the list at the last minute."

Later, when I was talking with my lawyers, Steve told me what had happened. Apparently, while I was in Guantanamo, some bureaucrats in Bosnia had discovered a technical problem with the citizenship application I filed when I moved there in 1997. Obviously, I hadn't been able to go into their office to sort out the technicality, so the bureaucrats had revoked my citizenship. And since I was no longer a Bosnian citizen, I was no longer allowed in Bosnia.

According to Steve, several members of the Bosnian parliament had been willing to reinstate my citizenship so I could come home, but a hardline Orthodox Serb politician who opposed my return had taken steps to block them.

I was furious.

"To hell with Bosnia," I told Steve. "Why would I want to go back there anyway? They were the ones who sold me to America. Maybe next time they'll sell me to China. Their citizenship wouldn't even be useful as toilet paper."

After Mustafa, Mohamed, and Hadj were flown to Bosnia, and I was left behind, despair set in once more. I had been found innocent, and yet still I had no idea if I would ever be allowed to leave.

In the meantime, I decided, I would demand to be treated with respect. I told one of the guards that I wanted to talk to an officer, and when the officer arrived at my cell, I tried to reason with him.

"Listen," I said. "I'm not a troublemaker. Other people cause problems and throw their feces. So far, I haven't done anything like that. And I'm sure you've heard that the judge found me innocent?"

"No," he answered.

"You should have," I told him. "It's been on the news, in the paper, everywhere. The judge found me innocent a month ago. And look, I don't want anything special—I'm not going to ask you to get me food from McDonald's to celebrate. I just want my basic rights. I want a pillow and a real mattress. This isomat is something a mechanic would kneel on to fix a car. I am a human being. I want a mattress for human beings. And I want a cushion to sit on in the feeding chair. And a toothbrush and toothpaste, and soap and shampoo."

"You can have those things," the officer said, "in Camp Four. All you have to do is end your hunger strike."

"I can't do that."

"Then I can't help you."

"Okay," I told him. "Prepare your IRF people. I'm not going to another feeding until you give me my rights. If you want to feed me, you'll have to IRF me."

And that's what happened. Two times a day, a group of armored soldiers stormed into my cell, pinned me down, carried me to the room with the feeding chair, and strapped me into it. They fastened my head to the back of the chair, and no matter how much I wriggled and resisted, there was nothing I could do to prevent the tube from entering my throat. When the feeding was over, the IRF team forcefully carried me back to my cell. Four IRFings a day, because I had dared to insist that my innocence entitled me to a mattress.

After three weeks, the officer who had refused me a mattress returned to my cell to propose a compromise. I think the higher-ups must have realized—maybe with some help from my lawyers—that it would make them look bad if the public found out they were routinely IRFing an innocent man.

"Listen," the officer said. "We want to take you to Camp Iguana, where you'll get better treatment."

I had been to Camp Iguana before, both for meetings with my lawyers and for interrogation sessions. It was set at a distance from the other camps. I had heard from other prisoners that in the early days of Guantanamo, women and children as young as eight years old had been housed in Camp Iguana before they were returned to Afghanistan. And I knew that a large group of Uighurs had lived there in the months between when the government had said it would release them and when it actually did. I was confident that Iguana would be a step up from the hunger strike ward.

"And," the officer added, "you don't have to end your strike if you don't want to. You just need to come to your feedings voluntarily without being IRFed."

"I'll think about it," I told him.

"I need an answer now," he demanded.

"No," I shot back. "You need to go now. It's my decision to make, and I'll tell you once I've made it."

After the officer left, I talked with my neighbors.

"They want to take me to Camp Iguana," I told them. "But you are my brothers. I don't want to abandon you here."

"No," they said. "Don't be crazy. We want what's best for you. Get out of here."

We wished each other luck, and then I asked the guard to let the officer know that I was ready to leave.

After a short jeep ride, I was greeted by an officer who spoke to me in a polite, courteous tone.

"Welcome to Camp Iguana," he said. He told me that in this camp, I should feel free to go for rec walks or take a shower whenever

I wanted—I didn't need an escort. They would give me soap and shampoo and a toothbrush and toothpaste, and if I ever ran low I should ask for more. The officer showed me a kitchen with a coffee machine and told me that I could use it anytime.

"And are you sure," the officer asked, "you don't want us to bring you food?"

"I will eat," I told him, "when I get home."

"Okay," he said. "There's a small room here that we'll set up the feeding apparatus in. Will you please come to the feedings voluntarily?"

I appreciated that he was talking to me like an adult.

"Yes," I told him, "on one condition. Just feed me in a regular chair, not the torture chair, and I'll cooperate."

"Sure thing," he said.

And then they showed me to my cell. Through my window, I could see boats sailing past on the shimmering waters of the Caribbean. It would have been beautiful, if it hadn't been prison.

For the next several weeks, I was treated with civility, so I didn't cause trouble. I went to my feedings without complaint, and as they promised, they didn't use the torture chair. Instead, they used something resembling the chair at a dentist's office. Being force-fed was still uncomfortable, but it wasn't as painful now that there weren't restraints digging into my skin.

I passed time by talking to my two cellmates—Saber Lahmar, who had been moved to Camp Iguana shortly after me, and a young man from Chad named Youssef who had also been found innocent and was waiting to be released. There was also a small room with books, magazines, and a TV and videos, but I wasn't able to focus on anything but getting out. I found a pen and made myself a souvenir by inscribing the tally of my court cases on an undershirt: "Boumediene 2, Bush 0."

.   .   .

The most important difference between Camp Iguana and the other camps was that I was able to receive phone calls from Abassia. I had talked to her a few times in the past seven years, when my lawyers had arranged a call, but it was always in a crowded room with soldiers listening in. It was wonderful to be able to have something closer to real conversations with my wife.

Abassia would give me updates on our daughters and on herself. The three of them were now living with Abassia's family in Algeria. They missed me, and day-to-day life was a struggle, but they were holding up as best they could. I reassured her that I would get out soon, Insha'Allah, and I promised that I would stay strong until then.

Whenever I heard her voice, I knew that I could.

In late December of 2008, after Bosnia had rejected me, one of my lawyers, Rob Kirsch, told me that he could look into the possibility of getting me released to Algeria. However, he warned me that negotiating with the Algerian government might take years.

"If we can find some other country," Rob asked, "would you go?"

"I'm willing to go to the moon," I told him. "I'll go to Somalia. I'll go anywhere. Just get me out of here."

In early 2009, Rob asked me what I thought of France.

"I'd be thrilled to go there," I told him. "But do you really think they'd be willing to take me?"

"We're going to work on it," he said.

Rob spent the next several weeks talking with diplomats at the French Embassy in Washington. In March, he called and told me that he was optimistic.

"How's your French?" he asked.

"Decent," I told him. I had learned French as a schoolchild in Algeria and in my classes in Yemen, although it had become a bit rusty after my efforts to learn Albanian, Bosnian, and enough English to get by in Guantanamo.

"Good," Rob said.

Rob told me that President Obama was traveling to Paris in early April to meet with President Sarkozy, and during that meeting, they were going to discuss whether France would accept any released prisoners from Guantanamo. It was hard to imagine that two world leaders would be having a conversation about me. But then, I had already held my own in the ring with President Bush.

On April 3rd, Rob called again. He told me that after their meeting, Obama and Sarkozy had held a press conference in which they announced that France was willing to take one freed Guantanamo detainee. They didn't say which prisoner it was going to be, but Rob believed that it would be me.

It was about ten days later when Rob called again. He had heard from the French Embassy.

"They gave me a name," Rob said. "It's going to be you. There are just a few more hoops to jump through."

I couldn't believe it. But I badly wanted to.

The next few weeks were about logistics.

Rob called me from the French Embassy in Washington and told me that the French ambassador wanted to talk with me. He wanted to make sure that I could speak the language. My French was worse than I would've hoped, but we still had a pleasant conversation. Afterward, I wrote the ambassador a letter in French expressing my gratitude to him.

There was also the matter of my visa. My lawyers asked the U.S. Government to turn over the documents it had seized from me, including my old passport, so that France could issue me a visa based on them. But the U.S. refused. All my documents, we were told, had been lost. The French wound up making me a visa using a picture that they found on the Internet.

Finally, there was Abassia. When it became clear that France would take me, my lawyers had asked if I wanted Abassia and the girls to arrive in France first.

"Yes," I said. "That would be better. I cannot go there and live without my wife, she in Algeria and me in France. What's the point?"

There were lots of hurdles to clear to make that happen. Algeria had a law prohibiting a mother from taking her children out of the country without the father's written consent, so I had to sign an authorization letter for my lawyers to deliver to the Algerian Embassy in Washington. And then we had to wait for it to be processed.

Abassia also had to get an Algerian passport. A kind diplomat from the French Consulate in Oran, Algeria, went with her to the administrative office, but the chief of the office refused to issue her a passport. Abassia wasn't sure why, but the chief was incredibly rude to her and the diplomat.

"Don't worry," the diplomat told her. "Go home, and I'll make some phone calls and get this sorted out."

And then everything happened all at once.

On Wednesday, May 13th, 2009, the French diplomat called Abassia. He told her that he had just spoken with the Algerian minister of the interior, and the passport issue had been taken care of. Abassia just needed to go back to the administrative office. When she went in, she encountered the same chief. This time, he sang a different tune, calling her "sister" and acting polite to the point of being obsequious. Abassia didn't even acknowledge him. She quietly accepted her passport and left.

When she got home, Abassia got another call from the French diplomat.

"Did you get your passport?" he asked.

"Yes. Thank you."

"Do you have enough money for plane tickets to Paris?"

"No."

"Okay," the diplomat said. "We'll get you plane tickets and a hotel room in Paris. Tomorrow morning, come to the consulate. Bring your daughters and your suitcases. We'll give you your visas and then we'll all go to the airport."

The diplomat was an unassuming man. And a true hero.

The next day, Rob and a diplomat from the French Embassy in Washington came to see me. For the first time, the guards allowed me to meet with other people without being shackled.

"Your wife and daughters," the diplomat told me, "are going to the airport right now. And tomorrow, you're going to be flown to France."

The diplomat told me I was going to be transported on a military plane in chains, which was why he and Rob couldn't accompany me. They were afraid their presence on the plane might make it seem like they approved of the way I was being treated.

"I understand," I told him. I wasn't excited about the prospect of a flight in chains, surrounded only by soldiers, but I knew I could survive it. And then I would never be shackled again.

After we talked a bit more, the diplomat offered me some food he had brought.

"I'm on a hunger strike," I told him.

"I know," he said. "And I respect that. But I'd advise you to eat something small, just to give you a bit more strength. Otherwise, the Americans might say that you aren't medically fit to travel."

His reasoning made sense, and I certainly didn't want anyone to have an excuse to keep me there. I brought the food—rice and beans—back to my room, where I ate a few bites and shared the rest with Youssef, the young man from Chad. I felt a bit queasy, but I was able to keep the food down.

Later in the day, I spoke with my brother, who had driven Abassia and the girls to the airport in Algeria. He had dropped her off, the diplomat from Oran had seen her to her flight, and they had both stayed to watch the plane take off. Abassia was on her way to France.

"Thank God," I said. "Tomorrow, Insha'Allah, I will be too."

. . .

That night, I was too excited to sleep. I spent the night outdoors in the rec yard, talking with Youssef about what we had been through. I couldn't believe that it might actually be coming to an end.

After several hours, a guard told me that it was almost time to go. As I hugged Youssef goodbye, I could see tears in his eyes.

"You'll get out soon, Insha'Allah," I told him. (And as it turned out, I was right. Youssef was flown to Chad just three weeks later.)

I took a quick shower and got dressed in brand new clothes that my lawyers had bought for me: a nice pair of slacks, a comfortable pair of shoes, and a dress shirt, under which I wore my "Boumediene 2, Bush 0" undershirt. *Maybe*, I thought, *I'll show it to the reporters when I land in France.*

I stood in my cell and waited. When a guard finally came to collect me, he was accompanied by a soldier carrying a video camera. That soldier was going to stay by my side, videotaping, until we landed in France. I guess the people in charge were afraid that I'd have a medical problem and didn't want to be blamed for it.

While the soldier videotaped, the guard cuffed and shackled me and led me outside. A large group of guards and officers were waiting. It seemed like practically all of the soldiers in Guantanamo were there. I had no idea why they needed that many people to escort one innocent man in chains.

Some of the guards led me onto a golf cart and drove me to a nearby camp, where a bus sat idling. When the guards ushered me onto the bus, I saw that the windows had been covered by black sheets of plastic to prevent me from looking at anything we drove past.

I took a seat, surrounded by about a dozen soldiers. We bumped along for a little while and then drove onto what felt like a ferry. I remembered my first ferry ride, more than seven years earlier. Now, I was sitting in a chair instead of on the hard floor. I didn't have a blindfold on or chains wrapped around me. But my hands were still cuffed and my legs were still shackled together.

I felt the bus drive back onto solid ground. Fifteen minutes later, we came to a stop and the soldiers escorted me off the bus. As I stepped down, I saw a huge plane, surrounded by still more soldiers, as well as some of my lawyers and some high-ranking military officers, including a general and a colonel. The cameraman filmed it all as he stepped off the bus behind me.

With the lawyers and officers looking on, the soldiers who had been with me on the bus led me toward the plane, where they handed me off to a new group of soldiers. The new soldiers gave me a thorough pat-down, touching me in inappropriate places in the process. I have no idea what they could have possibly been checking for. I had been in a prison cell, on a remote island, for almost a decade.

"You motherfuckers," I swore. "What are you going to do next, put your hands down my pants?"

As they led me onto the plane, I kept swearing. I cursed the soldiers, the general and the colonel, George Bush and Dick Cheney—all of the people involved in what had been done to me.

Before Guantanamo, I never would have talked like that to anyone. I used to be peaceful, polite, mild-mannered.

I still reject violence. It goes against everything my religion stands for, everything my parents taught me, and everything I hope to teach my children. But if I were given two minutes alone in a room with George Bush, I would spit in his face. His prison was a truly hateful place.

I took my seat on the plane, flanked by a soldier on either side. After the plane door closed, the plane gathered speed and lifted off the ground at a sharp angle. Guantanamo was behind me.

Even though I couldn't move—the chain connecting my shackles was fastened to the floor—a group of five soldiers kept watch over me, standing near my seat and not saying a word. When they grew weary, they were relieved by another group of soldiers, and then another. The three groups rotated turns for the entire flight.

The flight was interminable. All I could think was, *When will we land? When will I get to see my wife and daughters?* I stole glances at a soldier's wristwatch to see how long we had been airborne.

After several hours, the cameraman needed to use the bathroom, so he handed his video camera to another soldier.

"Keep taping until I get back," he said. "Give me a shout if anything happens."

Nothing did.

A few hours later, a soldier told me that there were about to be some bumps.

"Don't worry," he said. "Another plane is going to fly alongside and refuel us."

There were soldiers between the window and me, so I wasn't able to see the other plane approach, but I could feel our plane shudder for a few minutes as we were being refueled.

A while later, I needed to use the bathroom. I told a soldier, who unfastened my chain from the floor of the plane and guided me, still shackled, toward the bathroom. He opened the door and gestured to me to enter.

I realized, as I walked into the bathroom, that the soldier with the video camera was continuing to tape.

"Close the door," I said to the soldier who had brought me there.

"No."

"Then make him turn off the camera."

"No."

I stood over the toilet for a few moments, but I was unable to go to the bathroom while being videotaped. I returned to my seat, resigned to the fact that I would be uncomfortable for the rest of the flight.

When it was time for nighttime prayers, I took a bottle of water I had been given—I hadn't had any to drink—and used it for ablution.* Washing my feet while shackled required some contortions, but I was able to manage.

---

* Translator's Note: Before prayer, Muslims perform ritual washing of their face, arms, and feet. This is referred to as "ablution."

After I prayed, I looked at a soldier's watch and saw that we had been airborne for more than fifteen hours. *Surely*, I thought to myself, *we must be about to land.*

Another hour passed. And then another. And then I heard a soldier admiring the city lights below. We were over Paris.

As we descended, I wondered what Rahma would look like. She had been eighteen months old the last time I saw her, and now she was nine. I wondered about Abassia and Raja, and how the last seven-and-a-half years had changed them. When I felt the plane touch down on the runway, I thanked God that I was finally going to get to see them again.

Mustafa

WHEN HADJ, MOHAMED, AND I landed in Sarajevo, months before Lakhdar landed in Paris, there was a large crowd gathered at the airport. I was disoriented, because the airport had changed so much in the years since I had last been there.

Soldiers ushered us off the plane, still in chains. They loaded us directly into a waiting police car and accompanied us to a large police building in downtown Sarajevo. On the way, we drove through streets I had once known quite well. It looked so different now, seven years later, that I turned to one of the police officers and asked, "Are we really in Sarajevo?"

Outside the police building, another crowd was waiting to welcome us home. Once the soldiers brought us inside, one of them asked his commander, "What should we do with their chains?"

"That's it," he replied. "Remove them."

Police officers confirmed our identities and asked about our health. We each were given a bag containing some of the personal items that had been confiscated from us when we were first imprisoned back in 2001. All three of us noticed that the money we had been carrying was missing. My bag contained some of the clothing I had been wearing, but not all of it. The expensive suit I had worn for my Bosnian court appearances was gone, as were the pants from my track-suit. The shirt was still there. Mohamed Nechla found a passport in his bag, but it was not his; it belonged to someone from Sudan. No one had any idea how it got there.

After we were processed, it was time, at long last, to go home. The policeman assigned to drive me to my house asked me for my address.

"I don't know," I told him. My wife had moved to a new house with the boys while I was in Guantanamo. The policeman had to call the Intelligence Division to get my new address.

He started driving. It felt like an eternity as we wound through the streets of Sarajevo, streets that seemed at once both familiar and brand new to me. As we turned down a side street, the policeman told me that we were close. I looked out the window at my new neighborhood. And then I saw, standing in front of one of the houses, my oldest son. As the car pulled past Mohamed, toward our driveway, he started running after us.

There would be many joyful moments to come, and hardships too. But as we pulled into the driveway, as I looked out the car window at my boy running as fast as his legs could carry him, I was not thinking about the future that stretched before me or the past from which I will never be fully unshackled. For the first time in seven years, I could see my son. For the first time in seven years, I was about to see my wife. For the first time in seven years, I was home.

Lakhdar

AFTER WE LANDED IN PARIS, a soldier unfastened my chain from the plane floor but kept me cuffed and shackled. If no one had intervened, I probably would have still been in handcuffs and shackles when my wife and daughters saw me for the first time.

A tall, distinguished-looking Frenchman strode onto the plane and introduced himself. He was Eric Chevallier, the official spokesman for the French Ministry of Foreign Affairs.

"Are you all right?" he asked me.

"Yes."

"Can you walk?"

"Yes. I have a bad knee, but I can walk."

Eric turned to speak with the officer in charge about removing my handcuffs and shackles. After a few minutes of being stonewalled, Eric stepped off the plane, I think to call his superiors. When he came back, he quietly said a few more words to the officer. They were effective.

"Unchain him," the officer ordered, and a soldier took the shackles off my legs and the cuffs off my wrists.

I was a free man.

"Let's go," Eric said, and I followed him off the plane.

Walking down the steps toward the dimly lit tarmac, I was surprised to see that there were no reporters, and there was no crowd of supporters like there had been outside the prison in Bosnia when the Americans had first kidnapped me. The timing and location of my pre-dawn arrival in France, I later learned, had been kept a secret. I wouldn't have a chance to show off my "Boumediene 2, Bush 0" shirt.

In an instant, none of that mattered. I saw, some twenty feet away, a group of French officials standing near two cars and an ambulance. Next to them, huddled together and holding hands, were Abassia, Raja, and Rahma.

I walked toward them as quickly as my bad knee could carry me.

As we approached, Eric patted my shoulder.

"We'll give you some time with your family," he said, and he and the French officials who had been with Abassia blended into the background.

Just like that, the people I had dreamt about seeing for seven-and-a-half years were right in front of me. All four of us were in tears. We hugged each other and I tried to comfort my daughters.

"Hush," I said. "It's okay."

Raja was crying the hardest, since she remembered me from when she was five years old. Rahma was more bewildered. At one point, she turned to Abassia and said, "This man is too old to be my father."

I knew what she meant. It had been so long since I'd last seen my daughters that I didn't even recognize them. But I will never forget how good it felt to have them in my arms again.

We stayed like that, hugging and crying, for a long while. We were still in the shadow of the American plane, and I wouldn't be surprised if the soldier with the video camera kept taping us through the window the whole time.

Eventually, Eric and the other officials reappeared.

"We're going to take you to the airport clinic," Eric said, gesturing toward the ambulance. "Your wife and daughters will follow in that car," he pointed, "and we'll all meet up at the airport."

At the airport clinic, they ran a series of tests. My blood sugar was low, so they gave me glucose injections and IV fluids. And then it was time to go to the hospital—but first, they brought me to an airport café so that I could talk with Abassia and Raja and Rahma a bit longer.

For the first time in a long time, I enjoyed the simple pleasure of small talk. Abassia introduced me to the friendly Foreign Affairs officer who had been escorting her and the girls around Paris.

"Yesterday," Abassia told me, "she took us to the Eiffel Tower. We took pictures, and then we went to a nice restaurant."

The hospitality that the French Ministry of Foreign Affairs showed not only to me but also to Abassia and the girls, from their very first day in France, is something I'll always be grateful for.

I talked with Abassia and the girls for a long time. It felt unreal, and at the same time completely normal.

After a while, we got back in our vehicles—me in my ambulance, and Abassia and the girls in the car with their escort—and headed to Percy Hospital in West Paris. When we arrived, they told us that they needed to check me into the Intensive Care Unit and run a series of tests.

By then, it was getting late and the girls were getting tired.

"Let me take you back to your hotel," Abassia's escort said to her. Abassia was reluctant to leave.

"Don't worry," the escort reassured her. "I'll move you to a hotel closer to here, and you'll be able to visit as soon as he's out of the ICU."

Abassia relented, and she and the girls said goodbye.

"I'll see you soon," I told them.

They ran tests overnight, and the next morning they moved me from the ICU to a private room on an upper floor of the hospital. A friendly nurse called Abassia's hotel and told her she could visit anytime.

A short while later, Abassia and the girls were at my bedside. Abassia shared a heartwarming story about something that had happened on their walk from the hotel to the hospital. It was only a twenty-minute walk, but she had gotten a bit confused about her whereabouts, so she stopped in a convenience store to ask for directions and to buy some cookies and juice for the girls.

When she approached the shop-owner and asked how to get to

the hospital, speaking French with an Algerian accent, he did a double take.

"Don't tell me," he said. "Are you Boumediene's wife?"

The shop-owner was an Algerian man who closely followed the news and knew that I had just arrived in France. He didn't recognize Abassia as one of his regular customers, and when he heard her accent, saw her hijab, and found out she was going to the hospital, he put two and two together.

When Abassia nodded, the shop-owner gave her a sympathetic look.

"I'll drive you to the hospital," he said. He told his son to watch the shop while he was gone. And before he left, he grabbed a large paper grocery bag and filled it with candy and snacks for Raja and Rahma.

Abassia and the girls visited me in my hospital room for several hours every day. While the girls played in the room and on the balcony, Abassia told me more about what the past seven-and-a-half years had been like for the three of them.

Without me around, Abassia was unable to afford our rent, so she and the girls had no choice but to leave Bosnia and live with her family in Algeria. She found part-time work with the Algerian Illiteracy Eradication Program, teaching elderly people how to read and write.

Abassia's father worried that the reports about me were true. Maybe she should divorce me and marry a man who wasn't in prison?

"I know my husband," she told him. "He's innocent. He's a good man. I've lived with him for seven years, and he's never done anything immoral. He's been wronged, and I will stand by him. Even if he dies in Guantanamo, I will not marry another."

There were some Guantanamo wives who not only divorced their husbands but also refused to let their children see their husbands' families. Abassia did the opposite, bringing Raja and Rahma to see my parents during school vacations. She made sure that my parents didn't lose their grandchildren along with their son.

In addition to raising our girls and working at the Illiteracy Eradication Program, Abassia spent countless hours talking to my lawyers and watching the news for details about my case. She was my most steadfast supporter. I will never be able to thank her enough for everything she did.

Abassia told me that at first, when the girls asked where I was, she said that I was away on a business trip. That answer worked for a while, but as Raja grew older, it no longer satisfied her.

"Mommy," she asked one day, "why did Daddy leave us?"

Abassia didn't want Raja to think that I had chosen to abandon them, so she told the truth. That was when Raja started writing me letters.

"Daddy," she wrote, "I know you're being imprisoned unfairly. I want you to come home."

Abassia took pictures of Raja and Rahma and sent them with the letters. Not all of the letters had made it to me, but the ones that did had reminded me that no matter what, I could not give in to despair. I had to survive. I had to come home.

While Abassia shared her stories with me, the kind people at Percy Hospital nursed me back to health. They prepared meals designed to be gentle on my stomach, gave me medicine, and in general took good care of me. I was still frail and emaciated, at 5'9", 125 pounds, but I was beginning to feel human again.

After ten days in the hospital, I was healthy enough to be discharged. A French official suggested that I live in the nearby hotel with my family while the government made long-term housing arrangements for us. On May 25th, 2009, I walked out of the hospital with Abassia, Raja, and Rahma by my side.

On our way to the hotel, we stopped in the shop owned by the Algerian man who had been so kind to Abassia and the girls. I wanted to thank him myself.

The shop-owner recognized Abassia, and I introduced myself,

shook his hand, and expressed my gratitude. He invited us into his home—he lived above his shop—and as we sat in his living room, chatting over coffee and juice, he asked about my experience in Guantanamo. The more I told him, the more indignant he became.

"Seven-and-a-half years," he murmured. "What about the law? Isn't this America, which claims to respect human rights?"

After we talked for a while, Abassia and I got up to leave. As we exchanged goodbyes, he pressed some money into Raja and Rahma's hands. I tried to decline, but he insisted. He was a truly generous man.

That afternoon, we had lunch in a small pizzeria close to the hotel. It reminded me of The Fountain, the café we had regularly gone to in Sarajevo. After a few delicious bites, I turned to my wife and laughed.

"Pizza," I told her, "is sacred to Americans. The interrogators used to tell us that if we confessed we were in Al Qaeda, they would get us a pizza. For a pizza like this, someone could get in real trouble."

"Cretins," Abassia said, shaking her head.

The next morning, when I woke up, I checked to make sure it was a bed and not an isomat beneath me. I looked at the walls of the hotel room to make sure they weren't iron mesh. I asked myself, *Am I really not in Guantanamo?*

I stood up, walked over to the window, and pulled open the curtains. I gazed out on a busy street, with people walking on the sidewalk and cars speeding past. I don't know how long I just stood there, taking it all in, before Abassia appeared at my side.

"What's the matter?" she asked, seeing the look on my face.

"I just can't believe it," I said. "Am I truly free?"

For the next few months, I kept struggling to believe that I was a free man. Sometimes I would be sitting in a chair, having a conversation, and all of a sudden I would notice that I was gesturing with my hands—they weren't chained to the chair. Life outside of Guantanamo took some getting used to.

And in the seven-and-a-half years that I had been in Guantanamo, the rest of the world had changed. Before, only a few people had owned laptop computers, and now you couldn't walk past a coffee shop without seeing a dozen of them. Before, I had been one of the few people I knew who owned a cellphone, because of my job. Now, everyone had one. Even the cars were different: smaller, boxier, brighter.

Gradually, this free new world began to feel more normal. And I was fortunate to have Abassia and the girls to guide me through it. Every single day, I spent hours and hours with them, laughing and playing and appreciating how truly blessed I was to have them back in my life.

For the most part, Abassia and the girls and I kept to ourselves. We didn't know anyone in Paris, and except for the Algerian shop-owner, very few people knew who we were or recognized my name.

However, in the first few weeks after my release, several reporters asked to interview me about my experience. I agreed, hoping that sharing my story might keep it from happening to more people in the future. I spoke with journalists from *Le Monde*, *The Washington Post*, ABC News, Al Jazeera, and several other newspapers from around the world.

I hope that doing the interviews helped advance the cause of human rights in some small way. I was disappointed, though, that so many of the reporters didn't seem interested in learning about me or my family or what I'd really been through. They just wanted to get their stories and get out. One of them even borrowed some photos from one of Abassia's albums and never gave them back.

At one point, I had dinner with an old friend: Sami al-Hajj, the Al Jazeera journalist who had been released from Guantanamo a year before me. We reminisced about our experiences and fondly recalled his dramatic reading of *The Da Vinci Code*. As I lifted a fork to my mouth with an unchained hand, I thought about how remarkable it was that two men who had met in the hunger strike ward of an island prison were now enjoying a nice meal in a French restaurant.

In August of 2009, after I had been in Paris two-and-a-half months, a French official told me that the government had made long-term housing arrangements for us. We were going to live in an apartment near Nice, where one of Abassia's sisters lived. We were excited that we would have a place to call home.

Packing our belongings was easy. Abassia and the girls had only brought a few suitcases from Algeria, and I had arrived in Paris with even less. The Americans had returned a few items that had been on my person when they arrested me in Bosnia: my watch and about fifteen dollars worth of Bosnian marks. They never gave me back my wedding ring or my passport—but they returned a handful of currency from a country I will never set foot in again.

The soldiers had also given me two duffel bags filled with some travel items, including a blanket, a towel, a toothbrush and the foul-smelling Guantanamo toothpaste, a few bottles of shampoo, and a set of khaki-colored prison clothes. I gave the blanket to one of the house keepers in the hotel, a poor woman who said that she could make good use of it, but I kept everything else. The khaki prison uniform is hanging in my closet next to the "Boumediene 2, Bush 0" shirt.

EPILOGUE

Mustafa Ait Idir

AT FIRST, EVERYTHING WAS DIFFICULT. My youngest son, Abdullah, was afraid of me. I had been in Guantanamo for six months when he was born, so I was a complete stranger to him. It is an odd thing to meet your son for the first time when he is six-and-a-half years old. And my older sons, Mohamed and Hamza, who had been four and one, were now eleven and eight. They had grown up without me, and neither they nor my wife knew if I would be the same man I had been before Guantanamo.

I desperately wanted to show them that I had not changed, that my ordeal had not broken me. I put on a happy face. I did not talk about what I had been through, and I acted as though everything were fine. Eventually, it stopped being an act. Nowadays, I almost never think about Guantanamo. Like computers, everyone's brain has limited RAM (storage space), and I choose to use mine on the future, not the past.

In 2012, a friend of mine helped me raise funds to purchase a small copy shop. I named it "Respect," and it has been fairly successful. My customers tell me that even though I charge higher rates than some copy shops do, they come to my shop because they know that I care about delivering high-quality work and treating every customer well.

More recently, I hired an employee to help with the copy shop, which made it possible for me to obtain a position teaching at a private school. I teach computer classes and physical education, and some of my students are also members of a karate team I coach in the evenings. I get along well with my students and colleagues. They are aware of my time in Guantanamo, but none of them ever mentions it or treats me differently because of it. They know and respect the person that I actually am.

My oldest son recently started university, and my wife and I, praise God, recently had our fourth child, a boy named Bilal. Between being a father, a teacher, a shop-owner, and a coach, I do not have a lot of spare time. I sleep around five hours a night. My life is full, and happy. Guantanamo did not destroy me.

That does not mean that I forgive the people who put me there.

A short while after we were released from Guantanamo, Hadj Boudella and I met with former foreign minister Zlatko Lagumdžija, at his request. Sitting in his office, he expressed regret for handing us over to the Americans. He only did so, he said, because the Americans had forced him to. He asked us to excuse what he had done.

This was a man who had appeared on television and called me a terrorist, with absolutely no evidence. This was a man whose lack of spine cost me seven years of my life.

"There is no excuse," I told him, "for what you did."

Hadj added that even if he could forgive Lagumdžija, his wife and children never would.

After that meeting, I received several phone calls from Lagumdžija's office, but I stopped answering them. I do not know if he was genuinely remorseful or if he was merely afraid of a lawsuit, but either way, I have nothing to say to him. He had the power to stop an injustice, and instead he authorized it.

Everyone involved in what happened to me insists that it was someone else's fault. "The Americans made me do it," says Lagumdžija. "My supervisors made me do it," say the guards who abused me. And in some sense, I suppose, they are right. If the guards had not beaten me, belittled me, and denigrated my religion, they might have lost their jobs. If Lagumdžija had protected my basic rights as a citizen instead of acquiescing to the Americans, there could have been harsh consequences for him and perhaps even for Bosnia.

At a certain point, though, a man has to stand up. If the school principal threatened to fire me unless I tortured one of my students, I would quit, and it would not be a difficult decision. I can understand why men like Lagumdžija and the abusive guards chose the path of least resistance, but it is not a choice I can forgive. I believe that we should expect more of each other, and of ourselves.

There is a famous story in Islam about a man who decided to make a charitable gift. He gave money to three people, but later discovered that one of the recipients was a thief, another a prostitute, and the third a wealthy man. None of them were "deserving." At first the man felt remorse, but then in a dream, God told him that his gifts would result in a robber abstaining from theft, a prostitute abstaining from immorality, and a wealthy man seeing the importance of being charitable. The moral, we are told, is that it is important to be kind no matter who the recipient of your kindness is.

It is my sincere hope that more people will take this message to heart, and will be kind to everyone, not just those they deem "deserving." I recently saw a news story about a political rally in America where men were assaulting those who disagreed with them. And, of course, there are reports every day of people getting attacked because of their race or their religion. Having been subjected to such attacks, I would like to humbly plead and pray that we, all of us, find a way to recognize the basic humanity in one another, and treat each other with decency and respect. I have seen, heard, and felt people acting out their very worst impulses, and I know we can be better than we have been.

Lakhdar Boumediene

I LIVE WITH MY FAMILY in a mid-sized fourth-floor apartment in a small town near Nice. We have lived here for the last several years, rebuilding our life together.

At first, our new life was hard on Raja and Rahma. They had to improve their French, make new friends, adapt to new schools, and get used to receiving instructions from two parents instead of one. It was especially difficult for Rahma, who hadn't seen me since she was eighteen months old. Unlike Raja, she had never really known me, except for some pictures that Abassia had shown her. I was a stranger in her house. And she had shared a bed with Abassia while I was in Guantanamo. She wasn't happy about suddenly having to sleep in her own bed all by herself.

To make matters worse, I am not as calm or as lighthearted as I used to be. Since Guantanamo, I have been quicker to anger. The smallest provocations can set me off. Once I was trying to talk to someone on the phone and I couldn't hear him because the girls had the volume on the TV too high, so I flung the phone to the ground and yelled at the girls to turn it down. They know that I would never hurt them, but too often I have been too harsh with them.

My wife understands. She explains to the girls that this isn't who I am, it is a wound that I'm healing from. And when my temper flares, she and the girls give me my space for a few minutes until I calm down.

I told Abassia, shortly after we were reunited, that Guantanamo had changed me.

"I am not the person you knew before prison," I told her. "I lived for seven years in a place made of metal. The floor was made of metal. The ceiling was made of metal. The walls were made of metal. So my heart became like metal—a hard heart. Please be patient with me."

And, thanks be to God, she and the girls have been.

With time, my anger hasn't subsided, but I've become better at controlling it. Now when I feel rage welling up inside me, I keep my composure and remove myself from the situation. Recently, I went to an administrative office in Nice to fill out some required paperwork and was told that there was an error in my file. Instead of shouting, I simply walked out, went home, and waited until the next day to come back and sort things out. It meant an extra hour on the bus, but it was well worth it. And I hope that as time passes, I will become even less quick-tempered, less hard-hearted, more like the person I used to be.

I am certainly healing physically. At first, I limped around Nice, my left knee still damaged from the concrete steps. But I made a point to walk for several hours a day—the Mediterranean climate means the weather is usually pleasant—and now I'm able to walk without pain.

And unlike when I first got to France and could only eat gentle foods, now I'm able to eat whatever I want. Raja is an adventurous cook, and sometimes she likes to experiment with recipes that she finds online. I've told her that I'll happily try anything she wants to make. Usually, her first attempt is so-so, the second try is pretty good, and by the third time it's excellent. She's become especially good at baking bread and making pizza.

Unfortunately, although I'm getting healthier, I haven't been able to find a job yet. For now, I receive a welfare check each month, but it's just enough for our family to live on. And regardless of money, I want to find a job. I miss the sense of purpose and fulfillment that my work brought me when I was helping people in Pakistan, Albania, and Bosnia.

Most days I get up, eat breakfast, and then go online and read two newspapers: one in Arabic and one in French. It's a good way to improve my French and to stay informed about what's going on in the world. Sometimes, though, I'll come across an article about Guantanamo, or even just a related word, like "Cuba," and my mind is instantly overtaken by a flood of painful memories and images.

After reading the newspapers, I go to a few different websites and search for employment opportunities. If anything looks promising, I apply online, and then I play some games on the computer. After that, there's usually something to get me out of the apartment in the afternoon: seeing my doctor, going to the grocery store, or visiting an administrative office to fill out forms.

There's also a little mosque in town that I go to on Fridays. The crowds for afternoon prayers are smaller than they had been in the other places I had lived—including Guantanamo—but it's a nice atmosphere and I'm grateful for it.

Other than my family, I don't have close friends here. When I meet people, I don't tell them about Guantanamo, both because it's difficult to talk about and because I want my wife and daughters to lead a normal life. I worry that they'll be treated differently if people here know about my past. So far, neither Raja nor Rahma has ever had a teacher or classmate ask them about my time in Guantanamo, and I don't want that to change.

Once in a while, though, I do get recognized. The other day, for example, I was buying meat at the butcher shop I usually go to. The butcher told me that he had been searching online for a friend of his who was also named Boumediene, and dozens of articles had popped up with my picture next to them. Out of curiosity, he had clicked on a few of the articles and found stories about my time in Guantanamo.

"Did that really happen to you?" he asked.

"Yes."

"How were you able to bear it?"

"I had to."

The butcher wished me a good recovery. I appreciate his kindness, and that of the few other people who've recognized me, but I always keep the conversation short. It's a strange conversation to have.

The only person I've been able to really talk about Guantanamo with is Abassia. Sometimes Raja and Rahma ask me questions, but I just change the subject. I'm not able to have that conversation with them yet.

Although I haven't made new friends in Nice, I've been able to get in touch with some old ones. I talk on Skype with Mustafa and his wife and children in Sarajevo. I've also contacted some of the families I had worked with in Sarajevo, including the mother of the two eight-year-old candy pilferers. They're young men now, she tells me, and leading successful lives.

We received a visit from my lawyer, Steve Oleskey, not long after we moved to Nice. He brought his wife and kids with him, and we were thrilled to be able to host them in our home. When Steve and I had first met, he had been in tears and I had been in chains, and now here we were, sitting together and talking as free men while our wives and children laughed and played around us.

More recently, I've been trying to contact Houriyya, the kind widow who had been like a mother to Abassia and me in Albania. I called the Red Crescent office in Albania and got the phone number they have on file for her, but when I dial it, the phone just rings and rings and no one answers. I'll keep trying, though. Every time I call, I imagine hearing Houriyya's voice and I think back fondly on my life in Albania, where Abassia and I had begun building our wonderful family together.

In the spring of 2010, a year after I had been freed, Abassia and I joyously welcomed a new addition to our family.

In Guantanamo, some of the guards and nurses had mocked me by saying that the medicine I was being forced to take would make me sterile.

"When you leave here," they said, "you won't be able to have children. You won't be a real man anymore."

So when Abassia told me that she wanted to have another child—she had always wanted to have a son—I wasn't sure it would be possible. But months later, when Abassia told me that she thought she was pregnant, I was hopeful. When our doctor confirmed it, I was overjoyed. And at the six-month checkup, when we saw our son on the sonogram and the doctor told us that he appeared to be in good health, I was deeply relieved.

"Thank God," I said.

Raja and Rahma were delighted when we told them that they were going to have a baby brother. They suggested we name him Youssef.

"How come?" I asked. It was a somewhat unusual name. Most Muslim boys have Abdul or Mohamed in their name.

"Well," Raja said, "We read about him in the Qur'an. He was a prophet. And he was in prison unfairly, just like you."

Abassia's brother proposed a more common name, Abdullah, which we passed along to Raja and Rahma.

"We'll leave the decision up to you," we told them.

Youssef it was.

During the eighth month of Abassia's pregnancy, our doctor asked her who she wanted in the delivery room with her.

"Your mother? Your sister? Your husband?"

"My husband," Abassia said.

It was a long, difficult delivery. It was exhausting for Abassia, but once again she showed what a strong, brave person she is.

After Youssef was born, a nurse brought him into another room and gave him a warm bath while I watched. The nurse put some medication in his eyes, dressed him, and said, "You can hold him now."

Cradling Youssef in my arms, I walked back to the delivery room and showed Abassia our baby son. We were deliriously happy. Youssef calmly lay in my arms for the next hour and a half.

To express my gratitude to God for my son, I sent some money to a friend in Sarajevo who agreed to help me perform my *'aqiiqah*. He slaughtered a lamb and gave the meat to some of the orphans I had worked with and other people in need.

After three days in the hospital, I brought Abassia and Youssef home. The girls were delighted to meet their brother.

"I'm going to take care of him!" Raja exclaimed.

"No, I am!" Rahma said.

And in fact, they have both been wonderful with him. They make a very efficient diaper-changing team, one of them holding him still while the other one changes him. And Rahma often entertains Youssef for hours on end, clambering around on the floor with him and our small collection of baby toys.

When Youssef was five months old, my mother came to visit. It was wonderful to see her and to introduce her to my son. I would like for my father to meet Youssef too, but he hasn't been able to make it yet. Hopefully someday it will be possible for us to visit him in Algeria, but I doubt I'll be able to get a visa.

In the meantime, we talk on Skype. My parents don't have a computer, but they often go to my brother's house and use his computer so they can see their grandchildren. Youssef's infectious laugh brings them so much joy. He fills our whole household with light.

I used to think, when I was in Guantanamo, that I would be able to erase the worst memories after I got out. *Once I'm back to my normal life*, I told myself, *I will forget all about this place.* But it isn't easy for a human to forget. Instead, I am simply doing my best to recover.

It would help if the American government would apologize and explain its mistake. I still have no idea why anyone ever thought that

I was a terrorist. Even now, even after everything I've been through, I would never support the use of violence against innocent people.

Of course, no apology can make up for the pain and humiliation I endured. Nothing can give me back my daughters' childhoods. But it would be the right thing to do. And it would make a difference.

It would also help if Guantanamo were closed, and if the American government and the American people would take steps to make sure nothing like this ever happens to an innocent man again.

I am hopeful for the future. I would like to start a small business so that we would have a regular source of income. I would like to buy a small house and tell my mother we have a room for her if she ever needs it. I would like to put away some money for Raja and Rahma's education. Raja recently spent ten days working as an intern at a neighbor's pharmacy, and she's interested in going to school to become a pharmacist. Rahma says she wants to be a doctor when she grows up, "so I can take care of you and mom."

I want to be able to provide smaller things, too, the types of things that I was able to provide to my wife and children back in Bosnia. Rahma has had her eye on a doll for several months. Raja wants a cellphone. And I want to take Abassia out to a restaurant, like the McDonald's at the bottom of the hill.

Abassia tells me not to worry about it.

"I don't want money," she told me, just a few days ago. "I don't want gold. All I want is for my husband to be near me, to never go away again."

And, Insha'Allah, I never will. With Abassia by my side, I am truly blessed, no matter what else happens. I may have spent seven-and-a-half years in a hateful place, but one thing I've learned is that nothing—nothing—is stronger than love.

ADDITIONAL MATERIAL

The Sura of Youssef

A Summary by Kathleen List

When Youssef was young, God blessed him with inspired visions in his dreams. His father warned him not to stir up his brothers' jealousy by telling them about these dreams. But his brothers sensed that their father had a special affection for Youssef, and they hated Youssef for it. They said to each other:

> "Slay ye Youssef or cast him out to some unknown land, that the favor of your father may be given to you alone: there will be time enough for you to be righteous after that!" (*Qur'an*, 12:8–9)

These weak, selfish brothers threw Youssef to the bottom of a well, and brought a bloodstained garment home to their father. Weeping false tears, they told him his beloved son had been devoured by a wolf. But he never believed them, and never gave up hope of being reunited with his son.

God had plans for Youssef—beyond the well, beyond even the land of his birth. A passing caravan stopped at the well, drew him out of it, and sold him as a slave in Egypt, where he worked in the house of a wealthy and powerful man. Youssef grew wise and strong and remained faithful to God. Even when the wealthy man's wife falsely accused Youssef of seeking to harm her, and he was thrown into prison, his devotion to God remained unshakeable. He never gave in to despair.

In prison, Youssef would interpret his fellow prisoners' dreams and teach them about God. So great was his reputation for wisdom that even the king eventually sought his counsel. But Youssef didn't just want to have a comfortable life in the king's employ—he was a righteous man. He told the king that he wanted his name cleared. So the king spoke to the woman who had falsely accused Youssef, and she admitted her treachery. The king made Youssef the guardian of all the storehouses of Egypt, and he proved himself a good and sincere steward. Youssef's faith in God had carried him from the king's dungeon to the king's right hand:

> "We established Youssef in the land to settle therein wherever he willed. We touch with Our mercy whom We will, and We do not allow to be lost the reward of those who do good." (*Qur'an*, 12:56)

God even saw fit to bring about a great reunion between Youssef and his family. The father who had never lost hope saw his son again, and Youssef found within himself the strength and love to forgive his brothers who had once betrayed him.

The Decision to Arrest the "Algerian Six"

(October 2001)

In a sworn affidavit signed October 6th, 2008, Bosnia's former prime minister Alija Behmen offered details about the arrests of Lakhdar, Mustafa, and four other Algerian men living in Bosnia.

¶10. On 8 October 2001, an individual by the name of Belkacem Bensayah was arrested in Zenica. I was informed that a piece of paper with the number of a senior officer of Al Qaeda was found at his home.

¶11. After that, I was informed by the U.S. Embassy that they suspected security threats to the U.S. and U.K. Embassies. . . . [T]he U.S. and U.K. Embassies were closed down on 17 October 2001.

¶12. On the day of closure of the U.S. and U.K. Embassies, I had a meeting with representatives of the U.S. Embassy, led by Deputy U.S. Ambassador and Charge d'Affaires Mr. Christopher Hoh. . . . During the meeting, [t]he representatives of the U.S. Embassy insisted on the arrest of additional suspects because of the threats against the aforementioned embassies. The representatives of the U.S. Embassy especially emphasized that they had reasons for justified suspicions regarding the members of the so-called Algerian Group as possible perpetrators of these threats. Although they did not present any evidence to us, the representatives of the U.S. Embassy left an impression that they had firm evidence for their suspicions. Also, the representatives of the U.S. Embassy made it unequivocally clear that unless the authorities of Bosnia and Herzegovina arrested the persons whom the U.S. suspected, the [U.S.] would withdraw all Embassy personnel and would stop any further U.S. support to Bosnia and Herzegovina. I remember that Mr. Hoh told me then something like "and then let God protect Bosnia and Herzegovina."

¶13. I informed Mr. Lagumdžija, who was Chairman of the national Council of Ministers at the time, on the content of this meeting, and we consulted about what actions to take. . . .

¶14. Shortly after my meeting with Mr. Hoh, the Federation police arrested the remaining members of the Algerian Group. I was informed that arrests occurred peacefully and that the suspects did not try to resist or flee. . . .*

* Prime Minister Behmen's affidavit is available at www.WitnessesBook.com.

The Investigation by Bosnian Authorities

(October 2001–January 2002)

In his affidavit, Prime Minister Behmen went on to discuss the subsequent investigation of Lakhdar, Mustafa, and the other members of the "Algerian Six."

¶15. The investigation by the Federation Prosecutor and Investigative Judge of the Federation Supreme Court, which was launched on the basis of initial information provided by the United States, lasted for three months. During that time, Federation authorities conducted searches, interviewed witnesses, conducted forensic analyses, and cooperated with the U.S. Embassy, the FBI, the European Union, and Interpol. Via my assistants I regularly received word that there was no firm evidence that linked the suspects to an act of terrorism. My assistants from the police expressed their frustration that, during the investigation, they were not provided with the recordings of allegedly intercepted communications between the suspects and senior officials of Al Qaeda outside Bosnia and Herzegovina.

¶16. After the investigation was completed, the Investigative Judge and Prosecutor found no firm evidence that the suspects were involved in terrorist activities. . . . Due to the lack of evidence for the charges against these men, the investigative bodies suggested that the suspects be released from detention.*

---

* *Id.*

Release & Rendition

(January 17, 2002)

After three months of investigation, the Bosnian Supreme Court ruled that the Algerian Six "shall be immediately released," due to the prosecutor's acknowledgment that "the grounds and circumstances on which the custody was ordered . . . have ceased to exist."* Fearing that they might be handed over to American forces, their lawyer sought and obtained the following court order from Bosnia's Human Rights Chamber:

> The Human Rights Chamber for Bosnia and Herzegovina . . .
>
> Considering that it appears likely that if provisional measures are not ordered, the applicant will suffer harm which cannot subsequently be remedied;
>
> ORDER the respondent Parties, Bosnia and Herzegovina, and the Federation of Bosnia and Herzegovina, to take all necessary steps to prevent that the applicants are taken out of Bosnia and Herzegovina by the use of force. . . .†

However, as Prime Minister Behman's affidavit explains, Bosnian authorities made the decision to deliver the "Algerian Six" to an American military base:

> ¶7. [U]nder the Dayton Peace Agreement, the international military troops stationed in Bosnia as the NATO Stabilization Force ("SFOR") were set up beyond the constitutional order of Bosnia and Herzegovina. That means that they were authorized to act autonomously in the territory of Bosnia . . . if they assessed that certain individuals or even institutions threatened the Dayton Peace Agreement or SFOR.
>
> ¶18. [O]n 8 January 2002, a meeting took place in my office . . . with representatives of the U.S. Embassy and SFOR. In addition to myself and my assistant Ms. Asja Rasavac, the meeting was attended by the Deputy U.S. Ambassador and Charge d'Affaires

---

* Judge Zdenko Eterovic's legal opinion is available at www.WitnessesBook.com.
† The complete text of the court order is available at www.WitnessesBook.com.

Christopher Hoh; General John Sylvester, the U.S. Commander of SFOR; General David Petraeus, then with SFOR; Mr. Robert Kendra, Mr. Mark Fray, and Ms. Vildana Aljovic from the U.S. Embassy. The reason for meeting was, among other things, to inform me of a briefing that had taken place at the White House. At that briefing, the U.S. President had been informed that there was a risk that persons arrested in Bosnia, namely the six members of the so-called "Algerian Group," may be released from detention due to lack of evidence for charges against them. After consultations among the U.S. President, Vice President, and Defense Secretary, the order was issued that, in the event that the six men were released, SFOR should take direct action to seize the men and extradite them to their countries of origin. General Sylvester told me that he held the view that the direct involvement of SFOR in this case would be a serious mistake, and he suggested that efforts be taken so that the problem be resolved by the authorities of Bosnia and Herzegovina, without direct involvement of SFOR. Nonetheless, he informed me that he had a direct order from the top level of his command to use SFOR troops to re-arrest the six men if necessary. I forwarded the Minutes of this meeting to the Chairman of the Council of Ministers, Mr. Zlarko Lagumdžija, for information and further action.

¶19. It was unequivocally clear that the United States was determined to take these six men into custody and even to use force if the authorities of Bosnia and Herzegovina did not secure their transfer to SFOR troops. Such a development would have been characterized as a lack of support on Bosnia's part for the fight against terrorism and, ultimately, would have put an end to U.S. support for further democratic development of Bosnia and Herzegovina. That would have caused unforeseeable negative consequences for Bosnia and Herzegovina.

¶20. On 17 January 2002, due to a lack of evidence for the accusations of terrorism, the Supreme Court ordered the suspects, the so-called Algerian Group, released from detention.

¶21. The operational data from the Coordinating Team and from the Police showed that civilians, friends or supporters of the Algerian Group, having learned of the decision of the Supreme Court regarding their release on 17 January 2002, formed a circle around the prison on the evening of 17 January 2002. Some of them had radio devices for communication, and some of them were even armed. A local radio station was covering live the dramatic situation around the prison, inviting citizens to prevent the hand-over of the detainees. At the same time, SFOR troops were also present around the prison, ready to act in accordance with the orders that General Sylvester had received from the United States.

¶22. I was informed that on 17 January 2002, the Council of Ministers unanimously accepted a Report on the Coordinating Team's activities, supported its work, and decided to hand over the members of the Algerian Group to the custody of SFOR. I am of the opinion that, by doing so, the authorities of Bosnia and Herzegovina averted certain confrontation and bloodshed between the members of SFOR and the gathered individuals who were supporting the Algerian Group.

¶23. The Federation Police took custody of the six men after the order on their release from detention. In the presence of appropriate representatives of the IPTF [International Police Task Force], the six individuals were handed over to SFOR troops. As far as I know, all six men were handed over to representatives of the U.S. component of SFOR at the Butmir military base in Sarajevo. At that time we did not have information or indications that those men would be taken out of Bosnia and Herzegovina for purposes of investigation. Only later was I informed that, shortly after they were taken into custody by the U.S. forces, these forces transported them out of Bosnia and Herzegovina to Guantanamo Bay.*

---

* The complete text of the affidavit is available at www.WitnessesBook.com.

State of the Union Address

(January 29, 2002)

In his State of the Union Address, President George W. Bush specifically mentioned the alleged plot to bomb the American Embassy in Sarajevo:

> While the most visible military action is in Afghanistan, America is acting elsewhere. We now have troops in the Philippines, helping to train that country's armed forces to go after terrorist cells. . . . Our soldiers, working with the Bosnian government, seized terrorists who were plotting to bomb our embassy. . . .
>
> My hope is that all nations will heed our call, and eliminate the terrorist parasites who threaten their countries and our own. Many nations are acting forcefully. . . . But some governments will be timid in the face of terror. And make no mistake about it: If they do not act, America will.*

---

* The complete text of President Bush's State of the Union Address is available at www.WitnessesBook. com.

Exculpatory Emails

(2002 or earlier)

The "exculpatory emails" referred to in the court filing below remain classified. However, the court filing itself—written by a lawyer with access to the classified emails—has been officially declassified and is available online.

Brief for Petitioner-Appellant Belkacem Bensayah

. . . The government initially alleged that Mr. Bensayah was the leader of a terrorist group . . . that was plotting to attack the U.S. Embassy in Sarajevo . . . The Embassy allegations were abandoned before trial when exculpatory emails surfaced indicating that military intelligence officers knew by 2002 that those allegations were "bullshit."*

---

* Brief for Petitioner-Appellant Belkacem Bensayah at 9, *Bensayah v. Obama*, No. 08-5537 (D.C. Cir. June 3, 2009), available at www.WitnessesBook.com.

Interview with Intelligence Analyst

(August 4, 2014)

When he was the U.S. Lead Counter-Terrorism Analyst in Bosnia, Michael, who prefers that we not use his last name, played a role in the investigation of Lakhdar and Mustafa. Years later, their paths crossed again when Michael was stationed in Guantanamo as an Interrogation Section Chief. Over the course of a two-hour conversation with Daniel Norland (DN) and Kathleen List (KL), presented below in abridged and edited form, Michael (M) shared his thoughts about what happened to Lakhdar and Mustafa. He was careful not to divulge any potentially classified information, and he stressed that he was not speaking on behalf of the United States Armed Forces, the Defense Intelligence Agency, or anyone other than himself.

DN: The two broad areas we have some questions about are, first, the things you can tell us about the investigation into the "Algerian Six," and then separately, the interactions you had with people at Guantanamo. In terms of the first, I don't know what you can and can't talk about, but something that Lakhdar and Mustafa have expressed curiosity about is what put them on the radar screen initially. And I know you were saying you're not sure, with the six—

M: Who's who. I mean, it's been a long time.

DN: Of course.

M: And I don't mean this in any—but at some point all these names blend together. It's unfortunate, but it's the reality. And most of my career has been focused on people in the Iraq area, so they were only part of my life for a very short time.

I was part of the analysis team in Bosnia, working with SFOR [the NATO Stabilization Force]. And I was pulling at strings that had not been previously pulled at. I decided to go at it through the NGOs.

I was the Lead Analyst for a brand new thing that was called the CAT— the Counter-terrorism Analysis Team—for SFOR. It was the first SFOR element ever to look at Islamic terrorist issues. Because really, where the threat had been previously in that region, was from the Serbians. There were these groups like the Drina Wolves, for example. They're a gang, or a KKK kind of a mentality, but they are Serbs and they would terrorize Bosniaks and others.

When we talked, as SFOR, about counter-terrorism operations, it was seen as very, very small—maybe one analyst, maybe two, almost entirely looking at Serbians, because that's really where the threat was. Well now, with 9/11, we had to sort of look elsewhere.

In Bosnia, we were trying to figure out what network was there, and we believed that this was—there's still a concern about this, but it was at fever-pitch at the time—that if Al Qaeda could recruit, train, and deploy a Bosniak Muslim to come to America, that would be really, really dangerous. Because many of these young men—first of all, they're white. They look like you and I. They don't look Middle Eastern. Two, a lot of them have been working as translators or working on military bases for the last ten years, since the war, and they speak English really well. Sometimes with an American accent.

And so there was a real concern that this would be a prime recruiting area. And there was also reason to believe that if you did work with the Americans, there was a possibility that your visa application would be approved. So there was a lot of concern. Does Al Qaeda recognize the potentiality of the Bosnian Muslims? If so, are there efforts to recruit, train, and deploy them? If so, where does that operation meet the road, if you will, outside of Afghanistan? What does it look like here, in Bosnia? And that's kind of the mission I was asked to crack.

I decided to look at youth programs and NGOs. The AIO was a Muslim youth organization and NGO, and that's kind of where all of this started to take root. I started to see a lot of communication with organizations and individuals that were on lists that were known to be associated with, or even fronts of, Al Qaeda. And that seemed to be their entrée into the Balkans. And then from there I would take a look and see, who are the named operators who are operating under that particular NGO?

You may be more intimately familiar with details than I am, and perhaps you can tell me a little bit that will help jog my memory, but this was sort of the case that—from an intelligence perspective, not from a legal perspective—the men we called the "Algerian Four" were becoming persons of interest. And when I briefed it to the general, they wanted me to brief it to that general's boss, which at the time was General Sylvester, the three-star in charge of all of SFOR. I went down there, and also, ironically, there was a one-star by the name of David Petraeus, and I briefed him. And it was David Petraeus, actually, who said, "Sergeant, you've got it. This is it. I need you to brief the team."

So I met with the Special Operations team, and we provided as comprehensive a brief as we could, based on a lot of reporting—even reporting that was beyond my own.

DN: So that brief was focused on, at that time, the "Algerian Four"?

M: Four. It was never six.

DN: And just to be clear, the brief was essentially saying, "We have reason to believe these four are engaged in a plot against the American Embassy in Sarajevo"?

M: Yes. Exactly. That was the trigger thing. That was the thing that said there's an imminent threat, and we have to act. Before that point it was, "We think we've got the link, or we've got *a* link, to the mothership, Al Qaeda."

We weren't seeing a lot of threat streams early on. We were seeing a lot of movement of money, and movement of weapons, and some people, and we thought, "This is good intel. And you don't need to move in on them. You can monitor them, and you can learn their associates. By letting them live their life and do what they do, if they're under surveillance and so forth, theoretically, you can get potentially even bigger fish."

But when the threat stream started to play out, we started to see that there was more than one thing. It started to seem like, "There's something going on. There is a threat against the American Embassy. And this individual, these individuals, they are involved."

DN: So before the threat became something on the radar screen, in Fall 2001, you're surveilling these four individuals, and the idea is, "Based on their connections with different organizations, different individuals, we have reason to believe these four are characters we need to be tracking."

M: Right.

DN: Are you able to talk a little bit about—are their phones being tapped? How are they being monitored? Or is that something you—

M: Yeah, I'm not going to—I don't feel comfortable talking about sources and methods.

DN: Understood. So they're being surveilled in various ways, and initially the plan is, "We're just going to keep an eye on them."

M: Right. Minus the threat stream, that's probably all we would have done, at least at that point.

DN: But then, with the threat stream, the decision is made, "We're going to round these guys up." Can you talk a bit about how that decision was made?

M: I reported to the commander of Task Force Eagle, in Tuzla. When my reports got to—when there were enough dots to connect, and I was able to give sound analysis to say, "We know this, we know this, we know this. This connects to that. That connects to this." All of it down the line.

And you paint that picture. And you draw it as dispassionately as possible. My goal here is not to—I am beholden to the facts, not to a narrative. It needs to stay strictly to the facts. This is what we know, and then this is what you can extrapolate from that knowledge.

So, does this activity constitute a potential threat? It's a potential thing—so it's, "Yes, it does. The likelihood of an actual threat has gone up, because now you've got surveillance of the embassy, you've got an inside man, and what we know from other forms of communication, intelligence and whatnot, and connections with money and so forth. And it does start to look like something is imminent, and it does seem to be focusing around the American Embassy."

That was enough to sell my General, and he said, "Okay, we've got to get you down to Sarajevo, and you need to brief this to General Petraeus." So I did. So you brief General Petraeus, you put your best foot forward, and you bring out all the charts and maps and graphs and pictures, and you back up all your evidence. And General Petraeus said, "I'm convinced.

Let's take it to my boss." Which was General Sylvester. General Sylvester was a three-star, and General Sylvester was the one who ultimately had to sign off on any move against this group. And he did. Who he consulted, did he need the president or whatever, I don't know—I didn't brief anybody higher than him.

I did brief the special ops team. And I was part of a larger support element—I wasn't the only intel guy at that point. Now you have a lot of other intel people, who are providing a lot more detail. I gave the lead-up, and a lot of other people were providing granular details. That kind of granularity, I wasn't working on that. But when you get to that stage of an operation, that's the kind of operational intelligence you need.

So by that point, a lot of other analysts have been tuned into this. Now, whether or not they had also seen this in real time next to me, or whether or not I was the guy who—I'll never know. I won't know if I was the guy that put the first domino into effect, or if I was the corroborating guy. I was not involved with the raid itself, other than the briefing of the team. They went in, they got them. I did not see—I never met these individuals until I got to GTMO five years later.

DN: When you talk about the raid, are you talking about the—the six men are in prison in Bosnia, they initially were arrested by Bosnian police, were held for three months, and then on January 18, 2002—

M: They were rendered to the U.S.

DN: Exactly. So when you talk about the raid, you're referring to—you briefed the team who—

M: I briefed the team who coordinated the raid. I briefed Americans, not Bosnians. The fact that the police went in tells me that somebody in the American chain of command decided that they wanted to go in softer and make this a law enforcement issue, so they did that. A Foreign Disclosure Officer would have to decide what would be releasable intelligence to the Bosnians, and then the Bosnians would be asked to do something. I would imagine, given the fact that I was talking to special operators, special operations teams were involved with that raid, either as support or potentially in there as well. I don't know. But I have to assume, though, that there was at least a cordon which included American special operations, in case the Bosnian police failed.

DN: So the decision to arrest them initially was based on some of your intelligence, but you didn't brief Bosnian police. That was something that—

M: I never talked to anybody about this other than Americans.

DN: So when you briefed the American team, it was still the "Algerian Four" at that point?

M: Yes. I found out that it was six people with George Bush's State of the Union Address. And everybody's patting me on the back because I inadvertently made the news. Here I am, a sergeant, I find this threat stream, I develop it, I brief it, an operation is based upon it, and the President of the United States says that the war against terrorism is going well and we've just sent to Guantanamo six terrorists—the first ones not taken off of the Afghan battlefield.

So this seems to be a big moment for me and my career. My name is not at all associated publicly, but I know it, the people who were involved with me, they know it. So there's a lot of back-slapping going on, like "Hey, you made the news," as much as any intel person wants to make the news.

But then it was like—he used the number six in his address, and that was surprising to me. Up until that moment, I only had intel on four. These other two people were a surprise to me, and I'm like, "Where were they from?" I asked, and I was told that they were all gathered up at the same place. It was a surprise to me that there were six people.

And when I got to GTMO, my boss, Paul Rester, who is a trip—imagine, if you will, Christopher Walken having a love child with Yoda, and that's Paul Rester. He was an interrogator in Vietnam, he had four bronze stars. He was a little guy, and he kind of talked like Christopher Walken and he looked like Yoda, and he was brilliant. He was a really bright guy, and he would just talk and talk and talk and talk. You would go in there, and it could be an hour before you'd get out of there. He would sit you down and talk to you, and what are you going to do? He's the boss.

I remember when I first got to GTMO, he had been reading up on me, and he said, "I see here that you were one of the guys responsible for sending us the Algerians." I said, "Yes, sir." He said, "What can you tell me about these other two?" I said, "Nothing. I didn't even know who they were until it was announced they were here."

Paul Rester had been at GTMO for years. I think he left for a while and came back. He was on again, off again at GTMO all the time. And he didn't have anything. He had access to interrogation reports, I would imagine since the time they got there, and he's thinking that there's very little on any of these guys, beyond what I provided, and nothing on these other two. They didn't show up with any intel. These other guys at least had a couple of reports, particularly Belkacem, but there was nothing on these other two.

Now I don't really know, so this is maybe where you can tell me a bit more—were they all together in the same house when they were arrested?

DN: No, they were each arrested individually by the Bosnian police. When the American team took them it was all in one fell swoop, but when the Bosnian police arrested them, they were at their—

M: Their homes.

DN: Or their workplace. I know that at least Lakhdar was at work.

KL: Do you recall anything about—the connection with Lakhdar was that he paid for an attorney for Belkacem. Belkacem's wife came to his place of work, which was the Red Crescent, and begged him to help, so he went and paid for an attorney and left his card with the attorney. And that was the connection—

M: Maybe that's what I'm thinking. I remember—I'm a big fan of Cat Stevens, and after [the "Algerian Six"] had left Bosnia under American custody, Cuba-bound, a concert was held in Sarajevo. And Yusuf Islam—Cat Stevens—actually came to perform at the concert.

KL: Wow.

M: And it was part of raising money for the widows of the war, but also, he brought up on stage Belkacem's wife and a couple other wives of these people. And so he brought a little attention to their plight. I begged—I said to the General, "I really should go to that concert, there's a real intel opportunity there." He was like, "Good try. You're not going."

Cat Stevens ended up on our no-fly list now, for that. His management company is New York–based, or was—I'm not sure if it still is—and he was flying into America. He was on a flight from London. And I don't believe that Cat Stevens is a nefarious individual. I believe that he is governed by the best of intentions, and I know that he has met with and been involved with some unsavory characters and some groups, but I don't think that he's involved with their nefarious activities. And he may or may not even be aware that he's meeting with somebody who's questionable status.

But nevertheless, when he did this concert, they said, "That's it. Okay, enough." So they actually had to stop the plane. They had the plane forced to land in Maine, and they took him off and they had to get him back to England, and he's on a list. So Cat Stevens is a casualty of this issue as well.

DN: Wow.

M: Now, I think he's probably changed his management. I don't know if he's resolved that, or if he moved his music management to London or whatever, or they could certainly go to London and see him. But he's very active, or at least he was very active, in a lot of charities, Islamic charities in particular. He's very anti-war. I really can't believe that he is in any way complicit with any act of terror. But he has been in the presence of organizations that are connected to—it's a daisy chain.

DN: Right. And that's at least—when Lakhdar talks about his connection with all this, that's how he describes it. He—

M: Where's he living now? Where are they living now?

DN: Mustafa went back to Sarajevo. Lakhdar, while he was in Guantanamo, his Bosnian citizenship expired. He didn't renew it, because he couldn't.

M: So is he back in Algeria?

DN: France actually agreed to take him, so he's now in France.

M: So what's your involvement in this? Are you one of the lawyers?

DN: I used to work at the law firm that represented these six men, WilmerHale. I wasn't involved in the case, but I learned a lot about it. Once Lakhdar and Mustafa were released, they wanted to tell their story to an American audience.

M: Like this [holding up *Enemy Combatant*, by Moazzam Begg]?

KL: Oh, I've read that one. Yes, like that.

M: This guy is before my time, but—I don't know a lot about Moazzam Begg, like I said, he was before my time, but he has become an instrument after Guantanamo. And he's been arrested a few times. When Republicans talk about recidivism, this counts. Writing this book is recidivist. I mention it because I wonder, if these fellows write a book, if they will be classified as recidivists, and if that will have any impact on their freedom.

DN: One thing that Lakhdar's talked about is that it's really important to him that he not write a book that is propaganda for Al Qaeda. He thinks it's important—and we think it's important—that Americans know what happened to him, what he went through, but he's very clear that he does not think the appropriate response to that is violence. I think he's certainly—I don't think he's a big fan of George W. Bush, say, but he's also certainly not a big fan of radical Islam. In fact, even before any of this happened—

M: That would be an important aspect of the story. At the same time, you've got to be careful that the other side, whoever the other side is—you also don't want it to be framed as, "Guantanamo served a purpose of rehabilitation."

DN: No, I don't think that's how it would come off.

KL: His biography pre-Guantanamo doesn't really lend itself to that interpretation.

M: So is he one of the two or one of the four?

DN: He would say his involvement was, one day, while he's sitting at his desk at the Red Crescent, he gets a phone call from a woman in tears who says, "My husband's been arrested. Can you please help?"

M: Which would be normal, because that's where you'd go.

DN: And so Lakhdar got in his car, drove to their town, and walked into a law office and said, "Hey, if I give you some money, can you represent this guy?" Left his business card, and then ten days later got arrested by the Bosnian police.

M: I also wonder where the intel on these two came from, particularly if they weren't rounded up in the same place. I did this all from Tuzla or Sarajevo. We brief the operation, and sometimes we're involved in the operation, but more often than not the intel person is not that intimately integrated into the operation. As was the case here.

I was tracking independently this intelligence, I did analysis, and briefed what I knew. And from that, an operation was put into effect, which incorporated my intelligence—but my intelligence did not include much on three of them, and none on two of them. I had associations—really, very, very little at all on what we called the henchmen. They were clearly associated but not necessarily involved in anything. And on the other two, I had nothing.

So based on (a) what I knew at the time I submitted my intelligence reports for briefing, and (b) what I learned when I was at GTMO, and I was the team leader looking at the interrogation reports against them. . . . And we weren't even collecting—I didn't have anybody going in to talk to them about any real intel.

We always tried to send an interrogator in periodically, for a variety of reasons. One, you want to maintain rapport. You don't want to just shut them out—they give you something, you use it, they're no longer useful to you, and then you don't go back in there for several months. And then several months later you go back in there and they go, "Why should I talk to you? You just forgot about me for months and months and months."

Remember, this is—they get time out of the cell, they get time away from the guards, they get a lot. The interrogators ply them with sweets and honey and peanut butter and cigarettes and all kinds of stuff they can't have back in the cell block. So it's like a—they live a rough life, but the interrogation is one of the highlights, believe it or not.

And there's always this contention between the interrogators and the guards. There's two categories of detainees: either cooperative or uncooperative, and compliant or noncompliant. And *cooperative* is an interrogation term, and *compliant* is a term for the guards.

So it's very possible that you can be a cooperative detainee, and as a cooperative detainee, you get benefits from me—I'm going to say you can have tea and sugar and honey and all these sorts of things, and you can have it at your cell. That's the reward for your cooperation. But you're not compliant. When you're back there, you're a dick. You're spitting on guards, raising hell, throwing feces, instigating trouble. And then the guards take away the things that I gave you. They say, okay, as punishment for your non-compliance, you lose the tea and the sugar and the honey and all that stuff. And then that has repercussions when you come back to me. Now you don't want to talk to me anymore. You're like, "Hey, you gave me this stuff, they took it away." Then I talk with the guards, and they say, "Hey, he's being a jerk, and we can't have it, so we have to punish him. And this is how we do it." It's that kind of a thing. And sometimes they can use that to play us against each other.

Anyway, I always tried to make sure that there was regular interrogator contact with the detainees. Also, remember, our interrogators swapped out every six months to a year, so we had to introduce new people and build rapport.

But really, we had no requirements [for gathering intelligence from the "Algerian Six"]. They had not provided enough intelligence when they were fresh and new and bright and shiny. They had not provided anything of value to where they would have a track record of having provided intelligence, to where analysts at CIA, at DIA, at CENTCOM, wherever, would say, "Hey, you know what, maybe this guy knows something. Can you ask him questions A, B, C, and D?"

Those requirements weren't coming in. We don't generate requirements at Guantanamo, typically. We have some standard requirements where we can talk about things like the road to radicalization, recruitment, things like that—which is good intel, just background stuff like that—

but it's not operational. It's not like, "What do you know? What's going to happen? Who's the next target?"

And so they were just sort of stagnating on the vine.

DN: When you arrived, did you learn much about what had happened in the course of their interrogations before you got there—how they were treated, what happened to them, that type of thing?

M: To a degree. Like I said, Paul Rester asked me if I could shed some light. He was very frustrated, because there was a lot of pressure from the legal teams, the *habeas* teams, and also from—potentially, I imagine—from Algeria. A lot of countries would say, "We want our guy back." And that goes through the proper channels—State Department and all of that—trickles down, and by the time it gets to GTMO, it ultimately ends up on Paul Rester's desk. And it's on Paul Rester to decide—to give feedback to the admiral in charge of GTMO, and all of it back up the chain, as to why or why not we can support a release.

And so he's looking at this, and he's like, "I don't have anything." I said, "I can tell you about Belkacem." That's really what I did. I was the guy that found Belkacem. And through Belkacem, I found three other people that he was in contact with, but I was still focused on Belkacem. Belkacem was my collection target. And these other two people, I didn't even know about them.

So Paul Rester was a little frustrated with me, because he thought, "Hey, I got the guy who brought us these six guys. He must know." And I'm like, "No. These other five people, I really don't know much about, and two of them I don't know anything about. At all."

So I looked at their interrogation reports. There was some history of restrictions and punishments and stuff like that.

DN: Yeah, at least a couple of them were considered "troublemakers."

M: I think all six of them were—but I think that that's also fairly normal. You know, when you're in captivity, I think acting out becomes your only sense of freedom. So I wouldn't take that as an indicator of innocence or guilt.

DN: Right. That's exactly how Lakhdar described it. He went on a hunger strike because it was the only thing he had any control of.

M: I also think that there's a lot of peer pressure in the environment. And there's pressure from both ends. The detainees have varying degrees of loyalty to Al Qaeda, and suspicion or distrust or even hate for us. That compounds because they can't get away from their more inculcated brethren. So they have to sort of toe the line, and there's the possibility of reprisals against them if they were to be seen talking and stuff like that.

They had to be very careful about how they managed their privileges. There's a game. They want to get their privileges, they want to move from one camp to another camp which is easier going. There's one camp, called Camp Four, which was great. They had gardens. It was open. And there's a jumpsuit—do you know about the jumpsuit color scheme?

DN: The orange and the white, I think?

M: Orange, white, and tan. If you're in orange, you're a bad guy—you're a troublemaker. Now, this goes to compliance. It has nothing to do with cooperation. It's a compliance thing—it's a guard mentality. The guards color code the detainees. If you're wearing an orange jumpsuit, you're going to have the most restrictions, because you're the most problematic from a compliance perspective. If you're wearing a tan jumpsuit, then you're kind of middle-of-the-road. Let's call that "average." You do sometimes act out, but sometimes you don't. And the white jumpsuits are the ones who are pretty much always on good behavior.

When you get to the white jumpsuit status, and there's an opening in Camp Four, that's the camp that you want to be at. But you've also got to be very careful about how fast you get there, right—it's a very delicate game, and I wouldn't even know all the nuances of it. Because you can get shivved—something bad could befall you, because obviously if you went from an orange jumpsuit to Camp Four, you must have given up the goods on somebody, and that makes you a traitor, a squeal.

But they had gardens, they could freely associate, they could go outside at will. It was caged, but it was the best status that you could have. We had a real, real problem when we closed that camp and we moved everybody into Camp Six, which is a hard-site facility. This was a real problem for the intel people, because now there was very little incentive for cooperation and compliance. In fact, you had compliant and cooperative people who were now neither, because everybody was moved into the hard-site facility. It's exactly the same standard as people who are non-compliant—so what's the incentive?

But as I recall, they were treated pretty well, and they were fairly average prisoners. And after—when they're bright and shiny new, and they first get there, everybody wants to talk to everybody. Even though we don't have existing intelligence on you, we've got to trust that somebody brought you here because of some reason. But as that didn't—you know, either these guys are very, very, very, very good resisters, or they just don't have anything to give. And it started to look like they didn't have anything to give.

DN: Now, in Lakhdar's account, by 2006–2007 he wasn't subjected to harsh treatment during interrogations. But he does talk about some harsh treatment during interrogations in the time period before that, 2003–2004.

M: Was he also in Camp X-Ray?

DN: He was in Camp X-Ray and then Camp Delta. He said the interrogations began shortly after he was put in Delta, but he lived in X-Ray for the period while Delta was being built.

M: X-Ray is really nothing more than dog kennels.

DN: That's how he described it.

M: I have a large dog. I have a huge—we call it a crate, but it's a cage. It's wire. I could sleep in it—it's huge. That's basically what X-Ray was. It was just a bunch of these dog kennels. Large dog kennels. You could not stand up in them. You have to be sitting or lying down.

I'm six feet tall. If I were to lie down in my dog's kennel, my feet would stick out. But if the door were shut, I'd have to be in a semi-fetal position. It's comfortable enough, but at some point you'll want to stretch out, and you wouldn't be able to. That's essentially what these guys were living in.

That site is all overgrown right now, but it cannot be dismantled because of evidentiary reasons. It would be seen as destroying evidence, so the military cannot dismantle it. At least, at the time I was there, they were not allowed to dismantle it. They didn't maintain it, so it was all grown up with ivy and stuff like that, but Camp X-Ray is still physically extant. But it looks like dog cages covered in ivy.

Delta looks like a *stalag*, or some sort of World War II–era camp, really. They are these long, long bays, and there are these large sections that are caged with a small, tight chain-link fence between them. Certainly, each cage has enough room to stand up, walk around, move around, stuff like that—it's not spacious, it's maybe about half of the size of my office.

They closed Delta because it was still pretty open, and we were worried about hurricanes. So we were building—and they had been building—these hard-site facilities that were based on maximum security prisons in Terre Haute, Indiana. If you look at the prison in Terre Haute, Indiana, an exact copy of that is at GTMO, floor for floor.

And so we're building these state-of-the-art hard-site facilities, really as a safety issue. It's safer for the guards, it's safer for the detainees. But it starts to feel like a prison. There was a sense of communality, and all of that went away—now it's a very antiseptic jail cell with a slamming door, a cell-block look. It looked like a prison. But I'm sorry, I'm not sure where exactly I was going with this. . . .

DN: We were asking about the interrogations in the early Delta days, and what those looked like. Lakhdar described some things that happened, and I don't know if that's something that's in the reports or something you maybe heard about?

M: When I was there, I was able to look back on a lot of interrogation records. There's a need-to-know—I'm in charge of all the detainees in these two teams, which he's one of, and I can request to see interrogation reports on any of my detainees, going back to the earliest ones. And I did. I looked at them, because Paul Rester was asking me for intel on these guys, and I was thinking, "Well, I don't have it, maybe the interrogators got it." So I did my due diligence, and I went back, and I didn't see anything.

The interrogations—another thing about Guantanamo, when you ask Joe Q. Public on the street, "Let's play the word association game. I'm going to say a word, you tell me the first thing that pops into your head." You say "cat," they say "dog." You say "Guantanamo," they might say "torture." That isn't probably the best word to pop into your head for the association. When you think about EITs [Enhanced Interrogation Techniques], you're really thinking about the CIA's approach. So if I were to ask that person, "Tell me more about torture," they'd say, "You know, water-boarding." But that's not something that happened—it didn't happen in GTMO at all. And that's because the DOD never had that authorized.

There were EITs for DOD, and some of them were the same, but some were different. Use of dogs, sleep deprivation, stress positions—these were all available to DOD. All of those sorts of things were used at GTMO, well before my time there, like in the 2002 timeframe. In Camp X-Ray in particular, they used a lot of dogs. There are a lot of pictures of guards with dogs in the compound. Not *around* the compound, which is acceptable, but *inside* the compound. That dog is now being used as an intimidation tool, not just as a disincentive to break through the wire.

So, Lakhdar very likely did experience some DOD/Rumsfeld-authorized EITs, either directly or secondhand by watching it happen to others.

I don't know exactly when—I want to say it was 2004—they started to change how they did business with regard to interrogations in GTMO. It started to get a little bit more on the up-and-up. And when I got there, I was a fairly senior interrogator in the pecking order, and the Army Field Manual had been codified by the law around that same time—so I was implementing real changes to interrogation at Guantanamo. Again, partially because of my view of what good interrogation tactics are, and partially because the law was changing too.

And so Lakhdar might have recognized a difference in the interrogations because of those things. I would not allow any kind of threatening or violent interrogation at all.

I would allow for some—there's a tactic that's completely acceptable called "fear up." There's "fear up mild" and "fear up harsh." Fear up is when—there's nothing saying that rapport has to be good. I don't have to make you think that I'm your friend. I just need to have a relationship with you. Maybe it's adversarial. Not necessarily intimidation—intimidation usually shuts somebody up. But maybe you think you're smarter than I am, you don't like me, I'm an arrogant prick—and I'm going to get you to give up the goods simply to prove me wrong. That's a relationship. That's a rapport.

But I wouldn't allow anything harsher than a fear up harsh. I can throw a chair against the wall. I can't throw a chair at you. And I wouldn't allow for a fear up harsh unless you really made the case of why you needed to do a fear up harsh. I also was training—most of my interrogators were fairly young, and I said, "What happens in the next interrogation after you've done a fear up harsh and you get nothing? How do you dial it back? If you fail at the fear up harsh, I have to swap you out. I have to."

And I would say the same thing about an EIT. How many times do you think KSM had to be water-boarded before he realized it wasn't going to kill him? And if that's the harshest thing we can do—if that's it—and I've survived it, not just once but several, several times, and I know the Americans aren't going to go any further than that, I've already won.

So you've got to be very judicious about using harsh techniques. Even a fear up harsh—a fear up harsh is not torture, but it's the harshest I would allow. And I would always sit down with the interrogator. He has to do an interrogation plan, and he has to tell me exactly what he's going in after, what information he hopes to get, and what approaches he intends to use. And if he starts off with fear up harsh, I want to know why.

If that's his contingency—"If this doesn't work, then I'm going to go to fear up harsh"—as soon as I see fear up harsh, I want to sit down with you. And I want you to tell me, "What happens if you don't get it on fear up harsh? At what point do you break contact, and then what happens next? Do you understand that I cannot send you back in there? Because it just looks like you've lost your cool, and he wins. I don't want him to win."

So, it doesn't surprise me that Lakhdar recognized a difference in the interrogation tactics from 2002 to 2006.

Again, I mean—interrogation has gotten a bad rap because of the bad interrogators. It really is a useful thing, but you have to do it judiciously, and you have to do it in a way—the best interrogation is when the detainee wants to talk to the interrogator. That's the best interrogation. When I was training my interrogators, I'd say, "Look, not every detainee is going to want to talk to you, I get that—but if you can't think about how you can get a detainee to at least want to talk to you, then you're in the wrong business." If they don't want to talk to you, you're pushing the boulder uphill.

DN: When you were there, did you have the opportunity to observe a lot of the guard interaction with detainees?

M: Yeah. Again, a very mixed bag. Most guards are good people, in a difficult job. And in many ways, they're as much prisoners as the detainees. They're on the other side of the cage, but they're still caged. They're all inside the wire, and they're all in the same cage, just on different sides of partitions. They can't go home until they're told to go home.

I mean, it's not quite analogous. They may or may not have been sent to Guantanamo of their own free will, but they did enlist of their own free will. And they also know that they're going to get off shift in a few hours, and they're going to be able to have a beer, and they're going to be able to go home at six months, whereas the detainee doesn't know if he's ever going to—he may die there, and never see his family again. They don't know.

But the guards do have a difficult job. And also, they have no information about one detainee to another. They don't know if this guy is senior Al Qaeda—I mean, they hear rumors, and they know certain people, but for the most part they don't know who's who in the zoo, as far as, "Are you a terrorist or are you just unlucky? I don't really know, so I have to treat you all the same."

And the detainees make it difficult on the guards. They throw these little cocktails made up of every bodily fluid you can imagine. Blood, semen, urine, feces. They call it a cocktail, and it's a biohazard if nothing else. It's disgusting. And these poor kids are getting—and they're young. So you have to guard against these sort of post-adolescent tempers. Somebody literally throws shit in your face, you kind of want to stomp on 'em. That's a normal reaction. The thing is, they can't. They can't. So you've got to make sure that they understand that, and you train them not to do that, and you give them other outlets.

So, it's a very difficult job. Everybody in Guantanamo is under duress. Everybody. Interrogators, guards, detainees, everybody. It's a difficult, difficult situation. And the detainees don't make it easier on anybody.

There are also guards who are abusive, vindictive, sadistic—and it's sickening to me. But it does happen. We tend to be pretty harsh on them when we catch that. Unfortunately, the interrogations do not happen in where the guards are, so we don't really see that very often. I had a little bit more entrée, because I was able to go into the detention facilities. Most interrogators do not. They go into the wire, but then there's a hut where the interrogation booths are, and the detainee is brought to them.

And the guards stay outside the room, or maybe in the room, depending on how you want to set up the room as an interrogator. Maybe your detainee is shackled. A lot of times what I would do, when I would have an interrogation—the standard protocol is the guard will bring you in, shackle your foot to a floor shackle, and usually have your wrists shackled as well. And the first thing I would do is tell the guard, "Unshackle him." The guards don't want to unshackle the foot, and I usually didn't ask them to do that, because it's a safety issue—but I always had them unshackle the wrists. And then I always asked the guard to step outside.

My reason for doing that is, there's a little bit of power there. I have the power to tell the guards what to do. But I also wanted the detainee to see that I don't want to treat them like an animal. I want to treat them like a person.

And I very often would address that floor shackle and explain that there are protocols that even I can't undo. Unless I really—if I know you pretty well at this stage and you're cooperative and you're compliant and you're talking with me, I might have that undone. But if I just met you—first, second, even fifth interrogation—I might explain, "For my safety, you have to understand that I don't have the power to do that. But I'm going to give you as much freedom as I can. I'm going to take you to an area where the guard can't hear you. You can speak freely."

Even in the observation rooms that were between the—guards were not allowed in there either. Unless we wanted to. Sometimes some rooms were mic'd, so we could sometimes allow the guards to hear it—but that was only if I requested it, like if I thought I needed to call for a guard.

[Telephone rings. M answers and has brief conversation before interview resumes.]

DN: This has been really helpful.

M: So, a couple things for you guys to know. I'm willing to be on the record for you, if that's useful to you. And I'd like to help as best I can. I have perspective on two important aspects of their lives. The conditions that led to their arrest, and the conditions that were part of their interrogation and captivity.

I like this project, on the face of it, because a lot of things happened in the days and weeks and months—even in the first year or two—after 9/11, where a lot of innocent people got caught up in a vortex. This counter-terrorism vortex. And I think it's understandable. And because it's so humanly understandable, given the context of the world we lived in and what we had just gone through, and the fear and the uncertainty of everything, maybe it was even justifiable to a degree. But what has been inexcusable is that we were so late, and we still are too late, to make any adjustments to try to undo—to recognize that mistakes were made, and that our dragnet approach was not judicious. And it ends up hurting us in the end.

I don't know that it was inappropriate to arrest these people. But to send them to Guantanamo without having the intelligence—and I can tell you that they didn't.

You could say, "Well, maybe there was intelligence, Michael, but you just didn't know about it." Well, okay. And I was willing to accept that when I heard the president talk about six people. I wasn't the only intelligence guy in the room that day. So maybe somebody else found some intel, or maybe the Bosnians provided intel.

But what I can say is this. When I got to Guantanamo, the guy in charge of all—Paul Rester's title was Director, Joint Intelligence Group. That's the guy in charge of all the intelligence in Guantanamo. All the interrogations, all the analysis, everything. Everybody works for him. And he reports directly to the admiral. He didn't have any intel on them, and he'd been at Guantanamo for years. He was there well before I got there, and he was there well after I left.

Paul Rester, for better or for worse, is very much associated with Guantanamo. He is very much part of Guantanamo's history, much more so than any of us. And he didn't know. He asked me, when I first got there—he said, "I am so glad to see you, Lieutenant, because maybe you can fill in some information for me which I have been racking my brains on." And I couldn't. So, why is it that so—how many years were they in captivity before they decided to send these guys home?

DN: Seven years.

M: Seven years. That's inexcusable. The government knew they didn't have the intelligence on them. They interrogated them. They didn't get intelligence on them. They interrogated other people, and didn't get intelligence that would implicate their involvement. And they still held onto them for seven years. That doesn't make any sense.

And at what cost? How many people, who don't necessarily know these individuals, were radicalized and became a threat because of the injustice that they perceived was done—that was truly done—on some innocent people? I mean, Guantanamo was a rally cry for people who really are terrorists. That was the thing that got them into that camp.

Who knows? Maybe if Guantanamo didn't happen, maybe—who's a latter-day terrorist? Let's say Major Nidal Hasan. I don't know all the story of his radicalization, but just for the sake of argument—maybe he doesn't become the gunman at Fort Hood if this injustice didn't happen.

If we were able to say that only known terrorists with corroborated and confirmed intelligence went to Guantanamo, and we did the due diligence—or even if we said, "You know what? In the early days, we did this dragnet approach, but we quickly resolved that and we've fine-tuned our process." But we didn't. So that's why I think this book is important.

DN: Well, this has been immensely helpful. Thank you for your time.

M: I'm honored to be part of this. And I'm eager to be on the record for you, because I want my story to be told as well. Part of my story is that I was involved in Bosnia. Part of my story is that I was involved in GTMO. And I want to be able to lend credence to their story by saying, "Yeah, it's true. We didn't have intelligence on these guys. This was a wrong time, wrong place kind of a thing." And we can argue about whether or not that was an acceptable, appropriate, justifiable thing to do. But what certainly is not up for debate is that it should not have taken seven years to rectify that problem.

ACKNOWLEDGMENTS

This book would not have been possible without tremendous emotional, intellectual, and logistical support from the Boumediene and Ait Idir families, and from Jen Barkley, Ellie Norland, Cam Norland, Phil List, Yvette Luxenberg, Jasper Rose, Akiva Rose, Mary Hartnett, Richard Norland, Sue Rose, Paul Barkley, Leta Holley, Steve Hartnett, and Joshua Gomez.

Additionally, Raja Ben Hammed, Mohamed Wajdi Ben Hammed, and Felice Bezri provided exceptional translation assistance, and Kim Miner was an outstanding research assistant. Olivia Martin, Remy Reya, Ward Farnsworth, Chris Bryan, Elsa Hart, Robbie Hart, Blair Overstreet, Cortney Golub, Jonathan Shulman, Harry Thomas, Jonathan Herman, and Debby Couture offered helpful suggestions at various stages of the project. Josette Welsh and Jackie Salazar delivered office support with good cheer, welcome encouragement, and quiet, friendly competence. Michelle Lipinski, Stanford University Press editor extraordinaire, provided invaluable guidance, as did editorial assistant Nora Spiegel, copyeditor David Horne, publicist Ryan Furtkamp, Editor-in-Chief Kate Wahl, and the dedicated production team spearheaded by Gigi Mark.

Finally, the legal team at WilmerHale spent more than 17,000 *pro bono* hours litigating the case of *Boumediene v. Bush*, work that would have cost paying clients more than $35 million.